CLEP
Humanities
Exam

SECRETS

Study Guide
Your Key to Exam Success

**CLEP Test Review for the
College Level Examination Program**

Dear Future Exam Success Story:

First of all, **THANK YOU** for purchasing Mometrix study materials!

Second, congratulations! You are one of the few determined test-takers who are committed to doing whatever it takes to excel on your exam. **You have come to the right place.** We developed these study materials with one goal in mind: to deliver you the information you need in a format that's concise and easy to use.

In addition to optimizing your guide for the content of the test, we've outlined our recommended steps for breaking down the preparation process into small, attainable goals so you can make sure you stay on track.

We've also analyzed the entire test-taking process, identifying the most common pitfalls and showing how you can overcome them and be ready for any curveball the test throws you.

Standardized testing is one of the biggest obstacles on your road to success, which only increases the importance of doing well in the high-pressure, high-stakes environment of test day. Your results on this test could have a significant impact on your future, and this guide provides the information and practical advice to help you achieve your full potential on test day.

Your success is our success

We would love to hear from you! If you would like to share the story of your exam success or if you have any questions or comments in regard to our products, please contact us at **800-673-8175** or **support@mometrix.com**.

Thanks again for your business and we wish you continued success!

Sincerely,
The Mometrix Test Preparation Team

Need more help? Check out our flashcards at: http://MometrixFlashcards.com/CLEP

TABLE OF CONTENTS

Introduction

Thank you for purchasing this resource! You have made the choice to prepare yourself for a test that could have a huge impact on your future, and this guide is designed to help you be fully ready for test day. Obviously, it's important to have a solid understanding of the test material, but you also need to be prepared for the unique environment and stressors of the test, so that you can perform to the best of your abilities.

For this purpose, the first section that appears in this guide is the **Secret Keys**. We've devoted countless hours to meticulously researching what works and what doesn't, and we've boiled down our findings to the five most impactful steps you can take to improve your performance on the test. We start at the beginning with study planning and move through the preparation process, all the way to the testing strategies that will help you get the most out of what you know when you're finally sitting in front of the test.

We recommend that you start preparing for your test as far in advance as possible. However, if you've bought this guide as a last-minute study resource and only have a few days before your test, we recommend that you skip over the first two Secret Keys since they address a long-term study plan.

If you struggle with **test anxiety**, we strongly encourage you to check out our recommendations for how you can overcome it. Test anxiety is a formidable foe, but it can be beaten, and we want to make sure you have the tools you need to defeat it.

Secret Key #1 – Plan Big, Study Small

There's a lot riding on your performance. If you want to ace this test, you're going to need to keep your skills sharp and the material fresh in your mind. You need a plan that lets you review everything you need to know while still fitting in your schedule. We'll break this strategy down into three categories.

Information Organization

Start with the information you already have: the official test outline. From this, you can make a complete list of all the concepts you need to cover before the test. Organize these concepts into groups that can be studied together, and create a list of any related vocabulary you need to learn so you can brush up on any difficult terms. You'll want to keep this vocabulary list handy once you actually start studying since you may need to add to it along the way.

Time Management

Once you have your set of study concepts, decide how to spread them out over the time you have left before the test. Break your study plan into small, clear goals so you have a manageable task for each day and know exactly what you're doing. Then just focus on one small step at a time. When you manage your time this way, you don't need to spend hours at a time studying. Studying a small block of content for a short period each day helps you retain information better and avoid stressing over how much you have left to do. You can relax knowing that you have a plan to cover everything in time. In order for this strategy to be effective though, you have to start studying early and stick to your schedule. Avoid the exhaustion and futility that comes from last-minute cramming!

Study Environment

The environment you study in has a big impact on your learning. Studying in a coffee shop, while probably more enjoyable, is not likely to be as fruitful as studying in a quiet room. It's important to keep distractions to a minimum. You're only planning to study for a short block of time, so make the most of it. Don't pause to check your phone or get up to find a snack. It's also important to **avoid multitasking**. Research has consistently shown that multitasking will make your studying dramatically less effective. Your study area should also be comfortable and well-lit so you don't have the distraction of straining your eyes or sitting on an uncomfortable chair.

The time of day you study is also important. You want to be rested and alert. Don't wait until just before bedtime. Study when you'll be most likely to comprehend and remember. Even better, if you know what time of day your test will be, set that time aside for study. That way your brain will be used to working on that subject at that specific time and you'll have a better chance of recalling information.

Finally, it can be helpful to team up with others who are studying for the same test. Your actual studying should be done in as isolated an environment as possible, but the work of organizing the information and setting up the study plan can be divided up. In between study sessions, you can discuss with your teammates the concepts that you're all studying and quiz each other on the details. Just be sure that your teammates are as serious about the test as you are. If you find that your study time is being replaced with social time, you might need to find a new team.

Secret Key #2 – Make Your Studying Count

You're devoting a lot of time and effort to preparing for this test, so you want to be absolutely certain it will pay off. This means doing more than just reading the content and hoping you can remember it on test day. It's important to make every minute of study count. There are two main areas you can focus on to make your studying count:

Retention

It doesn't matter how much time you study if you can't remember the material. You need to make sure you are retaining the concepts. To check your retention of the information you're learning, try recalling it at later times with minimal prompting. Try carrying around flashcards and glance at one or two from time to time or ask a friend who's also studying for the test to quiz you.

To enhance your retention, look for ways to put the information into practice so that you can apply it rather than simply recalling it. If you're using the information in practical ways, it will be much easier to remember. Similarly, it helps to solidify a concept in your mind if you're not only reading it to yourself but also explaining it to someone else. Ask a friend to let you teach them about a concept you're a little shaky on (or speak aloud to an imaginary audience if necessary). As you try to summarize, define, give examples, and answer your friend's questions, you'll understand the concepts better and they will stay with you longer. Finally, step back for a big picture view and ask yourself how each piece of information fits with the whole subject. When you link the different concepts together and see them working together as a whole, it's easier to remember the individual components.

Finally, practice showing your work on any multi-step problems, even if you're just studying. Writing out each step you take to solve a problem will help solidify the process in your mind, and you'll be more likely to remember it during the test.

Modality

Modality simply refers to the means or method by which you study. Choosing a study modality that fits your own individual learning style is crucial. No two people learn best in exactly the same way, so it's important to know your strengths and use them to your advantage.

For example, if you learn best by visualization, focus on visualizing a concept in your mind and draw an image or a diagram. Try color-coding your notes, illustrating them, or creating symbols that will trigger your mind to recall a learned concept. If you learn best by hearing or discussing information, find a study partner who learns the same way or read aloud to yourself. Think about how to put the information in your own words. Imagine that you are giving a lecture on the topic and record yourself so you can listen to it later.

For any learning style, flashcards can be helpful. Organize the information so you can take advantage of spare moments to review. Underline key words or phrases. Use different colors for different categories. Mnemonic devices (such as creating a short list in which every item starts with the same letter) can also help with retention. Find what works best for you and use it to store the information in your mind most effectively and easily.

Secret Key #3 – Practice the Right Way

Your success on test day depends not only on how many hours you put into preparing, but also on whether you prepared the right way. It's good to check along the way to see if your studying is paying off. One of the most effective ways to do this is by taking practice tests to evaluate your progress. Practice tests are useful because they show exactly where you need to improve. Every time you take a practice test, pay special attention to these three groups of questions:

- The questions you got wrong
- The questions you had to guess on, even if you guessed right
- The questions you found difficult or slow to work through

This will show you exactly what your weak areas are, and where you need to devote more study time. Ask yourself why each of these questions gave you trouble. Was it because you didn't understand the material? Was it because you didn't remember the vocabulary? Do you need more repetitions on this type of question to build speed and confidence? Dig into those questions and figure out how you can strengthen your weak areas as you go back to review the material.

Additionally, many practice tests have a section explaining the answer choices. It can be tempting to read the explanation and think that you now have a good understanding of the concept. However, an explanation likely only covers part of the question's broader context. Even if the explanation makes sense, **go back and investigate** every concept related to the question until you're positive you have a thorough understanding.

As you go along, keep in mind that the practice test is just that: practice. Memorizing these questions and answers will not be very helpful on the actual test because it is unlikely to have any of the same exact questions. If you only know the right answers to the sample questions, you won't be prepared for the real thing. **Study the concepts** until you understand them fully, and then you'll be able to answer any question that shows up on the test.

It's important to wait on the practice tests until you're ready. If you take a test on your first day of study, you may be overwhelmed by the amount of material covered and how much you need to learn. Work up to it gradually.

On test day, you'll need to be prepared for answering questions, managing your time, and using the test-taking strategies you've learned. It's a lot to balance, like a mental marathon that will have a big impact on your future. Like training for a marathon, you'll need to start slowly and work your way up. When test day arrives, you'll be ready.

Start with the strategies you've read in the first two Secret Keys—plan your course and study in the way that works best for you. If you have time, consider using multiple study resources to get different approaches to the same concepts. It can be helpful to see difficult concepts from more than one angle. Then find a good source for practice tests. Many times, the test website will suggest potential study resources or provide sample tests.

Practice Test Strategy

When you're ready to start taking practice tests, follow this strategy:

Untimed and Open-Book Practice

Take the first test with no time constraints and with your notes and study guide handy. Take your time and focus on applying the strategies you've learned.

Timed and Open-Book Practice

Take the second practice test open-book as well, but set a timer and practice pacing yourself to finish in time.

Timed and Closed-Book Practice

Take any other practice tests as if it were test day. Set a timer and put away your study materials. Sit at a table or desk in a quiet room, imagine yourself at the testing center, and answer questions as quickly and accurately as possible.

Keep repeating timed and closed-book tests on a regular basis until you run out of practice tests or it's time for the actual test. Your mind will be ready for the schedule and stress of test day, and you'll be able to focus on recalling the material you've learned.

Secret Key #4 – Pace Yourself

Once you're fully prepared for the material on the test, your biggest challenge on test day will be managing your time. Just knowing that the clock is ticking can make you panic even if you have plenty of time left. Work on pacing yourself so you can build confidence against the time constraints of the exam. Pacing is a difficult skill to master, especially in a high-pressure environment, so **practice is vital**.

Set time expectations for your pace based on how much time is available. For example, if a section has 60 questions and the time limit is 30 minutes, you know you have to average 30 seconds or less per question in order to answer them all. Although 30 seconds is the hard limit, set 25 seconds per question as your goal, so you reserve extra time to spend on harder questions. When you budget extra time for the harder questions, you no longer have any reason to stress when those questions take longer to answer.

Don't let this time expectation distract you from working through the test at a calm, steady pace, but keep it in mind so you don't spend too much time on any one question. Recognize that taking extra time on one question you don't understand may keep you from answering two that you do understand later in the test. If your time limit for a question is up and you're still not sure of the answer, mark it and move on, and come back to it later if the time and the test format allow. If the testing format doesn't allow you to return to earlier questions, just make an educated guess; then put it out of your mind and move on.

On the easier questions, be careful not to rush. It may seem wise to hurry through them so you have more time for the challenging ones, but it's not worth missing one if you know the concept and just didn't take the time to read the question fully. Work efficiently but make sure you understand the question and have looked at all of the answer choices, since more than one may seem right at first.

Even if you're paying attention to the time, you may find yourself a little behind at some point. You should speed up to get back on track, but do so wisely. Don't panic; just take a few seconds less on each question until you're caught up. Don't guess without thinking, but do look through the answer choices and eliminate any you know are wrong. If you can get down to two choices, it is often worthwhile to guess from those. Once you've chosen an answer, move on and don't dwell on any that you skipped or had to hurry through. If a question was taking too long, chances are it was one of the harder ones, so you weren't as likely to get it right anyway.

On the other hand, if you find yourself getting ahead of schedule, it may be beneficial to slow down a little. The more quickly you work, the more likely you are to make a careless mistake that will affect your score. You've budgeted time for each question, so don't be afraid to spend that time. Practice an efficient but careful pace to get the most out of the time you have.

Secret Key #5 – Have a Plan for Guessing

When you're taking the test, you may find yourself stuck on a question. Some of the answer choices seem better than others, but you don't see the one answer choice that is obviously correct. What do you do?

The scenario described above is very common, yet most test takers have not effectively prepared for it. Developing and practicing a plan for guessing may be one of the single most effective uses of your time as you get ready for the exam.

In developing your plan for guessing, there are three questions to address:

- When should you start the guessing process?
- How should you narrow down the choices?
- Which answer should you choose?

When to Start the Guessing Process

Unless your plan for guessing is to select C every time (which, despite its merits, is not what we recommend), you need to leave yourself enough time to apply your answer elimination strategies. Since you have a limited amount of time for each question, that means that if you're going to give yourself the best shot at guessing correctly, you have to decide quickly whether or not you will guess.

Of course, the best-case scenario is that you don't have to guess at all, so first, see if you can answer the question based on your knowledge of the subject and basic reasoning skills. Focus on the key words in the question and try to jog your memory of related topics. Give yourself a chance to bring the knowledge to mind, but once you realize that you don't have (or you can't access) the knowledge you need to answer the question, it's time to start the guessing process.

It's almost always better to start the guessing process too early than too late. It only takes a few seconds to remember something and answer the question from knowledge. Carefully eliminating wrong answer choices takes longer. Plus, going through the process of eliminating answer choices can actually help jog your memory.

Summary: Start the guessing process as soon as you decide that you can't answer the question based on your knowledge.

How to Narrow Down the Choices

The next chapter in this book (**Test-Taking Strategies**) includes a wide range of strategies for how to approach questions and how to look for answer choices to eliminate. You will definitely want to read those carefully, practice them, and figure out which ones work best for you. Here though, we're going to address a mindset rather than a particular strategy.

Your chances of guessing an answer correctly depend on how many options you are choosing from.

How many choices you have	How likely you are to guess correctly
5	20%
4	25%
3	33%
2	50%
1	100%

You can see from this chart just how valuable it is to be able to eliminate incorrect answers and make an educated guess, but there are two things that many test takers do that cause them to miss out on the benefits of guessing:

- Accidentally eliminating the correct answer
- Selecting an answer based on an impression

We'll look at the first one here, and the second one in the next section.

To avoid accidentally eliminating the correct answer, we recommend a thought exercise called **the $5 challenge**. In this challenge, you only eliminate an answer choice from contention if you are willing to bet $5 on it being wrong. Why $5? Five dollars is a small but not insignificant amount of money. It's an amount you could afford to lose but wouldn't want to throw away. And while losing $5 once might not hurt too much, doing it twenty times will set you back $100. In the same way, each small decision you make—eliminating a choice here, guessing on a question there—won't by itself impact your score very much, but when you put them all together, they can make a big difference. By holding each answer choice elimination decision to a higher standard, you can reduce the risk of accidentally eliminating the correct answer.

The $5 challenge can also be applied in a positive sense: If you are willing to bet $5 that an answer choice *is* correct, go ahead and mark it as correct.

Summary: Only eliminate an answer choice if you are willing to bet $5 that it is wrong.

Which Answer to Choose

You're taking the test. You've run into a hard question and decided you'll have to guess. You've eliminated all the answer choices you're willing to bet $5 on. Now you have to pick an answer. Why do we even need to talk about this? Why can't you just pick whichever one you feel like when the time comes?

The answer to these questions is that if you don't come into the test with a plan, you'll rely on your impression to select an answer choice, and if you do that, you risk falling into a trap. The test writers know that everyone who takes their test will be guessing on some of the questions, so they intentionally write wrong answer choices to seem plausible. You still have to pick an answer though, and if the wrong answer choices are designed to look right, how can you ever be sure that you're not falling for their trap? The best solution we've found to this dilemma is to take the decision out of your hands entirely. Here is the process we recommend:

Once you've eliminated any choices that you are confident (willing to bet $5) are wrong, select the first remaining choice as your answer.

Whether you choose to select the first remaining choice, the second, or the last, the important thing is that you use some preselected standard. Using this approach guarantees that you will not be enticed into selecting an answer choice that looks right, because you are not basing your decision on how the answer choices look.

This is not meant to make you question your knowledge. Instead, it is to help you recognize the difference between your knowledge and your impressions. There's a huge difference between thinking an answer is right because of what you know, and thinking an answer is right because it looks or sounds like it should be right.

Summary: To ensure that your selection is appropriately random, make a predetermined selection from among all answer choices you have not eliminated.

Test-Taking Strategies

This section contains a list of test-taking strategies that you may find helpful as you work through the test. By taking what you know and applying logical thought, you can maximize your chances of answering any question correctly!

It is very important to realize that every question is different and every person is different: no single strategy will work on every question, and no single strategy will work for every person. That's why we've included all of them here, so you can try them out and determine which ones work best for different types of questions and which ones work best for you.

Question Strategies

Read Carefully

Read the question and answer choices carefully. Don't miss the question because you misread the terms. You have plenty of time to read each question thoroughly and make sure you understand what is being asked. Yet a happy medium must be attained, so don't waste too much time. You must read carefully, but efficiently.

Contextual Clues

Look for contextual clues. If the question includes a word you are not familiar with, look at the immediate context for some indication of what the word might mean. Contextual clues can often give you all the information you need to decipher the meaning of an unfamiliar word. Even if you can't determine the meaning, you may be able to narrow down the possibilities enough to make a solid guess at the answer to the question.

Prefixes

If you're having trouble with a word in the question or answer choices, try dissecting it. Take advantage of every clue that the word might include. Prefixes and suffixes can be a huge help. Usually they allow you to determine a basic meaning. Pre- means before, post- means after, pro - is positive, de- is negative. From prefixes and suffixes, you can get an idea of the general meaning of the word and try to put it into context.

Hedge Words

Watch out for critical hedge words, such as *likely, may, can, sometimes, often, almost, mostly, usually, generally, rarely*, and *sometimes*. Question writers insert these hedge phrases to cover every possibility. Often an answer choice will be wrong simply because it leaves no room for exception. Be on guard for answer choices that have definitive words such as *exactly* and *always*.

Switchback Words

Stay alert for *switchbacks*. These are the words and phrases frequently used to alert you to shifts in thought. The most common switchback words are *but, although*, and *however*. Others include *nevertheless, on the other hand, even though, while, in spite of, despite, regardless of*. Switchback words are important to catch because they can change the direction of the question or an answer choice.

Face Value

When in doubt, use common sense. Accept the situation in the problem at face value. Don't read too much into it. These problems will not require you to make wild assumptions. If you have to go beyond creativity and warp time or space in order to have an answer choice fit the question, then you should move on and consider the other answer choices. These are normal problems rooted in reality. The applicable relationship or explanation may not be readily apparent, but it is there for you to figure out. Use your common sense to interpret anything that isn't clear.

Answer Choice Strategies

Answer Selection

The most thorough way to pick an answer choice is to identify and eliminate wrong answers until only one is left, then confirm it is the correct answer. Sometimes an answer choice may immediately seem right, but be careful. The test writers will usually put more than one reasonable answer choice on each question, so take a second to read all of them and make sure that the other choices are not equally obvious. As long as you have time left, it is better to read every answer choice than to pick the first one that looks right without checking the others.

Answer Choice Families

An answer choice family consists of two (in rare cases, three) answer choices that are very similar in construction and cannot all be true at the same time. If you see two answer choices that are direct opposites or parallels, one of them is usually the correct answer. For instance, if one answer choice says that quantity x increases and another either says that quantity x decreases (opposite) or says that quantity y increases (parallel), then those answer choices would fall into the same family. An answer choice that doesn't match the construction of the answer choice family is more likely to be incorrect. Most questions will not have answer choice families, but when they do appear, you should be prepared to recognize them.

Eliminate Answers

Eliminate answer choices as soon as you realize they are wrong, but make sure you consider all possibilities. If you are eliminating answer choices and realize that the last one you are left with is also wrong, don't panic. Start over and consider each choice again. There may be something you missed the first time that you will realize on the second pass.

Avoid Fact Traps

Don't be distracted by an answer choice that is factually true but doesn't answer the question. You are looking for the choice that answers the question. Stay focused on what the question is asking for so you don't accidentally pick an answer that is true but incorrect. Always go back to the question and make sure the answer choice you've selected actually answers the question and is not merely a true statement.

Extreme Statements

In general, you should avoid answers that put forth extreme actions as standard practice or proclaim controversial ideas as established fact. An answer choice that states the "process should be used in certain situations, if..." is much more likely to be correct than one that states the "process should be discontinued completely." The first is a calm rational statement and doesn't even make a definitive, uncompromising stance, using a hedge word *if* to provide wiggle room, whereas the second choice is a radical idea and far more extreme.

Benchmark

As you read through the answer choices and you come across one that seems to answer the question well, mentally select that answer choice. This is not your final answer, but it's the one that will help you evaluate the other answer choices. The one that you selected is your benchmark or standard for judging each of the other answer choices. Every other answer choice must be compared to your benchmark. That choice is correct until proven otherwise by another answer choice beating it. If you find a better answer, then that one becomes your new benchmark. Once you've decided that no other choice answers the question as well as your benchmark, you have your final answer.

Predict the Answer

Before you even start looking at the answer choices, it is often best to try to predict the answer. When you come up with the answer on your own, it is easier to avoid distractions and traps because you will know exactly what to look for. The right answer choice is unlikely to be word-for-word what you came up with, but it should be a close match. Even if you are confident that you have the right answer, you should still take the time to read each option before moving on.

General Strategies

Tough Questions

If you are stumped on a problem or it appears too hard or too difficult, don't waste time. Move on! Remember though, if you can quickly check for obviously incorrect answer choices, your chances of guessing correctly are greatly improved. Before you completely give up, at least try to knock out a couple of possible answers. Eliminate what you can and then guess at the remaining answer choices before moving on.

Check Your Work

Since you will probably not know every term listed and the answer to every question, it is important that you get credit for the ones that you do know. Don't miss any questions through careless mistakes. If at all possible, try to take a second to look back over your answer selection and make sure you've selected the correct answer choice and haven't made a costly careless mistake (such as marking an answer choice that you didn't mean to mark). This quick double check should more than pay for itself in caught mistakes for the time it costs.

Pace Yourself

It's easy to be overwhelmed when you're looking at a page full of questions; your mind is confused and full of random thoughts, and the clock is ticking down faster than you would like. Calm down and maintain the pace that you have set for yourself. Especially as you get down to the last few minutes of the test, don't let the small numbers on the clock make you panic. As long as you are on track by monitoring your pace, you are guaranteed to have time for each question.

Don't Rush

It is very easy to make errors when you are in a hurry. Maintaining a fast pace in answering questions is pointless if it makes you miss questions that you would have gotten right otherwise. Test writers like to include distracting information and wrong answers that seem right. Taking a little extra time to avoid careless mistakes can make all the difference in your test score. Find a pace that allows you to be confident in the answers that you select.

Keep Moving

Panicking will not help you pass the test, so do your best to stay calm and keep moving. Taking deep breaths and going through the answer elimination steps you practiced can help to break through a stress barrier and keep your pace.

Final Notes

The combination of a solid foundation of content knowledge and the confidence that comes from practicing your plan for applying that knowledge is the key to maximizing your performance on test day. As your foundation of content knowledge is built up and strengthened, you'll find that the strategies included in this chapter become more and more effective in helping you quickly sift through the distractions and traps of the test to isolate the correct answer.

Now it's time to move on to the test content chapters of this book, but be sure to keep your goal in mind. As you read, think about how you will be able to apply this information on the test. If you've already seen sample questions for the test and you have an idea of the question format and style, try to come up with questions of your own that you can answer based on what you're reading. This will give you valuable practice applying your knowledge in the same ways you can expect to on test day.

Good luck and good studying!

Literature

William Shakespeare

William Shakespeare lived in England from 1564-1616. He was a poet and playwright of the Renaissance period in Western culture. He is generally considered the foremost dramatist in world literature, and the greatest author to write in the English language. He wrote many poems, particularly sonnets, of which 154 survive today, and approximately 38 plays. Though his sonnets were larger in number and are very famous, he is best known for his plays, including comedies, tragedies, tragicomedies and historical plays. His play titles include: *All's Well That Ends Well, As You Like It, The Comedy of Errors, Love's Labour's Lost, Measure for Measure, The Merchant of Venice, The Merry Wives of Windsor, A Midsummer Night's Dream, Much Ado About Nothing, The Taming of the Shrew, The Tempest, Twelfth Night, The Two Gentlemen of Verona, The Winter's Tale, King John, Richard II, Henry IV, Henry V, Richard III, Romeo and Juliet, Coriolanus, Titus Andronicus, Julius Caesar, Macbeth, Hamlet, Troilus and Cressida, King Lear, Othello, Antony and Cleopatra*, and *Cymbeline*.

William Faulkner

William Faulkner lived in the state of Mississippi in the United States of America from 1897-1962. He is known as one of the greatest authors of Southern literature in America, and of American literature in general. Faulkner wrote one play, poems, essays, screenplays, and especially novels and short stories. He based his writing on his experience living in Mississippi during the early 20th century. Many of his short stories and novels are set in a fictional Southern county modeled on the two counties where he lived. Faulkner was awarded the 1949 Nobel Prize for Literature and two Pulitzer Prizes for Fiction, both for novels: one for *A Fable* in 1954, and another for *The Reivers*, his final novel, in 1962. Titles of some of his best-known works include the novels *The Sound and the Fury; As I Lay Dying; Light in August; Absalom, Absalom!;* and the short story *A Rose for Emily*.

Geoffrey Chaucer

The Canterbury Tales

Medieval poet Geoffrey Chaucer (c. 1343-1400), called the "Father of English Literature," chiefly wrote long narrative poems, including *The Book of the Duchess, Anelida and Arcite, The House of Fame, The Parlement of Foules, The Legend of Good Women,* and *Troilus and Criseyde.* His most famous work is *The Canterbury Tales.* Its historical and cultural context is life during the Middle Ages, representing a cross-section of society—tradespeople, professionals, nobility, clergy, and housewives, among others, and religious pilgrimages, a common practice of the time. Its literary context is a frame-tale, that is, a story within a story. Chaucer described a varied group of pilgrims all on their way to Canterbury, taking turns telling stories to amuse the others. Tales encompass a broad range of subjects: bawdy comedy, chivalry, romance, and religion. These include *The Knight's Tale, The Miller's Tale, The Reeve's Tale, The Cook's Tale, The Man of Law's Tale, The Wife of Bath's Tale, The Friar's Tale, The Summoner's Tale, The Clerk's Tale, The Merchant's Tale, The Squire's Tale, The Franklin's Tale, The Physician's Tale, The Pardoner's Tale, The Nun's Priest's Tale,* and others.

The Parlement of Foules

In the brief preface to his poem "The Parlement of Foules," Geoffrey Chaucer refers to ancient Classical Roman author Cicero's "The Dream of Scipio." This was a philosophical dialogue Cicero wrote as a kind of epilogue to his famous longer book, *De re publica* ("*The Republic*"). It narrates that Roman senator and general Scipio the Younger dreams that his grandfather, the renowned general Scipio Africanus, visits him and escorts him to heaven. While viewing the spheres, he tells his grandson how the afterlife is the true life, earthly virtue earns the reward of Heaven, and earthly delights are less important. This reflects Stoic philosophy: Romans adapted Platonic ideals from the Greeks. Whereas "The Dream of Scipio" is a dream-vision on the nature of the universe as macrocosm, Chaucer's poem is a dream-vision on a smaller part of the universe as microcosm. He describes reading "The Dream of Scipio," then also dreaming of a visit from Scipio Africanus, who praises him and promises to reward him for reading Cicero's work.

Influence of Cicero's "Dream of Scipio": During Geoffrey Chaucer's lifetime (1300s), Cicero's philosophical dialogue "The Dream of Scipio," found at the end of his major work *De re publica* (*The Republic*) was a very popular, admired, and influential work. Medieval Christians appreciated Greek and Latin Stoic philosophies for their assigning more importance to spiritual virtues than materialism. They adapted these easily to Christianity for their similarity to Christian values, as they did with many other pagan traditions. Chaucer wrote several dream-vision poems influenced by the Classics, including "The House of Fame," influenced by Virgil's *Aeneid,* and "The Book of the Duchess," influenced by Ovid's *Metamorphoses.* He introduces *The Parlement of Foules* by recounting "The Dream of Scipio," and his own similar dream from the influence of reading this work, as homage to Cicero. He then segues to writing that though personally unsuccessful in love, he writes about love. He contrasts the brevity of life with the lengthiness of learning the poetic art. He concludes his preface asking help from Venus, Roman Goddess of Love.

Drama

Early development

Interestingly, early English drama originally developed from religious ritual. Early Christians established traditions of presenting pageants or mystery plays, each traveling on wagons and carts through the streets of its city, depicting events of the Judeo-Christian Old and New Testaments. Medieval tradition assigned responsibility for performing specific plays to the different guilds. In Middle English, "mystery" meant both religious ritual/truth, and craft/trade. Historically, mystery plays were to be reproduced exactly the same every time as religious rituals. However, by human nature, some performers introduced individual interpretations of roles and/or even improvised. Thus drama was born. Narrative detail and nuanced acting were evident in mystery cycles by the Middle Ages. As individualized performance evolved, plays on other subjects also developed. Middle English mystery plays extant include the York Cycle, Coventry Cycle, Chester Mystery Plays, N-Town Plays, and Towneley/Wakefield Plays. Mystery plays have been revived in the 20th and 21st centuries. Dame Judi Dench (born in York) and other actors began their careers in mystery play revivals.

Defining characteristics

In the Middle Ages, it was common to compose plays in verse. Early Christian mystery plays were always written in verse. By the time of the Renaissance, Shakespeare and other dramatists wrote plays that mixed prose, rhymed verse, and blank verse. Shakespeare also often used rhyming couplets in his plays. The traditions of costumes and masks were seen in ancient Greek drama, medieval mystery plays, and Renaissance drama. Conventions like asides, wherein actors make comments directly to the audience unheard by other characters, and soliloquies, i.e., dramatic monologues, were also common during Shakespeare's Elizabethan dramatic period. Monologues dated back to ancient Greek drama. Elizabethan dialogue tended to use colloquial prose for lower-class characters' speech and stylized verse for upper-class characters. Another Elizabethan convention was the play-within-a-play, like in *Hamlet.* As drama moved toward realism, dialogue became less poetic and more conversational, as in most modern English-language plays.

Contemporary drama, both onstage and onscreen, includes a convention of breaking the fourth wall, wherein actors directly face and address audiences.

Poetry

Unlike prose, which traditionally (except in forms like stream of consciousness) consists of complete sentences connected into paragraphs, poetry is written in verses. These may form complete sentences, clauses, or phrases. Poetry may be written in rhyming verses or unrhymed verse. It can be metered, i.e., following a particular rhythmic pattern, such as iambic, dactylic, spondaic, trochaic, or anapestic, or without regular meter. The terms iamb and trochee, among others, identify stressed and unstressed syllables in each verse. Meter is also described by the number of beats or stressed syllables per verse: dimeter (2), trimeter (3), tetrameter (4), pentameter (5), and so forth. With $\cup$ = unstressed, /= stressed, iambic = $\cup$/; trochaic = /$\cup$; spondaic =//; dactylic =/$\cup\cup$; anapestic =$\cup\cup$/. Poetry with neither rhyme nor meter is called free verse. Poems may be in free verse, metered but unrhymed, rhymed but without meter, or using both rhyme and meter. In English, the most common meter is iambic pentameter. Unrhymed iambic pentameter is called blank verse. Rhyme schemes identify which lines rhyme, such as ABAB, ABCA, AABA, and so on.

Major forms

The ballad is a form historically and currently used in both musical songs and poems. The *ballade* was very popular in 14th- and 15th-century France; ballads were also common in traditional English and American folk songs and poems. Poetry ballads often are rhymed and metered and cover subjects like love, death, murder, or religious topics. In dramatic monologue poems, the poet speaks in the voice of a character/persona. Elegies are mourning poems, traditionally with three parts: a lament, praise of the deceased, and solace for loss. Epic poems are long, recount heroic deeds and adventures, use very stylized language, and combine dramatic and lyrical conventions. Epigrams are memorable, one- or two-line rhymes. Epistolary poems are written and read as letters. Odes evolved from early poems with music and dance to Romantic poems expressing strong feelings and contemplative thoughts. Pastoral poems (and novels) idealize nature and country living. Limericks typically are two lines of iambic trimeter, two lines of iambic dimeter, and one line of iambic trimeter, usually humorous and/or bawdy.

Haiku

Haiku was originally a Japanese poetry form. In the 13th century, haiku was the opening phrase of renga, a 100-stanza oral poem. By the 16th century, haiku diverged into a separate short poem. When Western writers discovered haiku, the form became popular in English and other languages. A haiku has 17 syllables, traditionally distributed across three verses as 5/7/5, with a pause after the first or second line. Haiku are syllabic and unrhymed. Haiku philosophy and technique are that brevity's compression forces writers to express images concisely, depict a moment in time, and evoke illumination and enlightenment. An example is 17th-century haiku master Matsuo Basho's classic: "Oh, old pond! / A frog jumps in— / the sound of water." Modern American poet Ezra Pound revealed the influence of haiku in his two-line poem "In a Station of the Metro"—line 1 has 5+7 syllables, line 2 has 7, but it still preserves haiku's philosophy and imagistic technique: "The apparition of these faces in the crowd; / Petals on a wet, black bough."

Sonnets

The sonnet traditionally has 14 lines of iambic pentameter, tightly organized around a theme. The Petrarchan sonnet, named for 14th-century Italian poet Petrarch, has an eight-line stanza, the octave, and a six-line stanza, the sestet. There is a change or turn, known as the volta, between the eighth and ninth verses setting up the sestet's answer or summary. The rhyme scheme is ABBA/ABBA/CDECDE or CDCDCD. The Petrarchan sonnet was introduced to 16th-century England by Sir Thomas Wyatt. The English or Shakespearean sonnet has three quatrains and one couplet, with the rhyme scheme ABAB/CDCD/EFEF/GG. This format better suits English, which has fewer rhymes than Italian. The final couplet often contrasts sharply with the preceding quatrains, as in Shakespeare's sonnets—for example, Sonnet 130, "My mistress' eyes are nothing like the sun." Variations on these two forms include 16th-century Edmund Spenser's Spenserian sonnet; 17th-century John Milton's Miltonic sonnet; and sonnet sequences, as used by 17th-century poet John Donne in *La Corona*, 19th-century poet Elizabeth Barrett Browning in *Sonnets from the Portuguese*, 19th-20th-century poet Rainer Maria Rilke, and 20th-century poets Robert Lowell and John Berryman.

Literary terminology

In works of prose such as novels, a group of connected sentences covering one main topic is termed a paragraph. In works of poetry, a group of verses similarly connected is called a stanza. In drama, when early works used verse, these were also divided into stanzas or couplets. Drama evolved to use predominantly prose. Overall, whether prose or verse, the conversation in a play is called dialogue. Large sections of dialogue spoken by one actor are called soliloquies or monologues. Dialogue that informs audiences but is unheard by other characters is called an aside. Novels and plays share certain common elements, such as characters—the people in the story; plot—the action of the story; a climax—when action and/or dramatic tension reaches its highest point; and denouement—the resolution following the climax. Sections dividing novels are called chapters, while sections of plays are called acts. Subsections of plays' acts are called scenes. Novels' chapters are usually not subdivided, although some novels have larger sections divided into groups of chapters.

Novels

Major forms

Historical novels set fiction in particular historical periods—including prehistoric and mythological—and contain historical, prehistoric, or mythological themes. Examples include Walter Scott's *Rob Roy* and *Ivanhoe*; Leo Tolstoy's *War and Peace*; Robert Graves' *I, Claudius*; Mary Renault's *The King Must Die* and *The Bull from the Sea* (an historical novel using Greek mythology); Virginia Woolf's *Orlando* and *Between the Acts*; and John Dos Passos's *U.S.A* trilogy. Picaresque novels recount episodic adventures of a rogue protagonist or *pícaro*, like Miguel de Cervantes' *Don Quixote* or Henry Fielding's *Tom Jones*. Gothic novels originated as a reaction against 18th-century Enlightenment rationalism, featuring horror, mystery, superstition, madness, supernatural elements, and revenge. Early examples include Horace Walpole's *Castle of Otranto*, Matthew Gregory Lewis' *Monk*, Mary Shelley's *Frankenstein*, and Bram Stoker's *Dracula*. In America, Edgar Allan Poe wrote many Gothic works. Contemporary novelist Anne Rice has penned many Gothic novels under the pseudonym A. N. Roquelaure. Psychological novels, originating in 17th-century France, explore characters' motivations. Examples include Abbé Prévost's *Manon Lescaut*; George Eliot's novels; Fyodor Dostoyevsky's *Crime and Punishment*; Tolstoy's *Anna Karenina*; Gustave Flaubert's *Madame Bovary*; and the novels of Henry James, James Joyce, and Vladimir Nabokov.

Novel of manners

Novels of manners are fictional stories that observe, explore, and analyze the social behaviors of a specific time and place. While deep psychological themes are more universal across different historical periods and countries, the manners of a particular society are shorter-lived and more varied; the novel of manners captures these societal details. Novels of manners can also be regarded as symbolically representing, in artistic form, certain established and secure social orders. Characteristics of novels of manners include descriptions of a society with defined behavioral codes; the use of standardized, impersonal formulas in their language; and inhibition of emotional expression, as contrasted with the strong emotions expressed in romantic or sentimental novels. The novels of Jane Austen are examples of some of the finest novels of manners ever produced. In the 20th century, Evelyn Waugh's *Handful of Dust* is a novel of social manners, and his *Sword of Honour* trilogy is a novel of military manners. Another 20th-century example is *The Unbearable Bassington* by Saki (the pen name of writer H. H. Munro), focusing on Edwardian society.

Western-world sentimental novels

Sentimental love novels originated in the movement of Romanticism. Eighteenth-century examples of novels that depict emotional rather than only physical love include Samuel Richardson's *Pamela* (1740) in English, and Jean-Jacques Rousseau's *Nouvelle Héloïse* (1761) in French. Also in the 18th century, Laurence Sterne's novel *Tristram Shandy* (1760-1767) is an example of a novel with elements of sentimentality. The Victorian era's rejection of emotionalism caused the term "sentimental" to have undesirable connotations. In the 19th century, William Makepeace Thackeray and Charles Dickens, while not considered sentimental novelists by any means, both included sentimental elements in some of their novels: for example, in Dickens' *A Christmas Carol.* A 19th-century author of genuinely sentimental novels was Mrs. Henry Wood (e.g., *East Lynne,* 1861). In the 20th century, Erich Segal's sentimental novel *Love Story* (1970) was a popular bestseller, staying on the New York Times Best Seller List for 41 weeks, and was adapted into a movie (also released in 1970) which was also well received by both movie audiences and film critics, receiving numerous award nominations.

Epistolary novel

Epistolary novels are told in the form of letters written by their characters rather than in narrative form. Samuel Richardson, the best-known author of epistolary novels like *Pamela* (1740) and *Clarissa* (1748), widely influenced early Romantic epistolary novels throughout Europe that freely expressed emotions. Richardson, a printer, published technical manuals on letter-writing for young gentlewomen; his epistolary novels were natural fictional extensions of those nonfictional instructional books. Nineteenth-century English author Wilkie Collins' *The Moonstone* (1868) was a mystery written in epistolary form. By the 20th century, the format of well-composed written letters came to be regarded as artificial and outmoded. English novelist Christopher Isherwood tried to revive the form in *Meeting by the River* (1967), but this was criticized for using chatty and informal letters to tell a story with a serious religious theme. A 20th-century evolution of letters was tape-recording transcripts in French playwright Samuel Beckett's drama *Krapp's Last Tape.* Though evoking modern alienation, Beckett still created a sense of fictional characters' direct communication without author intervention as Richardson had.

Pastoral novels

Pastoral novels and fiction (as well as poetry) lyrically idealize country life as idyllic and utopian, akin to the Garden of Eden. *Daphnis and Chloe*, written by Greek novelist Longus around the second or third century, was pastoral and influenced Elizabethan pastoral romances like Philip Sidney's *Arcadia* and Thomas Lodge's *Rosalynde* (both 1590). William Shakespeare based his play *As You Like It* on *Rosalynde.* Jacques-Henri Bernardin de St. Pierre's French work *Paul et Virginie* (1787) demonstrated the early Romantic view of the innocence and goodness of nature. Later non-pastoral novels like *The Rainbow* (1915) and *Lady Chatterley's Lover* (1928), both by D. H. Lawrence, contain pastoral elements. Growing realism transformed pastoral writing into less ideal and more dystopian, distasteful and ironic depictions of country life in George Eliot's and Thomas Hardy's novels. Saul Bellow's novel *Herzog* (1964) may demonstrate how urban ills highlight an alternative pastoral ideal. Some scholars feel the pastoral satire *Cold Comfort Farm* (1932) by Stella Gibbons (also adapted into a movie) has made British novelists less able to take the pastoral tradition's lyricism seriously.

<u>Bildungsroman</u>

Bildungsroman is German, literally meaning "education novel." This term is also used in English to describe "apprenticeship" novels focusing on coming-of-age stories, including youth's struggles and searches for things such as identity, spiritual understanding, or the meaning in life. Johann Wolfgang von Goethe's *Wilhelm Meisters Lehrjahre* (1796) is credited as the origin. Charles Dickens' two novels *David Copperfield* (1850) and *Great Expectations* (1861) also fit this form. H. G. Wells wrote *bildungsromans* about questing for apprenticeships to address modern life's complications in *Joan and Peter* (1918), and from a Utopian perspective in *The Dream* (1924). School *bildungsromans* include Thomas Hughes' *Tom Brown's School Days* (1857) and Alain-Fournier's *Le Grand Meaulnes* (1913). Many Hermann Hesse novels, including *Demian, Steppenwolf, Siddhartha, Magister Ludi,* and *Under the Wheel* are *bildungsromans* about struggling/searching youth. Samuel Butler's *The Way of All Flesh* (written in 1885 and published in 1903) and James Joyce's *A Portrait of the Artist as a Young Man* (1916) are two outstanding modern examples. Variations include J. D. Salinger's *The Catcher in the Rye* (1951), set both within and beyond school, and William Golding's *Lord of the Flies* (1955), a novel not set in a school but one that is a coming-of-age story nonetheless.

Roman à clef

Roman à clef, French for "novel with a key," means the story needs a real-life frame of reference, or key, for full comprehension. In Geoffrey Chaucer's *Canterbury Tales,* the Nun's Priest's Tale contains details that confuse readers unaware of history about the Earl of Bolingbroke's involvement in an assassination plot. Other literary works fitting this form include John Dryden's political satirical poem *Absalom and Achitophel* (1681), Jonathan Swift's satire *A Tale of a Tub* (1704), and George Orwell's political allegory *Animal Farm* (1945), all of which cannot be understood completely without knowing their camouflaged historical contents. *Roman à clefs* disguise truths too dangerous for authors to state directly. Readers must know about D. H. Lawrence's enemies to comprehend *Aaron's Rod* (1922). To appreciate Aldous Huxley's *Point Counter Point* (1928), readers must realize that the characters Mark Rampion and Denis Burlap respectively represent author Huxley and real-life critic John Middleton Murry. Marcel Proust's *Remembrance of Things Past (À la recherché du temps perdu,* 1871-1922) is informed by his social context. James Joyce's *Finnegans Wake* is an enormous *roman à clef* via multitudinous personal references.

Realism

Realism is a literary form whose goal is to represent reality as faithfully as possible. Its genesis in Western literature was a reaction against the sentimentality and extreme emotionalism of the works written in the literary movement of Romanticism, which championed feelings and their expression. Realists focused in great detail on immediacy of time and place, on specific actions of their characters, and the justifiable consequences of those actions. Some techniques of realism include writing in the vernacular, i.e., the characters' ordinary conversational language; writing in specific dialects used by some characters; and emphasizing the analysis and development of characters more than the analysis and development of plots. Realistic literature often addresses various ethical issues. Historically, realistic works have often concentrated on the middle classes of the authors' societies. Realists eschew treatments that are too dramatic or sensationalistic as exaggerations of the reality that they strive to portray as closely as they are able.

Satire

Satire uses sarcasm, irony, and/or humor as social criticism to lampoon human folly. Unlike realism, which intends to depict reality as it exists without exaggeration, satire often involves creating situations or ideas deliberately exaggerating reality to be ridiculous to illuminate flawed behaviors. Ancient Roman satirists included Horace and Juvenal. Alexander Pope's poem "The Rape of the Lock" satirized the values of fashionable members of the 18th-century upper-middle class, which Pope found shallow and trivial. The theft of a lock of hair from a young woman is blown out of proportion: the poem's characters regard it as seriously as they would a rape. Irishman Jonathan Swift satirized British society, politics, and religion in works like *A Tale of a Tub.* In *A Modest Proposal,* Swift used essay form and mock-serious tone, satirically "proposing" cannibalism of babies and children as a solution to poverty and overpopulation. He satirized petty political disputes in *Gulliver's Travels.* Swift was known as a master of the ancient Roman Horatian and Juvenalian satirical styles.

Historical context of change between Middle Ages and Renaissance

The ancient Greek Athenian elite were a highly educated society, developing philosophies and writing about principles for creating poetry and drama. During the Roman Empire, the Romans assimilated and adapted the culture of the Greeks they conquered into their own society. For example, the gods of Roman mythology were essentially the same as in Greek myth, only renamed in Latin. However, after the fall of the Roman Empire, the many European countries formerly united under Roman rule became fragmented. There followed a 1,000-year period of general public ignorance and illiteracy—called the Dark Ages as well as the Middle Ages. Only the Church remained a bastion of literacy: monks and priests laboriously copied manuscripts one at a time by hand. Johannes Gutenberg's 1450 invention of the movable-type printing press changed everything: multiple copies of books could be printed much faster. This enabled a public return to literacy, leading to the Renaissance, or "rebirth"—reviving access and interest for Greek and Roman Classics, and generating a creative explosion in all arts.

Christopher Marlowe

Christopher Marlowe was born the same year as William Shakespeare (1564), but died at the age of 29. Some people have proposed Marlowe could have falsified his death and continued writing under Shakespeare's name. Most scholars reject this theory. In the 19th century, an anonymous author also suggested Shakespeare temporarily wrote under the name Christopher Marlowe. In *As You Like It,* Shakespeare pays homage to Marlowe, quoting "Hero and Leander"; in Touchstone's dialogue, mentioning death over a "reckoning," thought to allude to Marlowe's presumed murder over money he owed; and including "in a little room," words from Marlowe's *Jew of Malta.* Shakespeare recycled Marlowe's themes from *Dido* in *Antony and Cleopatra,* from *Jew of Malta* in *The Merchant of Venice,* from *Edward II* in *Richard II,* and from *Dr. Faustus* in *Macbeth.* A speech in *Hamlet* echoes *Dido.* Shakespeare's character Marcadé in *Love's Labour's Lost* acknowledges the god Mercury in Marlowe's play *The Massacre at Paris,* with whom Marlowe identified himself in his poem "Hero and Leander."

Comedy

Today, most people equate the idea of comedy with something funny, and of tragedy with something sad. However, the ancient Greeks defined these differently. Comedy needed not be humorous or amusing: it needed only a happy ending. The Classical definition of comedy, as included in Aristotle's works, is any work that tells the story of a sympathetic main character's rise in fortune. According to Aristotle, protagonists needed not be heroic or exemplary: he described them as not evil or worthless, but as ordinary people—"average to below average" morally. Comic figures who were sympathetic were usually of humble origins, proving their "natural nobility" through their actions as their characters were tested, rather than characters born into nobility— who were often satirized as self-important or pompous. Comedy's mirror-image was tragedy, portraying a hero's fall in fortune. While by Classical definitions, tragedies could be sad, Aristotle went further, requiring their depicting suffering and pain to cause "terror and pity" in audiences; that tragic heroes be basically good, admirable, and/or noble; and that their downfalls be through personal action, choice, or error, not by bad luck or accident.

Shakespearean comedy

Aristotle defined comedy not as a humorous drama, but as one in which the protagonist experiences a rise in fortune, and which has a happy ending. Such Classical definitions of drama were very popular during the Renaissance and the Elizabethan period within it, when William Shakespeare was writing. All of Shakespeare's comedies, as opposed to his tragedies, had happy endings. Not all of them are equally funny, although many are. His play *A Comedy of Errors* fits the comedic genre of the farce. Based and expanding on a Classical Roman comedy, it includes slapstick humor and mistaken identity—not deliberate, but accidental, and is generally light and "fluffy," with disturbing topics only hinted at but soon dissolved in laughter and love. Shakespeare's *Much Ado About Nothing* is a romantic comedy. It incorporates some more serious themes, including social mores; perceived infidelity; marriage's duality as both trap and ideal; and honor and its loss, public shame, and deception, but also much witty dialogue and a happy ending.

Dramatic comedies

Three types of dramas classified as comedy include the farce, the romantic comedy, and the satirical comedy. The farce is a zany, goofy type of comedy that includes pratfalls and other forms of slapstick humor. The characters appearing in a farce tend to be ridiculous or fantastical in nature, markedly more so than characters in other types of comedies. Another aspect of farce is inclusion in the plot of situations so improbable as to be unbelievable—albeit still highly entertaining. Farcical plots frequently feature complications and twists that can go on almost indefinitely. They also often include wildly incredible coincidences that rarely if ever would occur in real life. Mistaken identity, deceptions, and disguises are common devices used in farcical comedies. Shakespeare's play *The Comedy of Errors,* with its cases of accidental mistaken identity and slapstick, is an example of farce. Contemporary examples of farce include the Marx Brothers' movies, the Three Stooges movies and TV episodes, and the *Pink Panther* movie series.

Romantic comedy

Romantic comedies are probably the most popular of the types of comedy, in both live theater performances and movies. They include not only humor and a happy ending, but also love. In the typical plot of a romantic comedy, two people well suited to one another are either brought together for the first time, or reconciled after being separated. They are usually both sympathetic characters, and seem destined to be together yet separated by some intervening complication— such as an ex-lover(s), interfering parents or friends, or differences in social class. The happy ending is achieved through the lovers' overcoming all these obstacles. William Shakespeare's *Much Ado About Nothing;* Walt Disney's version of *Cinderella* (1950); Broadway musical *Guys and Dolls* (1955); and movies *When Harry Met Sally* (1989), starring Billy Crystal and Meg Ryan, written by Nora Ephron; *Sleepless in Seattle* (1993) and *You've Got Mail* (1998), both directed by Nora Ephron and starring Tom Hanks and Meg Ryan; and *Forget Paris* (1995), co-written, produced, directed by and starring Billy Crystal, are examples of romantic comedies.

<u>Satirical comedy and black comedy</u>

Satires generally mock and lampoon human foolishness and vices. Satirical comedies fit the classical definition of comedy by depicting a main character's rise in fortune, but they also fit the definition of satire by making that main character either a fool, morally corrupt, or cynical in attitude. All or most of the other characters in the satirical comedy display similar foibles. These include cuckolded spouses, dupes, and other gullible types; tricksters, con artists, and criminals; hypocrites; fortune seekers; and other deceptive types who prey on the latter, who are their willing and unwitting victims. Some classical examples of satirical comedies include *The Birds* by ancient Greek comedic playwright Aristophanes, and *Volpone* by 17th-century poet and playwright Ben Jonson, who made the comedy of humors popular. When satirical comedy is extended to extremes, it becomes black comedy, wherein the comedic occurrences are grotesque or terrible. Contemporary movie examples include Quentin Tarantino's *Pulp Fiction* (1994) and the Coen brothers' *Fargo* (1996).

Metaphysical poets

Dr. Samuel Johnson, a famous 18th-century figure, who wrote philosophy, poetry, and authoritative essays on literature, coined the term "Metaphysical Poets" to describe a number of mainly 17th-century lyric poets who shared certain elements of content and style in common. The poets included John Donne (considered the founder of the Metaphysical Poets), George Herbert, Andrew Marvell, Abraham Cowley, John Cleveland, Richard Crashaw, Thomas Traherne, and Henry Vaughan. These poets encouraged readers to see the world from new and unaccustomed perspectives by shocking and surprising them through their use of paradoxes; contradictory imagery; original syntax; combinations of religious, philosophical, and artistic images; subtle argumentation; and extended metaphors called conceits. Unlike their contemporaries, they did not allude to classical mythology or nature imagery in their poetry, but to current geographical and scientific discoveries. Some, like Donne, showed Neo-Platonist influences—like the idea that a lover's beauty reflected Eternity's perfect beauty. They were called metaphysical for their transcendence—Donne in particular—of typical 17th-century rationalism's hierarchical organization through their adventurous exploration of religion, ideas, emotions, and language.

Sir Thomas Browne

Sir Thomas Browne (1605-1682) was a British polymath, a practicing medical physician, scientist, religious philosopher, and author. His writing style was extraordinary and varied widely across his works. Browne was knighted in 1671 by King Charles II in recognition of his accomplishments. Among English-language writers, he has received widespread regard for his high originality. His thinking was paradoxical in that his interests embraced mysticism and other ancient esoteric disciplines, yet also a strong Christian religiosity and the nascent field of inductive scientific reasoning. His original mind produced many fresh ideas and perspectives, expressed with great complexity of both thought and language. Today he is less known and understood than many great authors, due not only to his advanced ideas and wording, but also to his many references to Biblical, Classical, and esoteric sources. The Oxford English Dictionary credits him with coining over 100 new English vocabulary words, most of which are commonly recognized today. Famous authors have consistently admired and cited him across all four centuries since his death.

Sir Thomas Browne's writing style influenced the literary world from his lifetime in the 17th century through the 21st century today. Eighteenth-century literary authority Dr. Samuel Johnson noted Browne's diverse linguistic sources, as well as his transfer of terminology among different artistic disciplines. He credited Browne with having "augmented our philosophical diction"; defended Browne's "uncommon words and expressions," observing that "he had uncommon sentiments"; and

- 23 -

explained that Browne coined new vocabulary because he "was not content to express, in many words, that idea for which any language could supply a single term." The Oxford English Dictionary lists Browne as number 70 of top-cited sources; contains 803 Browne entries; quotes him in 3,636 entries; and credits him with originating over 100 English words, including the following 38: ambidextrous, analogous, approximate, ascetic, anomalous, carnivorous, coexistence, coma, compensate, computer, cryptography, cylindrical, disruption, electricity, exhaustion, ferocious, follicle, generator, gymnastic, herbaceous, insecurity, indigenous, jocularity, literary, locomotion, medical, migrant, mucous, prairie, prostate, polarity, precocious, pubescent, therapeutic, suicide, ulterior, ultimate, and veterinarian. (Hilton, OED, 8/12)

Romanticism

The height of the Romantic movement occurred in the first half of the 19th century. It identified with and gained momentum from the French Revolution (1789) against the political and social standards of the aristocracy and its overthrowing of them. Romanticism was also part of the Counter-Enlightenment, a reaction of backlash against the Enlightenment's insistence on rationalism, scientific treatment of nature, and denial of emotionalism. Though expressed most overtly in the creative arts, Romanticism also affected politics, historiography, natural sciences, and education. Though often associated with radical, progressive, and liberal politics, it also included conservatism, especially in its influences on increased nationalism in many countries. The Romantics championed individual heroes, artists, and pioneers; freedom of expression; the exotic; and the power of the individual imagination. American authors Edgar Allan Poe and Nathaniel Hawthorne, Laurence Sterne in England, and Johann Wolfgang von Goethe in Germany were included among well-known Romantic authors. The six major English Romantic poets were William Blake, William Wordsworth, Samuel Taylor Coleridge, Lord Byron, Percy Bysshe Shelley, and John Keats.

William Blake

William Blake (1757-1827) is considered one of the major English Romantic poets. He was also an artist and printmaker. In addition to his brilliant poetry, he produced paintings, drawings, and notably, engravings and etchings, impressive for their technical expertise, artistic beauty, and spiritual subject matter. Because he held many idiosyncratic opinions, and moreover because he was subject to visions, reporting that he saw angels in the trees and other unusual claims, Blake was often thought crazy by others during his life, though others believed him angelic and/or blessed. His work's creative, expressive character, and its mystical and philosophical elements, led people to consider him both precursor to and member of Romanticism, and a singular, original, unclassifiable artist at the same time. Blake illustrated most of his poetry with his own hand-colored, illuminated printing. He also partially illustrated Dante's *Divine Comedy* a year before dying; the small portion he completed was highly praised. His best-known poetry includes *Songs of Innocence and of Experience, The Book of Thel, The Marriage of Heaven and Hell*, and *Jerusalem*.

William Wordsworth

William Wordsworth (1770-1850) was instrumental in establishing Romanticism when he and Samuel Taylor Coleridge, another major English Romantic poet, collaboratively published *Lyrical Ballads* (1798). Wordsworth's "Preface to Lyrical Ballads" is considered a manifesto of English Romantic literary theory and criticism. In it, Wordsworth described the elements of a new kind of poetry, which he characterized as using "real language of men" rather than traditional 18th-century poetic style. In this Preface he also defined poetry as "the spontaneous overflow of powerful feelings [which] takes its origin from emotion recollected in tranquility." *Lyrical Ballads* included the famous works "The Rime of the Ancient Mariner" by Coleridge, and "Tintern Abbey" by Wordsworth. His semi-autobiographical poem, known during his life as "the poem to Coleridge," was published posthumously, entitled *The Prelude* and regarded as his major work. Wordsworth was England's Poet Laureate from 1843-1850. Among many others, his poems included "Tintern Abbey," "I Wandered Lonely as a Cloud" (often called "Daffodils"), "Ode: Intimations of Immortality," "Westminster Bridge," and "The World Is Too Much with Us."

Samuel Taylor Coleridge

One of the six major Romantic English Poets, Samuel Taylor Coleridge (1772-1834) was also a philosopher and literary critic, and close friends fellow Romantic poet William Wordsworth, with whom he collaborated in publishing *Lyrical Ballads,* launching the Romantic movement. He wrote very influential literary criticism, including the major two-volume autobiographical, meditative discourse *Biographia Literaria* (1817). Coleridge acquainted English-language intellectuals with the German idealist philosophy. He also coined many now familiar philosophical and literary terms, like "the willing suspension of disbelief," meaning that readers would voluntarily withhold judgment of implausible stories if their authors could impart "human interest and a semblance of truth" to them. He strongly influenced the American Transcendentalists, including Ralph Waldo Emerson. Coleridge's poem *Love,* a ballad (written to Sara Hutchinson), inspired John Keats' poem "La Belle Dame Sans Merci." He is credited with the origin of "Conversational Poetry" and Wordsworth's adoption of it. Some of his best-known works include "The Rime of the Ancient Mariner," "Christabel," "Kubla Khan," "The Nightingale," "Dejection: An Ode," and "To William Wordsworth."

John Keats

John Keats (1795-1821), despite his short life, was a major English Romantic poet. He is known for his six Odes: "Ode on a Grecian Urn," "Ode on Indolence," "Ode on Melancholy," "Ode to a Nightingale," "Ode to Psyche," and "To Autumn." Other notable works include the sonnet "O Solitude," "Endymion," "La Belle Dame Sans Merci," "Hyperion," and the collection *Lamia, Isabella, The Eve of St. Agnes and Other Poems*. The intensity and maturity he achieved in his poetry within a period of only around six years are often remarked since his death, though during life he felt he accomplished nothing lasting. He wrote a year before dying, "I have left no immortal work behind me—nothing to make my friends proud of my memory—but I have lov'd the principle of beauty in all things, and if I had had time I would have made myself remember'd." He was proven wrong. His verse from "Ode on a Grecian Urn" is renowned: "'Beauty is truth, truth beauty'—that is all / Ye know on earth, and all ye need to know."

George Gordon, Lord Byron

George Gordon Byron, commonly known as Lord Byron (1788-1824) was a major English Romantic poet. He is known for long narrative poems "Don Juan," "Childe Harold's Pilgrimage," and the shorter lyric poem "She Walks in Beauty." The aristocratic Byron travelled throughout Europe, living in Italy for seven years. He fought in the Greek War of Independence against the Ottoman Empire, making him a national hero in Greece, before dying a year later from a fever contracted there. He was the most notoriously profligate and flamboyant Romantic poet, with reckless behaviors including multiple bisexual love affairs, adultery, rumored incest, self-exile, and incurring enormous debts. He became friends with fellow Romantic writers Percy Bysshe Shelley, the future Mary Shelley, and John Polidori. Their shared fantasy writing at a Swiss villa the summer of 1816 resulted in Mary Shelley's *Frankenstein*, Byron's *Fragment of a Novel*, and was the inspiration for Polidori's *The Vampyre* establishing the romantic vampire genre. Byron also wrote linguistic volumes on American and Armenian grammars. He loved and kept many animals. His name is synonymous today with the mercurial Romantic.

Percy Bysshe Shelley

Percy Bysshe Shelley (1792-1822), a major English Romantic poet, was not famous during life but became so after death, particularly for his lyric poetry. His best-known works include "Ozymandias," "Ode to the West Wind," "To a Skylark," "Music," "When Soft Voices Die," "The Cloud," "The Masque of Anarchy"; longer poems "Queen Mab"/"The Daemon of the World" and "Adonaïs"; and the verse drama *Prometheus Unbound.* Shelley's second wife, Mary Shelley, was the daughter of his mentor William Godwin and the famous feminist Mary Wollstonecraft (*A Vindication of the Rights of Woman*), and became famous for her Gothic novel *Frankenstein.* Early in his career Shelley was influenced by William Wordsworth's Romantic poetry, and wrote the long poem *Alastor, or the Spirit of Solitude.* Soon thereafter he met Lord Byron, and was inspired to write "Hymn to Intellectual Beauty". He composed "Mont Blanc," inspired by touring the French Alpine commune Chamonix-Mont-Blanc. Shelley also encouraged Byron to compose his epic poem *Don Juan.* Shelley inspired Henry David Thoreau, Mahatma Gandhi, and others to civil disobedience, nonviolent resistance, vegetarianism, and animal rights.

William Butler Yeats

William Butler Yeats (1865-1939) was among the greatest influences in 20th-century English literature. He was instrumental in the Celtic Revival/Irish Literary Revival, founding and initially running the Abbey Theatre, and was the first Irishman awarded the Nobel Prize for Literature (1923). An Irish Nationalist, he was passionately involved in politics. Yeats was believed transitional from Romanticism to Modernism. His earlier verses were lyrical, but later became realistic, symbolic, and apocalyptic. He was fascinated with Irish legend, occult subjects, and historical cycles—"gyres." He incorporated Irish folklore, mythology, and legends in "The Stolen Child," "The Wanderings of Oisin," "The Death of Cuchulain," "Who Goes with Fergus?" and "The Song of Wandering Aengus." Early collections included *The Secret Rose* and *The Wind Among the Reeds.* His later, most significant poetry collections include *The Green Helmet, Responsibilities, The Tower,* and *The Winding Stair.* Yeats's visionary, apocalyptic (1920) poem "The Second Coming" reflects his belief that his times were the anarchic end of the Christian cycle/gyre: "what rough beast, its hour come round at last, / Slouches toward Bethlehem to be born?"

Elizabethan literature

Elizabethan literature is English literature written during the reign of Elizabeth I. This includes the Early Tudor period and ends with the death of Shakespeare. Elizabethan literature reflects the national pride felt during the reign of the Virgin Queen. The language of the period is highly colored, rich, and ornamented. Elizabethan poetry saw the birth of the sonnet and the epic poem "The Faerie Queen," written by Edmund Spenser. The crowning achievement of the period was Elizabethan drama, which became hugely popular with the people. Authors such as Thomas Kyd and Christopher Marlowe ushered in this golden age of drama, followed by Thomas Dekker, George Chapman, and Thomas Heywood. William Shakespeare's elegant histories, comedies, and tragedies displayed the genius of this dramatic period. The death of the queen, followed closely by Shakespeare's passing, brought a close to this golden period of drama.

Geoffrey Chaucer

Geoffrey Chaucer is regarded as the greatest of the Middle English authors. Chaucer wrote works of narrative poetry, and his greatest achievement is "The Canterbury Tales." "The Canterbury Tales" presents 24 stories told by a group of pilgrims traveling to Canterbury. The tales range over many subjects, including romances, religious themes, and bawdy verses. The genius of the work is the rich characterization of the pilgrims, done with consummate skill, insight, and humor. Chaucer was influenced by Dante and Boccacio, whom he read on visits to Italy. Chaucer's writing expanded the scope of Middle English writing beyond provincial life and moral ideals to a more inclusive view of the world. Chaucer was born in England in 1343 and entered royal service in his teens. He held numerous political and diplomatic posts over the years, traveling and serving across Europe. Chaucer was widely read, and he incorporated much that he learned in his travels in his writing. Chaucer died in England in 1400.

Sir Thomas Malory

Sir Thomas Malory is thought to be Sir Thomas Malory of Warwickshire, although this is still the subject of academic debate. His major work, *Le Morte D'Arthur*, is a collection of prose stories based on Arthurian legend and oral traditions. These tales were the first collection of works on the legends of King Arthur and the Knights of the Round Table. They tell the stories of the kingdom of Camelot and the epic adventures of its characters. Famous characters—such as King Arthur, Sir Lancelot, Sir Gawain, and Queen Guinevere—have served as models for countless adaptations and are familiar figures in folk literature. The details of Thomas Malory's life are a mystery, but certain facts are known, chiefly from his works. Born in 1408 in England, Malory completed his literary masterpiece while imprisoned for criminal activity. Malory petitioned for release upon completion of his manuscript, but this was denied, and he died in jail in 1471. His great work was published posthumously in 1485.

Christopher Marlowe

Christopher Marlowe was an English author and playwright who produced a remarkable body of work in his short life. He gained acclaim as the most important Elizabethan dramatist before Shakespeare. His most successful plays include *Edward II, Tamburlaine the Great, Dr. Faustus*, and *The Jew of Malta*. Marlowe's writing is characterized by passionate protagonists, the strength of his verse, and his brilliant plotting. Scholars believe that some works attributed to Shakespeare may have been written in whole or part by Marlowe. Marlowe's poetry is accomplished, the best known being the verse that begins, "Come live with me and be my love." Marlowe, the son of a cobbler, was born in Canterbury in 1564 and educated at Cambridge. He lived a turbulent and sometimes violent life, engaging in criminal activity ranging from forgery to espionage. He was killed in 1593 at age 29 in a brawl over a tavern bill, cutting short a brilliant talent.

William Shakespeare

William Shakespeare, arguably the greatest playwright ever, has influenced world literature for the last 400 years. Shakespeare's genius was the ability to create works that capture the drama of human conflict and weakness while developing characters that suffer man's deepest existential anxieties. Master of drama and poetry alike, his writing is without peer in literary history. He wrote tragedies, histories, comedies, sonnets, and narrative poems. His works have been translated into scores of languages and adapted for film, opera, and ballet. Some of his best-known works include *Hamlet, Henry V, Romeo and Juliet*, and *Macbeth*. Shakespeare was born in Stratford-upon-Avon in 1564 and received a classical education. He married Anne Hathaway and spent most of his professional life in London, where he used the Globe Theatre as his base from 1599 on. He was well established as an actor and playwright as early as 1592 and wrote a series of brilliant sonnets in 1609. Shakespeare died in England in 1616 and is buried in Stratford.

Edmund Spenser

Edmund Spenser was one of the greatest Elizabethan poets, famed for his evocative sonnets and rich epic poetry. His most famous work is "The Faerie Queen," a heroic romance narrating the exploits of 12 knights. Published in 1596, it introduced a new poetic form, the Spenserian stanza based on an Italian poetic scheme. "The Faerie Queen" includes a moral allegory in an epic narrative. Spenser was a prolific author, penning sonnet sequences and notable short verse.

Born in London in 1552, Spenser was educated at Cambridge and joined the household of the Earl of Leicester, where he wrote his first work, *The Shepherdess Calendar,* comprised of 12 pastoral poems, in 1579. Spenser moved to Ireland in 1590, where he ran an estate in Cork. There he wrote an elegy for his friend Sir Philip Sidney called "Astrophel." Spenser returned to London, where he died in 1599, his place in literary history assured.

Samuel Pepys

Samuel Pepys's fame rests on his *Diary*, published in full in 1828. This work provides an insightful and unusually candid view of 17th-century court life. Pepys chronicled events in his own life as well as important historical occasions, such as the coronation of Charles II. Pepys left us the most dramatic account of the great fire in London and the Black Plague. His legacy is to provide a window into the history of his time through his *Diary*. Pepys was born in London in 1633, the son of a tailor. Educated at Cambridge, he served as a naval officer, member of Parliament, and president of The Royal Society. These positions gave him an entree into the high society of London, where he was feted and honored over the years. His personal life was marred by tragedy with the death of a beloved young wife. Pepys's *Diary* went undiscovered for over 100 years until it was found in Cambridge in 1825. Pepys died in London at age 70 in 1703, at the height of his fame.

John Dryden

John Dryden was a man for all seasons, a poet, playwright, and literary critic. He wrote a number of popular plays, the most important being *The Wild Gallant, All for Love, The Maiden Queen,* and *The Indian Queen.* Equally adept as a poet, Dryden won royal favor with his poem "To His Sacred Majesty," written for Charles II's restoration to the throne. His verse satires were considered masterpieces. He served as Poet Laureate of England from 1668 to 1688 and was revered in English society. Born in rural England in 1631, Dryden moved to London in 1655, where he remained for the rest of his life. He was appointed the royal historiographer in 1670. When James II was crowned, Dryden converted to Catholicism in the 1680s. His last years were spent translating several of the ancient classics. He died in London in 1700. His career was illustrious, and he became one of the most honored men in England.

John Bunyan

John Bunyan's literary reputation rests on his masterpiece, *The Pilgrim's Progress*, written in 1684. This work is a religious allegory that became the best seller of its day. Read by both Catholics and Protestants, it recounts the spiritual journey of humankind. Bunyan was born in 1628 in Bedford, in the English countryside, and served in Cromwell's army during the English Civil War. A spiritual maverick, he joined a nonconformist church in 1653 and became a popular preacher. In 1660, Bunyan was arrested for preaching without a permit and spent 12 years in prison. This was a time of productive writing for Bunyan, who penned *Grace Abounding to the Chief of Sinners, The Holy War,* and other spiritual tracts. Bunyan also began work on his magnum opus, *The Pilgrim's Progress*, while in prison. He was a vocal opponent of Quakerism, which he denounced in *A Vindication* in 1657. Bunyan was an active writer and preacher until his death in 1688.

Alexander Pope

Alexander Pope, the great English poet and satirist, was born in London in 1688. Pope's style features biting wit, excellent command of formal poetry, and a particular kind of verse that is both insightful and dramatic. Among his numerous works is his great satire, "The Rape of the Lock," narrating a feud started over a lock of hair. "An Essay on Criticism," Pope's poem about writing, launched his career in 1711. He was to produce a body of work noted chiefly for satire and brilliant essays, including translations of Homer's "Iliad" and "Odyssey." Pope also edited a controversial edition of Shakespeare, which won him notoriety. Pope had little formal education and was raised a Catholic at a time that anti-Catholic feeling ran high in England. He contracted an unknown illness when he was a child, leaving him a semi-invalid and stunting his growth. Despite these handicaps, Pope became one of the giants of English literature until his death in London in 1744.

Daniel Defoe

Daniel Defoe, born in London, had a varied and prolific literary career. He produced more than 500 books, the most important being *Robinson Crusoe* and *Moll Flanders*. Generally considered England's first novelist, Defoe was a keen observer of life and was able to translate this into riveting characters in his novels. Defoe was an eclectic author, writing essays and nonfiction, and working as a journalist during his productive years. His editorship of the *Review* from 1704 to 1713 made him the finest journalist of his day. Defoe was successful in both business and politics, becoming a strong supporter of William of Orange. His political pamphlets earned him a short term in prison. Rescued by a Tory politician, Defoe became a well-known political pamphleteer, writing arguments for the Tory party. Defoe died in London in 1731, at the apex of his journalistic career.

Jonathan Swift

Jonathan Swift, Irish satirist, wrote on a wide variety of subjects, including economics, politics, society, and manners. His legacy was established by *Gulliver's Travels*, his blistering satire on the human condition published in 1726. Other well-known works include *Tale of a Tub*, a satire on the church; *Drapier's Letters*, an influential tract on Irish politics; and *A Modest Proposal*, a suggestion that Irish children be fattened and used as food for the rich. Born in Dublin in 1667, Swift received an excellent education at Trinity College and Oxford. Ordained a priest in the Church of Ireland in 1694, Swift served for ten years before becoming secretary to a prominent diplomat. Swift lived for years in both London and Dublin, where his reputation as a satirist grew. His health began to decline in the 1730s, and he was declared incompetent and assigned a guardian. Upon his death in 1745, his estate granted a large sum to found a hospital for the mentally ill.

Henry Fielding

Henry Fielding, English novelist and playwright, is considered a pioneer in novel writing. Fielding wrote more than 25 plays before turning his talent to novels. His best-known work is *Tom Jones*, and other notable works include *Joseph Andrews, Amelia, Shamela*, and *The Life of Mr. Jonathan Wild the Great*. He also published a newspaper, *The Champion*, which was highly successful. He was adept in social satire and comedy, which are best exemplified by *Tom Jones*. Born in Somerset in 1707, Fielding became active in politics in his late twenties. His strong anti-Jacobite essays gained Fielding political favor, and he served for many years as a judge in London. When political favor turned against him, Fielding concentrated on his writing, producing several late novels of note. Fielding died in 1754.

Samuel Johnson

Samuel Johnson—the English poet, essayist, biographer, and lexicographer—dominated the literary period of mid-18th-century England. In 1746, he began to organize the first dictionary of the English language. He completed the task in 1755, and it was hailed as a major literary accomplishment and made Johnson's reputation. A prolific essayist and journalist, his prose was celebrated for its keen observation of human folly and frailty. Johnson's other major works include *Lives of the Poets*, *Rasselas*, and "The Vanity of Human Wishes," considered his greatest poem. "Irene," a verse tragedy, was produced for the stage in 1746. Johnson was born in Lichfield in 1709 and worked as a schoolmaster there for many years. He moved to London to become a writer and succeeded beyond his dreams. Johnson was immortalized by James Boswell, his friend and confidant, in *The Life of Samuel Johnson*. Johnson was such a giant literary figure that, upon his death in 1784, his era became known as the Age of Johnson.

Robert Burns

Robert Burns, the famed Scottish poet, became the most well-known literary figure in Scotland. Burns's work includes some of the best-known poetry in the English language, including "Auld Lang Syne," "A Red, Red, Rose," and the long narrative poem "Tam o' Shanter." His first anthology of poetry was *Poems, Chiefly in the Scottish Dialect*, which became an instant success and led to his long and distinguished career. Burns spent much of his life collecting and editing traditional Scottish airs. Born to a poor family in 1759, Burns spent much of his life working the land on the family farm. He was a rebel by nature and supported the French Revolution openly. Burns died in 1796, having lived only 37 years but enshrining his poetry in the hearts of all Scots. His reputation has grown over the generations, and Burns is recognized as a major poet who transcended his nationalistic feelings.

James Boswell

James Boswell was a Scottish biographer and essayist. His most important work is *The Life of Samuel Johnson*, still regarded as one of the finest biographies in the English language. He also wrote a political history, *An Account of Corsica*, which narrates that island's movement for independence. Boswell's diaries, which include astute observations on society and manners of his day, were published after his death. Born in Edinburgh in 1740, Boswell immigrated to England, where he met Samuel Johnson in 1763. Boswell neglected his own law practice to devote his life to Johnson and his biography. He spent much of the next 25 years traveling and living with Johnson. This was a unique friendship of two notable literary figures that resulted in a biography of great power and feeling. Boswell died at age 54, leaving a legacy for all future biographers.

William Blake

William Blake, poet and artist, launched his career in 1789 with the publication of *Songs of Innocence*. His most important prose work, *The Marriage of Heaven and Hell*, rejects rationalism in favor of mystical faith. His masterpiece, *Songs of Innocence and Experience*, was written in 1794. Blake pioneered what he termed prophetic books, which purport to predict the futures of America and Europe. His epic poem "Jerusalem" sought to imagine the existence of spirit after death.

Blake was a master illustrator and true mystic. Born in 1757, he had visions of angels, devils, and poets as a young child. His illustrations were extraordinary, and he worked on Dante's "Divine Comedy" and other major works. Blake's art and poetry are a heady mix of symbolism, mystic vision, and powerful emotion. Thought by many to be mad, Blake remained true to his vision and died in England in 1827 at the age of 69. Few men or women equaled Blake's extravagant perceptions and his ability to put them into words and art.

William Wordsworth

William Wordsworth was a catalyst for the Romantic movement in English literature. A close friendship with Samuel Taylor Coleridge resulted in the publication of a joint venture, *Lyrical Ballads*, which sounded a new voice in poetry. The neoclassical model then in vogue was renounced for poetry written in the manner in which people actually spoke. Wordsworth's best-known volumes include *Poems: in Two Volumes* and his greatest work, *The Prelude*, an epic based on the author's life. Wordsworth was born in the Lake District of England in 1770. Educated at Cambridge, he traveled extensively in Europe and became fired up with the spirit of the French Revolution. In his early thirties, Wordsworth married and retired to his home in Grasmere, where he lived the remainder of his life. He held the position of Poet Laureate of England from 1843 until his death in 1850. One of the most loved poems in the English language is "Tintern Abbey," published in his first slender volume of poems in 1798.

Samuel Taylor Coleridge

Samuel Taylor Coleridge was a leading figure in English Romanticism. His partnership with the young William Wordsworth blossomed with the publication of *Lyrical Ballads* in 1798. The first poem in this book is Coleridge's "The Rime of the Ancient Mariner," a spectacular start to a most successful career. Coleridge's creative ideas on poetic form and his original and striking use of language are his contributions to English literature. Other poems of this period include "Christobel" and "Kubla Kahn." Coleridge was a tragic figure in English literature. Born in the West Country in 1772, and educated at Cambridge, he married hastily and unhappily. In later life, he moved to the Lake District to be close to William Wordsworth, his lifetime friend. Coleridge became an opium addict and his marriage failed during this time. He had an unrequited love affair with Sara Hutchinson, the sister of Wordsworth's fiancée. These travails prevented Coleridge from creative work for many years, and his body of poetry is small. This unhappy but brilliant figure died in 1834.

Jane Austen

Jane Austen was an English novelist of enduring popularity. Considered by some to be a founder of the modern novel, Austen narrated the everyday life of country gentry in the latter part of the 18th century. She combined keen observation, sharp wit, and memorable characters to create a much-loved body of work. *Northanger Abbey, Sense and Sensibility*, and *Pride and Prejudice* were written in the 1790s but not published until 10 years later. *Emma, Mansfield Park*, and *Persuasion* were the fruits of her later work. Her parodies of Gothic romances and novels of courtship are unequaled in English literature. A brilliant plotter, her view of character relationships against the complex web of social manners and mores of the day is unequaled. Austen was born in 1775. She was educated at home in the Bath area, where she lived her entire life. All of her novels were published anonymously, and she wrote productively until her death in 1817. Austen's works were a critical success as well as being loved by the public. They have been adapted for the theatre, television, and the cinema.

Lord Byron

George Gordon Byron was an English poet who captured the imagination of the literary world. His most famous work is *Childe Harold's Pilgrimage*, a work of fiction set as a travelogue. Perhaps his masterpiece is the epic satire "Don Juan," a lengthy poem largely autobiographical. Later works of note include *The Prisoner of Chillon and other Poems*, "Manfred," and the satirical poem "Beppo."

Byron was born in 1788 in London and reared in Scotland. He was educated at Cambridge. He was unusually handsome but suffered from a clubfoot. Byron took his seat in the House of Lords briefly before setting out on travels in Europe. He left England for good in 1816, traveling widely in Switzerland, Italy, and Greece. Byron engaged in passionate love affairs, became a revolutionary, and generally captured the imagination of the literary world. He died of a fever in Greece in 1824, and his body was sent back to England for burial.

Sir Walter Scott

Sir Walter Scott was a Scottish poet and novelist. He began his literary career by collecting traditional ballads of Scotland and publishing them in an anthology. He specialized in narrative poetry with a romantic theme, usually set in medieval times. His breakthrough poems include "The Lady of the Lake" and "The Lay of the Last Minstrel." Scott is best known for his historical novels published as the *Waverley Novels*. Included in this group are *Rob Roy, Ivanhoe, Kenilworth*, and *The Bride of Lammermoor*. Scott was born in 1771 in Edinburgh and spent his early life there. His formal training was as a barrister, but he did not practice law for a living. He relied on his popular fiction for his income and was most successful at first. A publishing partnership failed, and Scott was burdened with large debts he spent most of his life repaying. He eventually became financially stable through his popular fiction and works of literary criticism. He died in Scotland in 1832.

Percy Shelley

Shelley was a renowned English poet who used the themes of love, romance, and imagination as his topics. Shelley had a powerful lyrical voice, and his best-known poems—"To a Skylark," "Prometheus Unbound," "Ode to the West Wind," and "Adonais"—exhibit this narrative power. He has remained an inspiration to Romantic poets for centuries. Born in England in 1792, Shelley attended Eton and Oxford before being expelled for publishing a tract on atheism. He traveled widely in Europe, sometimes in the company of Lord Byron. He had a passionate relationship with Mary Shelley, whom he would marry after the death of his first wife. Tragedy stalked Shelley, with the loss of two children and his wife's subsequent breakdown. Besieged by creditors, and in failing health, he continued to write productively until his death by drowning in Italy in 1822. His 29 years were filled with literary accomplishment and personal sorrow.

Mary Shelley

Mary Wollstonecraft Godwin (later Shelley) was an English novelist who won lasting fame with her Gothic horror story *Frankenstein*, published in 1818. This classic narrates the creation of a monster from human body parts. This work has been adapted countless times in many ways, always retaining the flavor of horror and responsibility. Shelley's later works include *Valperga, The Last Man*, and *Lodore*. She also edited numerous editions of Percy Shelley's prose and poetry.

Shelley was born in England in 1797, the only child of radical reformer William Godwin and feminist pioneer Mary Wollstonecraft. She eloped to Europe with Percy Shelley, whom she married in 1813. Mary Shelley suffered greatly from several miscarriages, the death of two children, and ultimately her husband's drowning. She continued to write effectively through these travails, but never again equaled the success of *Frankenstein*. She died in 1851.

John Keats

John Keats was an English poet of great imagination and a romantic nature. His work is best known for six odes written in 1819: "Ode to a Grecian Urn," "Ode to a Nightingale," "Ode to Psyche," "Ode on Melancholy," "Ode on Indolence," and "To Autumn." This poetry abounds in symbolism exploring the frailty of life and the power of creative art. They are felt to be some of the best English poetry extant. Keats's other notable works include "Lamia," "The Eve of St. Agnes," and "Hyperion."

Keats was born in London in 1795 and studied medicine for a time. He soon turned to poetry, mentored by the political radical and writer Leigh Hunt. In 1818, he published his first poetry, "Endymion," an epic based on Greek mythology. Keats contracted tuberculosis, and fell upon hard times. His engagement to Fanny Brawne would end as his health failed. As his disease advanced, Keats moved to Rome hoping the change would help heal him. He died there in 1821 at the tender age of 25.

Charles Dickens

Charles Dickens is thought by some to be England's greatest novelist. In 1837, *The Pickwick Papers*, a comic novel, launched his career. This was followed quickly by *Oliver Twist* (1838), *Nicholas Nickelby* (1839), and *A Christmas Carol* (1843). Dickens had a genius for creating memorable characters, and his ability to evoke a sense of 19th-century England is unmatched. His later works include *David Copperfield* (1850), *Great Expectations* (1861), and *A Tale of Two Cities* (1859).

Charles Dickens was born in Portsmouth in 1812. He worked as a journalist until the success of his novels. Dickens founded and edited several literary magazines, including *Household Words* and *All the Year Round*. Dickens gave reading tours in Europe and the United States that were very popular and drew large crowds. Dickens died in Gad's Hill Place in 1870 and is buried in Westminster Abbey.

Lord Alfred Tennyson

Tennyson was an important English poet of his day, publishing his first work, *Poems, Chiefly Lyrical* in 1830. His subsequent volumes of poetry include *Maud, and Other Poems* (1855), and *Idylls of the King* (1885), an epic poem based on the legend of King Arthur. Later works of note are *Enoch Arden* (1864) and *Demeter and Other Poems* (1889). His best-loved individual poems are "The Charge of the Light Brigade," "Crossing the Bar," and "Mariana." Tennyson wrote of history, honor, and faith, championing Victorian values and mastering the technical elements of poetry. Born in a small village in the north of England in 1809, he was educated at Cambridge and published his first book of verse there. Tennyson was named Poet Laureate of England by Queen Victoria in 1850, succeeding William Wordsworth. He died in England in 1892, his place in history secure.

Charlotte Brontë

Charlotte Brontë, beloved English novelist, wrote stories of independent women in a very personal voice. Her characters were enmeshed in romance and love affairs, even as they lived lives of creativity unusual for the period. Her first novel, *The Professor*, was not published until after her death. Her most powerful work is *Jane Eyre* (1847), a narrative of a young woman and her travails in love and society. Other works include *Shirley* (1849) and *Villete* (1853), based on her sister Emily's experiences living in Europe. Brontë was born in 1816, the daughter of a Yorkshire clergyman. She was sent to a boarding school with harsh living conditions and strict rules of behavior. She would later use the school as a model in *Jane Eyre*. The death of her three siblings in quick succession clouded her life with sadness. She died in England in 1855 at the tender age of 38.

Emily Brontë

Emily Brontë, sister of Charlotte Brontë, and English novelist and poet, produced only one novel in her lifetime. However, her novel *Wuthering Heights* (1847) stands as a testament to her literary talent. A harsh tale, it is the story of the passionate bond between Catherine and Heathcliff, in which two families are jealously destroyed. It is a signature novel of English Romanticism. Emily Brontë was a poet of some skill, her works appearing jointly with her sister's in *Poems by Currer, Ellis, and Acton Bell* (1846). Emily Brontë was born in 1818 in Yorkshire. A unique and mysterious personality, she had few friends except her sister Anne, with whom she maintained a strong bond. Together they created the world of Gondal, an imaginary society that she used extensively in her poetry. In Charlotte's words, "Emily was stronger than a man, simpler than a child." Emily contracted tuberculosis and died at age 30 in 1848.

William Makepeace Thackeray

William Thackeray was a gifted Victorian English novelist and satirist. He started his writing career doing satirical pieces for magazines and weeklies. *The Book of Snobs* (1848) and his masterwork, *Vanity Fair* (1849), both appeared first as serials in periodicals. *Vanity Fair* follows Becky Sharp as she attempts to climb the social ladder of English society. Thackeray's later work includes *Barry Lyndon* (1852), *The Virginians* (1859), and the fictional autobiography *Pendennis* (1850).

Thackeray was born in India, but returned to England for his education at Cambridge. Thackeray was a popular lecturer, and he toured England and America giving talks. His strength as a writer was his ability to describe the moralistic hypocrisy of British society. *Vanity Fair* is his lasting legacy and remains a popular vehicle for adaptations today. Thackeray died in London in 1863.

Anthony Trollope

Trollope was an English novelist of great dexterity. Famed for his evocation of Victorian life and his vivid characters, Trollope was one of the most popular writers of his day. His finest works were two novel sequences, *The Barsetshire Novels*, consisting of four volumes, and the politically themed *Palliser Novels*. His fiction created characters that have stood the test of time and remain fresh today. Trollope's stories have been adapted many times for film, television, and the stage.

Trollope was born in rural London in 1815 and reared there in modest circumstances. He became a civil servant, working for the Royal Mail for many years. He wrote with great energy during his life, producing prose collections, travel books, biographies, and 47 novels. His two-volume *Autobiography* appeared posthumously in 1883. Anthony Trollope died in 1882 at the age of 67.

Elizabeth Barrett Browning

Browning, the well-known poet of Victorian England, is best remembered for her lyrics of love in her *Sonnets from the Portuguese* published in 1850. Her verse "How do I love thee? Let me count the ways" has inspired lovers for over 150 years. Her other major works include "Aurora Leigh" (1857), a verse novel, clearly autobiographical, and *Last Poems* (1852). Browning's poetry evokes England and Italy, where she also lived, and has themes of social justice throughout. Browning was born in Hertfordshire in 1806 and reared on the family farm. Smothered by an overly protective father, the poet suffered poor health and was a semi-recluse. She met Robert Browning in 1845, and they wed the next year. The couple moved to Italy, where Browning improved both her health and disposition. She spent the next 16 years with Browning in a devoted and tender marriage. Elizabeth died in 1861 at age 55.

Robert Browning

Robert Browning was a major Victorian poet known for his skill in characterization, psychological nuances, and colorful and dramatic dialogue. His early work was not well received, but Browning persisted, publishing the successful *Dramatic Lyrics* in 1842. His next collection, *Dramatis Personae* (1864), was his most popular. His technical skill as a poet remains his greatest legacy. Browning was born in London in 1812 and was largely self-educated. He did not achieve public acclaim until later in life. In 1845, Browning began a correspondence with the reclusive Elizabeth Barrett. Against all odds, the couple married in 1846 and created one of the great literary romances. The pair lived a full and devoted life together until Elizabeth's death in 1861. Robert Browning survived and enjoyed his greatest success until his passing in 1889, 28 years after Elizabeth died.

Wilkie Collins

Willkie Collins, English novelist, is considered the pioneer of the mystery story and novel. His first novels were *Antonia, or The Fall of Rome* (1850) and *Basil* (1852), his first novel of suspense. Collins's reputation was made with the publication of *The Woman in White* in 1860. He followed this success with the hugely popular *The Moonstone* in 1868. His later works include *Armadale* (1866), *The New Magdalen* (1873), *The Haunted Hotel* (1879), and *Heart and Science* (1883).

Collins was born in London in 1824 and studied law in college. Although admitted to the bar, he never practiced and soon turned his energies to writing. Befriended by Charles Dickens, who published much of his early work serially in his literary magazines, Collins soon became popular, and the demand for mystery and suspense fiction has never waned. He died in London in 1889.

Christina Rossetti

Christina Rossetti was an accomplished English Victorian poet. Her best-known poetry is contained in *Goblin Market and other Poems* (1862) and *The Prince's Progress and other Poems* (1862). Rossetti published a successful book of children's poetry, *Sing-Song*, in 1872. Her later work is highlighted by *Time Flies*, published in 1885. In 1904, William Rossetti compiled his sister's *Poetical Works* followed by a collection of her letters. A devout high Anglican, her work often reflects her piety. Rossetti was born England in 1830 into a cultured and well-to-do family. After her initial successes, Rossetti was afflicted with Graves' disease and never really recovered her health. Increasingly reclusive, she devoted herself to melancholy religious prose. Rossetti never married, spurning several Catholic suitors, and died at her family home in 1894. She was 64 years old.

Lewis Carroll

Lewis Carroll is the pen name of Charles Lutwidge Dodgson, author of *Alice's Adventures in Wonderland* (1865) and its sequel *Through The Looking Glass* (1871). His literary reputation rests on these two children's books although he wrote several other works, including "The Hunting of the Snark" (1876), *A Tangled Tale* (1885), and *Sylvie and Bruno* (1889). Carroll also wrote several significant works on logic and mathematics. The character of Alice was inspired by his favorite child-friend, Alice Liddell, and her two sisters, to whom he related the story. Carroll was born in England in 1832 and became a mathematics teacher and resident scholar of Christ Church College, Oxford. He assumed his pen name to protect his academic reputation, which might have been affected by authoring children's books. *Alice* brought him instant celebrity and served as an entrée to Victorian society. Carroll remained at Guildford until his death in 1898.

Matthew Arnold

Matthew Arnold, English poet and critic, published six volumes of collected verse in his life, covering a wide range of subjects and moods. Much of his poetry evokes sadness and despair. Best remembered for "Dover Beach" (1867), a poem concerning the loss of faith in the modern age, Arnold was a critic of great importance. Arnold believed that literature and culture should be inculcated into society for moral and spiritual reasons. He was a prolific essayist, writing on religion, social issues, literature, and economics. His literary criticism was influential throughout the world. Arnold was born in Middlesex and educated at Rugby School and Oxford University. He worked for many years as an inspector of schools, a position he valued highly. In 1857, he became professor of poetry at Oxford, where he taught for ten years. His lectures at Oxford became the basis for many of his influential essays over the years. Arnold died in 1888.

W. S. Gilbert

Gilbert was an English playwright and humorist who teamed with Arthur Sullivan to produce the most popular light verse and comic opera in the English language. The partnership was formed in 1870, and they produced 17 operettas together. The most popular include *The Pirates of Penzance* (1879), *The Mikado* (1884), *H.M.S. Pinafore* (1878), and *The Yeoman of the Guard* (1888). Gilbert and Sullivan became the most successful writers of light opera ever. Gilbert was born in London in 1836 and educated at King's College. He began his writing career as a journalist, creating humorous pieces for magazines and weeklies. In 1866, he wrote his first play, *Dulcamara*, for a Christmas presentation. His partnership with Sullivan lasted 20 years and proved to be one of the most successful in music history. Gilbert died in London in 1911.

George Eliot

George Eliot, the pen name of Mary Ann Evans, English novelist and essayist, started her literary career with the publication of *Scenes of a Clerical Life* in 1858. Her most beloved novel is *Middlemarch* (1872), a richly evocative narration of life in an English country town. Her characters are vivid and memorable, particularly her protagonist Dorothea Brooke. Eliot went on to publish a number of fine novels, including *Silas Marner* (1861), *Daniel Deronda* (1876), and *The Mill on the Floss* (1860), thought to be largely autobiographical. Her writing was bold and powerful, and brought new prestige to the 19th-century English novel. Eliot was born in the English countryside in 1819. After her father's death, she served as an editor of *The Westminster Review*, a leading literary journal. Eliot was a free thinker who had a long relationship with a married man, causing a scandal in English society. She died in London in 1880.

Robert Louis Stevenson

Robert Louis Stevenson was a Scottish essayist, novelist, poet, and short-story writer. After writing for weeklies for a few years, his *Treasure Island* (1883) brought him acclaim and wealth. Stevenson followed this success with *Kidnapped* (1886), *The Strange Case of Dr. Jekyll and Mr. Hyde* (1886), and *The Master of Ballantrae* (1889), all critical and financial successes. Stevenson also wrote a book of verse for children, *A Child's Garden of Verses* (1885). His swashbuckling tales and colorful language engaged the fancy of the public, and he retired a wealthy man. Stevenson was born in Edinburgh in 1850 and educated in law. His life was tainted by chronic tuberculosis, and he sought cures and more healthy climates all over the world. Stevenson finally found the relief he sought in Samoa, where he settled and lived the last years of his life. He died there in 1894, at the young age of 44.

Sir Arthur Conan Doyle

Conan Doyle's contribution to literature was the enigmatic detective, Sherlock Holmes. Conan Doyle based his character on a former professor at the University of Edinburgh. Holmes first appeared in 1887 in "A Study in Scarlet," and more stories of the master of deductive reasoning appeared in magazines of the day. These stories were collected and published as *The Adventures of Sherlock Holmes* in 1892. Most memorable among the Holmes novels include *The Hound of the Baskervilles*

(1902), *The Valley of Fear* (1915), and *The Sign of Four* (1890). Conan Doyle also wrote a number of popular historical romances. Conan Doyle was born in Edinburgh in 1859 and educated at Edinburgh. He trained as a physician and practiced medicine in Southsea from 1882 to 1890. The success of his writing allowed him to largely retire from medicine.

Thomas Hardy

Hardy was an English novelist, playwright, and short-story writer. His dark works, often drawn from his own experience, include his first novel *Far from the Madding Crowd* (1874), a tale of a strong woman and her three lovers. Hardy followed this modest success with four powerful novels, *Jude the Obscure* (1895), *The Return of the Native* (1878), *Tess of the D'Urbervilles* (1891), and *The Mayor of Casterbridge* (1896). All these volumes showcase Hardy's skills as storyteller and creator of strong characters. Hardy's poetry is also considered some of the best of his time. Hardy was born in Dorchester in southwest England in 1840. He was trained as an architect, which he gave up for writing when he achieved success. Following the death of his wife, Hardy was guilt-ridden, and his grief fueled the writing of his greatest poetry, *Poems of 1912–13*. Hardy married again and lived until 1928.

Oscar Wilde

Oscar Wilde (originally named Fingal O'Flahertie Wills Wilde) was an Irish writer, poet, critic, and, playwright. Famed for his wit, repartee, and flamboyant lifestyle, Wilde's first success was *The Importance of Being Earnest*, produced in 1895. Some of Wilde's most famous works include *The Picture of Dorian Gray* (1891), a moral allegory, *An Ideal Husband* (1895), *The Happy Price* (1888), and a French drama *Salome* (1896). "De Profundis" (1905) was taken from a letter written in prison. His final work, "The Ballad of Reading Gaol" (1897), is his most famous poem. Wilde was born in Dublin in 1854 and had a classical education. He moved to London, becoming a leader in the Aesthetic movement. Wilde was imprisoned for his homosexual activity, after losing a libel suit against the father of his lover, and spent two years at hard labor. On his release from prison, he moved to France, where he resided until his death in 1900 at the age of 46.

H. G. Wells

H. G. Wells was an English journalist and novelist. Known as a founding father of science fiction, he is now best known for *The Time Machine* (1895), *The Island of Dr. Moreau* (1886), and *The War of the Worlds* (1898), futuristic novels that captured the fancy of the public. He was also admired in his day for his traditional novels, chief of which is *Tono-Bungay* (1909). Wells wrote the respected *The Outline of History* (1920), which is a warning to society to recognize and remedy its problems.

Wells was born in London in 1866 and attended the Normal School of Science. He incorporated his scientific knowledge in his work, which gave it a ring of truth. Wells was a socialist who believed the salvation of society would be its technology. He was active politically his entire life and became an influential advocate of socialism. Wells died in London in 1946, having witnessed the birth of the atomic age.

Bram Stoker

Bram Stoker, born Abraham Stoker, was an Irish novelist. His reputation is based on the creation of one of the most feared and imitated characters in literature, Count Dracula of Transylvania. Count Dracula was a polished and urbane aristocrat and a supernatural creature who feasted on human blood to transform his victims into monsters. The Gothic novel *Dracula*, published in 1897, is based on folklore and the historical figure Vlad the Impaler. Born in Dublin in 1847, Stoker received a classical education at Trinity College, Dublin. He worked in local government for a short time and then became secretary and manager of Sir Henry Irving, a prominent actor in London. Their association would last 27 years before Stoker retired to concentrate on his writing. Bram Stoker died in 1912, his legacy assured in the ever-popular figure of Dracula.

Rudyard Kipling

Kipling, the favorite writer of the British Empire, was a novelist, poet, and short-fiction writer of great skill. His novels of British imperialism, such as *Kim* (1901), carved a unique literary niche for Kipling. His poetry was much beloved; outstanding examples are "Gunga Din," "Mandalay," and "Danny Deever." Kipling's story collections for children include *The Jungle Book* (1894) and *Just So Stories* (1902). Kipling's descriptions of British colonial life became a window for the world to understand the glory and excesses of the empire. Kipling was born in Bombay in 1865 and educated in England. He returned to India for several years, working as a journalist and fledgling poet. Returning to England, his prose collection captured the fancy of the nation. Kipling lived for four productive years in Vermont and then went home for good. The first English writer to win a Nobel Prize for Literature, he died in England in 1936.

Joseph Conrad

Joseph Conrad, born Josef Teodor Konrad Korziniowski, was a Polish-born English novelist who found success with his early adventure novels of the sea, such as *Almayer's Folly* (1895), *Lord Jim* (1900), and *Typhoon* (1903). He is perhaps best known for his adventure and psychological thrillers, such as *Heart of Darkness* (1902) and *The Secret Agent* (1907). Conrad was noted for his treatment of moral questions and the adroit use of language in his work. Born in Poland in 1857, Conrad moved with his exiled family to Russia. Conrad went to sea with both the French Merchant Marine and the British Merchant Navy, eventually commanding a ship. His travels provided the raw material for his fiction, which is now highly regarded by critics. Conrad became a British subject and lived in Bishopsbourne until his death in 1924.

Samuel Butler

Samuel Butler, English essayist, critic, and novelist, is best known for his biting satire and savage wit. His first major work, *Erewhon*, published in 1872, was a satire on the public's belief in universal progress. He wrote two additional novels, *The Fair Haven* (1873), an attack on the Resurrection, and *Erewhon Revisited* (1901), before the publication of his best-known work, *The Way of All Flesh*, published posthumously in 1903. *The Way of All Flesh* is a largely autobiographical work describing Victorian middle-class life. Samuel Butler was born in Nottinghamshire in 1835 and educated at Cambridge. He emigrated to New Zealand and became a sheep farmer and occasional writer on scientific theory. Returning to England in 1864, he turned to writing full time, and produced most of his major work. Butler died in England in 1902.

Ford Madox Ford

Ford Madox Ford, born Ford Hermann Hueffer, was an English novelist and critic. His most honored work is *The Good Soldier*, published in 1915. *The Good Soldier* narrates an unhappy marriage in the English upper class. Ford collaborated on two novels with Joseph Conrad, *The Inheritors* (1901) and *Romance* (1903). His other major works include *Parade's End*, a trilogy of novels set in America and Europe. Editor and founder of the *Transatlantic Review*, a literary journal of excellent reputation, Ford spent his later productive years writing a general survey of world literature for lay readers.

Ford was born in England in 1873 and fought in France in World War I. He returned and settled in Paris after the war, where he was active in literary society. He lived for a time in America before returning to Europe. He died in 1939.

D. H. Lawrence

D. H. Lawrence, English novelist, poet, essayist, and short-fiction writer, brought an intensity to his work and life that sometimes scandalized his peers. His autobiographical novel, *Sons and Lovers*, was published in 1913. His greatest works, *The Rainbow* (1915), *Women in Love* (1921), and *Lady Chatterley's Lover* (1928) (banned in England and America for 30 years), focus on love, class, social standing, and sexuality. *The Complete Poems of D. H. Lawrence* (1964) is the best anthology of his verse. Lawrence was born in industrial England in 1885. His childhood was marred by an unhappy home. In 1915, Lawrence and his wife left England for good and traveled extensively. Suffering from tuberculosis, Lawrence sought a climate that would benefit his health. He died of the disease in 1930.

George Bernard Shaw

George Bernard Shaw was an Irish playwright and critic. Shaw published his collections of drama in *Plays Pleasant and Unpleasant* (1898), which included some of his best work, including his critical prefaces. Shaw's plays also include *Caesar and Cleopatra* (1901), *Major Barbara* (1907), *Pygmalion* (1913), and *St. Joan* (1924). He was awarded the Nobel Prize in literature in 1925. Shaw chose controversial topics for his dramas, stressing realistic social problems. He satirized social class and gender discrimination, but with a light touch that made its points without anger. Shaw was born in Dublin in 1856 and soon moved to London. An ardent progressive, he spoke and wrote passionately on the social issues of the day. He was renowned for his literary criticism, and was a major contributor to literary digests of his day. A leading figure in world literature, Shaw died in Hertfordshire in 1950.

James Joyce

James Joyce, Irish novelist and short-story writer, developed a style rich in innovative literary technique and creative language. His first major work was a collection of short stories, *The Dubliners* (1914), followed by an autobiographical novel, *A Portrait of the Artist as a Young Man* (1916), and a drama, *Exiles* (1918). Joyce published *Ulysses* in 1922 to critical acclaim. Joyce spent many years on his next novel, finally publishing *Finnegans Wake* in 1939. James Joyce was born in Dublin in 1882, and most of his fiction is set in that city. Rebelling against the constraints of Catholic society, Joyce left Ireland and lived in Europe most of his life. He lived in a number of European cities with his wife Nora Barnacle, often in poor circumstances and plagued by an eye disorder that caused near blindness. Joyce died in 1941.

Virginia Woolf

Virginia Woolf, born Adele Virginia Stephen—English novelist, short-fiction writer, essayist, and critic—was one of the most creative and influential writers of the 20th century. After publishing two traditional novels, Woolf wrote *Jacob's Room* (1922), using her stream of consciousness method of interior monologues to develop an absent character. She continued her experimentation in *Mrs. Dalloway* (1925), *To the Lighthouse* (1927), and *The Waves* (1931). Woolf was born in England in 1882 and educated by her father, a distinguished literary figure in his own right. After her father's death, she and her family moved to the Bloomsbury section of London, where their home became the center of the group of authors, artists, and thinkers known as the Bloomsbury

Group. She married Leonard Woolf, with whom she would found the Hogarth Press, a publisher of many important Modernist writers. Woolf committed suicide in 1941 by drowning.

Gerald Manley Hopkins

Gerald Manley Hopkins, English poet, published his first successful poem, "The Wreck of the Deutschland," in 1875. He followed this with a series of sonnets, including "The Windhover," "Pied Beauty," "God's Grandeur," and "Carrion Comfort." His later poems were written in a period of personal depression and religious doubt. He developed a style called sprung rhythm, which attempts to duplicate human speech. The first collection of his work, *Poems*, was published 30 years after his death. His reputation has grown over the decades, and he is now seen as a major influence on modern poetry. Hopkins was born in Stratford, Essex, in 1844. He attended Oxford where he received a classical education. Following his decision to convert to Catholicism and study for the priesthood, Hopkins abandoned poetry for seven years. Poverty and spiritual doubt haunted him the rest of his life. He died in England in 1889.

Wilfred Owen

Wilfred Owen is regarded as the greatest English poet of World War I. Owen's work is best known as a scathing indictment against war based on his experiences in France during 1917–18. Stylistically innovative, his language is starkly realistic in depicting the horrors of war. Most of Owen's work was published after his death, with the collected *Poems* introduced by Siegfried Sassoon, which include "Strange Meeting" and "Anthem for Doomed Youth." Owen's verse was used in Benjamin Britten's *War Requiem*, a powerful choral piece that became an instant classic.

Wilfred Owen was born in Shropshire and had a mundane education at Shrewsbury Technical College. He taught until 1915, when he enlisted in the army. Wounded in 1917, he was recovering in Scotland, where he met Sassoon, who encouraged his poetry. Returning to the front in 1918, he was killed only a week before the war ended.

Katherine Mansfield

Born Kathleen Mansfield Beauchamp, Mansfield was a New Zealand short story writer. Her first collection of short fiction, *In a German Pension* (1911), was well received. She was to publish a number of anthologies of her work, including *Bliss* (1920), *The Garden Party and Other Stories* (1922), and *Prelude* (1918). Her style and strength was the complex and subtle development of her characters, probing their psychological depths. She was a prolific contributor to magazines, working with her editor-husband, John Middleton Murry. He collected all of her letters and journals and published them after her death. Mansfield was born in New Zealand in 1888. She emigrated to England in 1907, where she would spend the rest of her life. Mansfield died in Fontainebleau in 1923.

Agatha Christie

Dame Agatha Christie, English novelist and playwright, is one of the most successful writers of all time. The author of more than 80 detective novels, her work has been translated into more than 100 languages. She created two memorable characters, the eccentric Hercule Poirot and the elderly spinster Miss Jane Marple, who are the protagonists of most of her books. Christie wrote and adapted many works for the stage, including her famous *The Mousetrap*, which is the longest running play in the history of drama. The play is still running in London, where it opened in 1952. Many of her works have been adapted for television and film. Born and raised in the West Country in 1890, she worked as a nurse and chemist in World War I, during which time she gained a working knowledge of poisons, which she utilized in her fiction. Christie died in Wallingford in 1976.

E. M. Forster

Edward Morgan Forster—English novelist, essayist, and critic—a major figure in modern literature, published his first four novels between 1905 and 1910: *Where Angels Fear To Tread* (1905), *The Longest Journey* (1907), *A Room With A View* (1908), and *Howard's End* (1910). Forster addressed subjects such as social justice, materialism and spirituality, and the dissolution of the English upper classes. His masterpiece, *A Passage to India* (1924), was inspired by several visits to India and Forster's service in Egypt in World War I. Forster also published volumes of literary criticism and essays. Forster was born in 1879 in London into an upper-middle-class household. He was educated at King's College, Cambridge, and became a contributor to a number of literary journals. His eclectic and prolific work made him a major figure in world literature. Forster died in England in 1970, at age 91.

William Butler Yeats

William Butler Yeats, Irish poet and playwright, originally made his name as a dramatist with such plays as *The Countess Cathleen* (1892), *The Land of Heart's Desire* (1894), and *Cathleen in Houlihan* (1902). The poetry of Yeats's later years shows a spare, realistic style, with much symbolism. Examples of this are "Easter 1916" (1916), celebrating the Easter rising in Dublin, and "The Second Coming" (1921). Yeats was awarded the Nobel Prize for Literature in 1923. Yeats was born in Dublin in 1865 and raised in London. He maintained a strong interest in Irish nationalism, folklore, mysticism, and painting his entire life. In love with the political activist Maud Gonne, he suffered when his love was not returned. Yeats was a founder of what became the Abbey Theatre in Dublin, a center of Irish literary life. Yeats died in France in 1939.

Aldous Huxley

Aldous Huxley, English novelist and social critic, created a hellish vision of the future in *Brave New World*, published in 1932. Describing a society based on technology and social control, *Brave New World* was the summation of a generation's fears about the future. Huxley's early novels are full of biting satire and criticism of society. His later works include *Island* (1962), reflecting his interest in Eastern spirituality and metaphysics. *After Many A Summer Dies The Swan* (1939) indicates Huxley's growing distrust of politics and social trends. Two later works discuss his experiments with hallucinogenic drugs. Huxley was born in Surrey, England, in 1894 and educated at Eton and Oxford. He emigrated to America in 1937, where he lived for the rest of his life. Huxley remained active as a teacher, writer, and social critic until his death in 1963.

W. H. Auden

Wystan Hugh Auden was an English-born man of letters, an accomplished poet, playwright, critic, editor, and translator. Perhaps best known for his verse, which was witty, musical, and innovative in the use of rhythms, Auden published a number of collections. *The Age of Anxiety* (1947) won him a Pulitzer Prize for Poetry. Other important works include *Another Time* (1940), *The Double Man* (1941), *Nuns* (1951), and the National Book Award winner *The Shield Of Achilles* (1955). An opera librettist of great skill, he worked with such luminaries as Britten and Stravinsky. Born in England in 1907, Auden was educated at Oxford, where he became a political activist for leftist movements. He moved to the United States, becoming a popular teacher and lecturer while producing work of the first order. Auden died in 1973 at the age of 65.

George Orwell

George Orwell, the pen name of Eric Arthur Blair—English novelist, critic, and playwright—is best known for his novels damning totalitarian regimes, and doing so with crushing satire. His two major works are *Animal Farm* (1945) and *1984* (1949), which established him as a leading satirist and novelist. His writing was fueled by his passionate economic and political views, and they are the keystones of his work. Aside from his two successful novels, he wrote several lesser ones, a collection of essays, and his four-volume *Collected Essays, Journalism, and Letters of George Orwell* (1968). Orwell was born Bengal, India in 1903 and educated at Eton. He then joined the Indian Imperial police in Burma but became disillusioned by imperialism and returned to Europe to live. Orwell fought for the Republicans in the Spanish Civil War and wrote of his experiences. After his success in the 1940s, he enjoyed an all too brief period of fame until his death in 1950.

Anthony Powell

Anthony Powell, English novelist, contributed to the staggering achievements of 20th-century fiction with his writing of the 12-volume opus *A Dance to the Music of Time*, published between 1951 and 1975. Grouped in three series of four novels each, it is the story of a man's life over 50 years, from public school through adulthood. His narration is sometimes humorous, often melodramatic, and it has been consistently overlooked by critics. His earlier works focus on satirizing the British upper class. After completing his master work, Powell remained productive, producing a four-volume memoir. Anthony Powell was born in London in 1905 and educated at Eton and Oxford. He worked for many years in journalism and publishing until his success allowed him to concentrate on his novels. He had a long and active career that ended with his death in 2000.

Samuel Beckett

Samuel Beckett was an Irish-French novelist, playwright, short-story writer, and poet. His work explores the degradation of modern man, with a focus on the essential meaninglessness and absurdity of life. Beckett's work contains little action, with meaning coming from dialogue and silences. His best-known work, the play *Waiting for Godot* (1953), is an allegory of life waiting only on death. Beckett was a prolific author, writing short fiction, drama, and prose for almost 50 years. He left a huge body of work behind that attests to his technical skills as a writer. He was awarded the Nobel Prize for Literature in 1969 for his contributions. Born in Ireland in 1906, Beckett was educated at Trinity College, Dublin. He moved to Paris, where he befriended James Joyce, who had an important influence on his work. He fought in the French Resistance during the war and was forced to flee Paris, to which he returned in 1945. He died in France in 1989.

Dylan Thomas

Dylan Thomas, Welsh poet and prose writer, was a figure bigger than life. Thomas produced his first volume of poetry in his twenties and won a reputation as a fresh voice in modern poetry. Later volumes include *Death And Embraces* (1946) and *In Country Sleep* (1952), which included his best-known verse, "Do Not Go Gentle Into That Good Night." Thomas was an eclectic writer, developing stories and radio scripts that were very successful. His short-story volumes include *Under Milk Wood* (1954) and *A Child's Christmas in Wales* (1955). Thomas was born in Swansea, Wales, in 1914, the son of a teacher. Perhaps best known by the public for his bouts of drinking, strife-ridden relationships, and flamboyant personality, his work is sometimes overshadowed by his personality. Thomas died of alcoholism on a poetry-reading tour in New York City in 1953 at the age of 39.

J. R. R. Tolkien

John Ronald Reuel Tolkien, English novelist, became famous for his mythological fantasies *The Hobbit* (1937), and *The Lord of the Rings* trilogy (1954–55). His fantasies were based on bedtime stories he told his children. At the urging of his friend and colleague C. S. Lewis, Tolkien wrote *The Hobbit* and spent the next 12 years writing the sequels, *The Lord of the Rings*. His own favorite among his novels was the Middle Earth romance *The Silmarillion*, published by his son after Tolkien's death. Tolkien was an academic, an Oxford professor of Anglo-Saxon and English language and literature. Born in South Africa in 1892, he attended Oxford on a scholarship and fought in World War I. His fantasies changed his life, but he continued his interest in medieval literature. Tolkien died in 1973 at age 81.

World literature from 1200 A.D. through Milton's Paradise Lost

1200 A.D. - European mystery plays combine biblical themes with social satire.

1297 A.D. - Marco Polo's "Travels" introduces Europeans to Asian culture.

1400 A.D. - Chaucer's "The Canterbury Tales" collects stories of pilgrims in a rich evocation of medieval life.

1450 A.D. - Gutenberg invents movable metal type and the printing press.

1516 A.D. - Martin Luther launches the Protestant Reformation in Wittenberg, Germany.

1558 A.D. - The reign of Elizabeth I begins the golden age of English literature.

1589 A.D. - William Shakespeare's first plays are produced in London.

1611 A.D. - The King James Bible is published and will have a lasting impact on English literature.

1660 A.D. - The Restoration Period of English literature begins.

1667 A.D. - Milton's "Paradise Lost" is published in blank verse in England.

Ben Jonson

Ben Jonson was a commanding figure in English letters. Playwright, poet, and critic, Jonson was famed for his elegant writing and brilliant intelligence. Jonson was the master of satires with his savage portrayals of human follies and corruption. The best known of these are <u>Valpone</u>, <u>Epicine</u>, and <u>The Alchemist</u>. Jonson also wrote epic poetry including the well known "Song to Celia" that was widely influential in the Restoration period. Jonson published his collected works in 1616 and was named Poet Laureate the same year. Born in London in 1572, Jonson had no formal education and went to war as a youth against the Spanish in Flanders. He became a popular writer of masques, a form of court entertainment that featured great spectacle, music, and poetry. Jonson was second only to Shakespeare in reputation among his peers. His followers, whom he served as a mentor, became known as "Sons of Ben."

Francis Bacon

Francis Bacon, Viscount St. Albans, Baron Verulam, was one of the greatest English essayists and philosophers. Bacon wrote primarily on science and scientific inquiry, championing the method of scientific investigation and empirical observation contrary to the scholastic philosophy favored by the Church. His greatest work was "Instaruratio Magna", a sweeping argument against the Renaissance and Scholastic philosophy. Bacon's "Essays," published in 1612, covered a wide range of subjects including English history, law, and society, and employed an aphoristic style. His vision of utopia was described in "New Atlantis" published in 1627. Bacon was born in London in 1561 and was active in politics, serving in Parliament several times. He served as Solicitor General under James I, but was charged with bribery in 1621 and barred from parliament. He remained an active writer until his death in London in 1626.

John Donne

John Donne, the greatest of the Metaphysical poets, wrote highly original verses on both religious and secular poetry. His love verses were written prior to his secret marriage to 17-year-old Ann More, of which the best known are "The Sunne Rising," "The Bait," and "To Catch a Falling Star." His reputation as a religious poet rests on "The Holy Sonnets" written in a period of spiritual search.

Donne was born into a Catholic family with strong ties to the Church. He converted to Anglicanism in 1614 after suffering a crisis of faith. Donne's marriage to Ann More without her father's consent caused a scandal for which he served a short prison sentence. His ambitions for a government career were dashed by this incident, and he turned to a career as an Anglican priest and dean of London's St. Paul's Cathedral. His reputation as a passionate preacher grew, but his poetry was not published until two years after his death. Donne wrote his own funeral sermon that was delivered in 1631.

John Milton

John Milton, the great English poet, wrote one of the great masterpieces of English literature in "Paradise Lost." This great Christian epic poem describing "mans first disobedience" was published in 1667. Milton followed this with the more severe "Paradise Regained", and his final work, the verse drama Samson Agonistes both published in 1671. Milton was born into a wealthy family and attended St. Paul's school and Cambridge before undertaking seven years of independent study. Several of his best known works including "L'Allegro" and "Il Penseroso" emerged from this period. Milton was a strong supporter of the Puritan and Commonwealth cause and wrote extensively defending civil freedom. He served as secretary in the Cromwell government but became severely disillusioned by the Restoration in 1660. Blind since 1652, he turned his power to the writing of his majestic work for which he is best remembered. Byron called him "the prince of poets" – a well deserved sobriquet.

World literature from 500 BC through Sappho's poems from the island of Lesbos

3500 bc: The first written language is developed by Sumerians in Mesopotamia.

3000 bc: The Egyptians begin using hieroglyphics on papyrus.

2000 bc: "Gilgamesh," an epic poem of Mesopotamia, is written.

1500 bc: The first alphabet is developed by the Phoenicians.

1200 bc: The Old Testament is written.

800 bc: Homer writes the epic poems the "Iliad" and the "Odyssey" on Greek heroism in the Trojan Wars.

800 bc: The Chinese spiritual text *The Way of Power* presents Taoist philosophy of harmonious living.

700 bc: Hesiod's "Theogony" presents the mythology of Greek gods.

610 bc: The earliest known record of Latin appears in Rome.

610 bc: Sappho's poems from the island of Lesbos are written.

World literature from Herodotus through 1100 ad

450 bc: Herodotus's history is the first historical work written.

430 bc: Sophocles, Euripides, and Aristophanes write Greek drama.

400 bc: The Indian epic the *Bhagavad Gita* is composed.

380 bc: Plato's *Republic* elaborates the teaching of Socrates and lays the foundation for Western philosophy.

100 ad: Papermaking is invented in China.

100 ad: The New Testament is written in Greek.

633 ad: The Koran is recorded in Arabic.

750 ad: The epic poem "Beowulf," the oldest extant work in English, is composed orally.

1045 ad: Movable type is invented in China.

1100 ad: Old English evolves into Middle English.

Homer

Homer is regarded as the greatest and earliest of the Greek epic poets and a literary giant whose innovations had lasting impact on Western culture. Very little is known of his life although it is generally agreed he was blind. He lived in the latter part of the eighth century bc, and his greatest works are the "Iliad" and the "Odyssey." The authorship and means of composition of both epics are a source of academic debate, and few facts can be verified. Both of these epic poems relate the events of the Trojan War and are clearly derived from oral traditions. Some scholars believe they were not written down until long after the death of Homer. Others feel that Homer may have been a bardic singer, and the poems were derived from his recitals. These epics were so influential that they were the foundation of education in classical Greece and Rome, and they remain a core of liberal arts today.

Sappho

Sappho was one of the earliest and most influential of the Greek poets. She lived on the island of Lesbos, from which the word *lesbian* is derived. On Lesbos, she is thought to have led a community of young women whom she tutored in music and poetry. Sappho's poetry is usually dedicated to these young women for whom she served as a mentor. Sappho's poetry is intimate in tone and often treats themes of love and friendship. Very little is known of her life, and her poetry survives only in fragments. Some scholars think she was exiled to Sicily by a repressive government on Lesbos. There is an apocryphal story about Sappho committing suicide by throwing herself off a cliff after a

- 45 -

tragic love affair. All such stories must be classed as speculation, but what is certain is her poetic skill and dedication to her students with whom she lived on Lesbos.

Sophocles

One of the greatest Greek playwrights, Sophocles wrote powerful tragedies that were considered the highest form of the art. He lived and wrote in the fourth century bc and was considered one of the leading citizens of Athens. His major works include *Oedipus the King, Antigone*, and *Electra*.

Although Sophocles wrote more than 100 plays, only seven complete dramas have survived. His tragic heroes value truth above all, even if it brings destruction and death. Sophocles was the master of writing tightly constructed plays and was an innovator in Greek drama. He added a third lead actor to the original two and produced self-contained plays rather than trilogies. Sophocles lived in Athens and was famous as a writer, musician, statesman, and priest. Aristotle considered Sophocles the greatest of the classical Greek dramatists, and his plays have been studied for centuries for their plotting and composition.

Euripides

Euripides is the author of 92 plays, of which only 19 survive. His greatest works are *Medea, Electra*, and *Hippolytus*. Euripides lived in Athens from 484 bc until the last two years of his life, which he spent at the court of King Archelaus of Macedonia. Little is known of his early life, and he built his reputation as a playwright by competing in the dramatic contests in Athens, which he won 22 times. Euripides was a master at creating complex characters with rich emotional lives. His characterization of women was particularly artful. In Euripides's dramas, the gods are indifferent to earthly problems, and he portrays human weakness as the cause of suffering. Many of his plays are about the foolishness of war, and he championed unpopular social causes, such as the equality of women in society. His personal reputation as a pundit inspired two dramatic parodies of him by his rival Aristophanes. Embittered by these attacks, Euripides left Athens for Macedonia, where he died in 406 bc.

Aristophanes

Aristophanes was a Greek playwright who was the greatest comedic writer of his time. His plays were noted for their brilliant dialogue, poetic choral lyrics, sharp parodies, and topical allusions. Eleven of his plays survive, the best known being *The Clouds, The Wasps*, and *The Birds*. Others include *Lysistrata* and *The Frogs*. He wrote in the style of old comedy, combining mime, fantasy, chorus, and bawdy humor, which delighted his audiences. He loved to satirize social institutions, public figures, and the gods. The details of his life are largely unknown, and most of the information comes from his work. A citizen of Athens all his life, Aristophanes launched his dramatic career in 427 bc. He wrote two parodies of Euripides's plays, which so incensed his rival that he left Athens. Aristophanes was a popular figure in Greece and his works are still occasionally staged today.

Virgil

Virgil was one of the greatest of Roman poets. He wrote the inscription for his own tomb, "One who sang of flocks and farms and heroes." Virgil's magnum opus is the epic poem the "Aeneid," which ranks as one of the most influential works in early classical literature. The "Aeneid" tells the tale of the adventures and triumphs of the Trojan hero Aeneas. Virgil's influence extends to the work of Dante, Spenser, Milton, and Shakespeare. His goal was to create works comparable to those of the Greek poets, and in this he succeeded. His work is uniquely his own and reflects his Roman culture.

Virgil was born in northern Italy and was well educated for a farmer's son. During the civil war of 41 bc, his farm was confiscated, and he moved to Rome to become part of the Emperor Augustus's circle of artists. His first published work was the "Eclogues," followed by "Georgics," and finally the "Aeneid." Much of his early work was about farm life and the joys of a bucolic existence. He became ill on a trip to Greece and died upon his return in 19 bc.

Ovid

Publius Ovidius Naso, known as Ovid, was a great Roman poet applauded for his passionate, technically skilled, and witty poetry. His influence is seen in the works of Chaucer, Milton, Dryden, and Shakespeare. His masterpiece, "Metamorphoses," is written on the theme of transformation in Greek and Roman myth and is widely respected as a seminal work in Roman literature. His love narratives, "Amores," were kept alive during the Middle Ages despite the opposition of the Church. Ovid also wrote an instruction manual on the art of love, which established him as a major writer.

Born in Sulmo in eastern Italy, Ovid moved to Rome to join the court of Emperor Augustus. He was exiled to the Black Sea for unknown reasons in 8 ad. Ovid's pleas for forgiveness were published as his *Sorrows and Letters from Pontus*, but he was not pardoned and remained in exile until his death in 17 ad. His legacy is one of the most influential in all of classical poetry.

Dante Alighieri

Dante Alighieri, the greatest of the Italian poets, was a major figure in the Renaissance revolution of arts and letters. His epic masterpiece, the "Divine Comedy," ranks as one of the truly great literary works in history. The "Divine Comedy" presents a panoramic view of man and his place in the cosmos, describing a man's journey through the divine realms of Hell, Purgatory, and Paradise. The traveler is helped first by Virgil then by Beatrice, who was based on Beatrice Portinari, a figure Dante idealized as a figure of divine love. Combining deeply religious themes with sharp commentaries on social and political institutions, the "Divine Comedy" uses Tuscan dialect, which had a great influence on the development of the modern Italian language. Dante was an aristocrat born in Florence in 1265, and his political activism led to his exile in 1302. Thereafter, he lived in different Italian cities, finally settling in Ravenna, on the Adriatic. He was a prolific writer, treating subjects as varied as uses of the Italian language and Christian political philosophy. Dante died in Ravenna in 1321.

Francois Rabelais

Francois Rabelais's major work was a five-volume masterpiece, *Gargantuan and Pantagreul*, published in Paris in 1564. This work is a unique combination of social satire, licentious comedy, and humanist philosophy. Shocked by this material, the Church placed the work on *Catholic Librium Prohibitorum*, and it was banned in France during his lifetime. His literature inspired the word *Rabelaisian*, which has come to mean a character with qualities of coarse humor, ribaldry, and boisterousness. His literary influence is seen in the works of Voltaire, Hugo, and Swift.

Rabelais was truly a Renaissance man, being a Benedictine monk, physician, teacher, and translator, and renowned for his knowledge in many fields. His role as a monk, no doubt, was part of the reason his work was seen as controversial by the church and banned. He died in France in 1553.

Michel de Montaigne

Michel de Montaigne's great contribution is the introduction of the essay to Western literature. His seminal work, *Essays*, introduced the genre, and the French term *essay*, meaning to try, was the name given the new form. *Essays* was published in three volumes from 1580 to 1588 and drew heavily from established literary forms, such as the treatise and religious confessions. Montaigne commented on social issues, as well as the human condition, in a brief, personal voice. His insights into major historical issues, such as religious conflict and exploration of the New World, were admired throughout Europe. The son of a wealthy landowner in southern France, Montaigne received a classical education and studied law. He counseled Parliament until 1571, when he retired to his family estate for study and writing. During the turbulent periods of civil war in France, he was drawn back to politics as a mediator and eventually became mayor of Bordeaux. He died on his family estate in 1592.

Jean-Jacques Rousseau

Jean-Jacques Rousseau was a Swiss-born novelist, essayist, philosopher, and intellect who was very influential in the affairs of nations. Written in French, Rousseau's most important work is *The Social Contract*, his polemic for changing society. The ideas expressed in this work helped ignite the French and American revolutions. He wrote two hugely successful novels, *Julie* and *Emile*, and numerous essays on a wide variety of topics. His autobiography *Confessions* is a candid self-examination and self-criticism. Born in Geneva in 1712, Rousseau moved to Paris and established his reputation as a writer with his essay "Discourse on the Science and Arts," which argued that science and art degraded the natural man. Rousseau's works became increasingly controversial, and he was derided and exiled from several countries. Finally, he found refuge in England, but his last years were marked by paranoia and mental illness. He died in Ermenonville in 1778, a largely broken man.

Johann Wolfgang von Goethe

Johann Wolfgang von Goethe was a German poet, novelist, and playwright. He was an initiator of the Sturm und Drang movement, which preceded German Romanticism. Goethe's best work includes the lyric poem "Hermann and Dorothea" and his drama *Faust*, which narrates the tale of the scholar who trades his soul for knowledge and pleasure. Goethe also wrote scientific essays and an autobiography, *Poetry and Truth*. One of his most popular works is the novel *The Sorrows of Young Werther*, which narrates the emotional pain of the protagonist/author. Goethe was born in Frankfurt in 1749 and served as a public official in Weimar for ten years. A long sojourn in Italy influenced his writing style and cultural outlook. Goethe developed a close friendship with the writer Friedrich von Schiller, and they remained confidants for many years. Goethe and Schiller shared many literary interests, and their relationship enriched both authors' work. Goethe remained active into old age and died in Weimar in 1832.

William Cullen Bryant

William Cullen Bryant was an American poet, critic, and prose writer. His most famous work is "Thanatopsis," a reverie on death, published in 1817. He enjoyed nature, and much of his work touches on natural beauty. "To a Waterfowl" (1821) is an example of his affection for the natural world. This poem became a milestone in American poetry, viewing nature as the guiding principle of life. Bryant was also a critic, and his volume *Early American Verse* was instrumental in building the foundation for the American literary tradition. Bryant was born in Massachusetts in 1794. He began a career as a lawyer but soon realized his interests were in writing. He moved to New York in 1825, where he served as editor of the *New York Evening Post*, a liberal newspaper dedicated to the abolition of slavery and workers' rights. Bryant became a champion of these causes, and much of his energy was used to advocate for them. He became the dean of American journalism and was active until his death in New York in 1878.

Washington Irving

Washington Irving was an American novelist, essayist, and short-story writer. Some of his best works are the now-familiar stories "Rip Van Winkle" and "The Legend of Sleepy Hollow," immortalized as children's fiction. Irving was an astute critic, essayist, and folklore expert. Irving's later works include *Tales of the Alhambra, Life and Voyages of Christopher Columbus*, and his impressions of the American west, *A Tour of the Prairies*. A well-known biographer, he wrote volumes about George Washington and Mohammed. Irving was born in 1783 and grew up in New York. Irving lived abroad for many years, serving as a diplomat in Spain for two separate periods of his life. He was a founder and co-publisher of a literary journal, *Salamagundi,* which was popular with American literary figures. He toured the American west several times and was an accurate observer of pioneer America. Upon his death in 1859, he was called "the first American man of letters."

James Fenimore Cooper

James Fenimore Cooper has a legitimate claim to being the first American novelist. Cooper was a prolific writer, and his best-known novels are *The Leatherstocking Tales*, which include *The Pioneers, The Last of the Mohicans, The Pathfinder*, and *The Deerslayer*. Cooper wrote a series of adventure novels in nautical settings, the most important being *The Pilot*. The three novels of *The Littlepage Manuscripts* address American social issues. His later work includes *The Sea Lions* and *Red Rover*, which enjoyed popular success. Cooper was born in New Jersey in 1789. Expelled from Yale University for unknown reasons, he spent eight years in the Navy, mustering out in 1809. Enriched by an inheritance from his father, Cooper devoted himself to politics and writing. Cooper's political writing embroiled him in many lawsuits, which he often won. He began a period of writing social criticism, including *The American Democrat* and *A Letter to His Countrymen* attacking American democracy. Cooper was active until the end of his life in 1851.

Victor Hugo

Victor Hugo—French playwright, novelist, and poet—was a giant figure in the Romantic revolution in the French arts. Best known for his great historical novels *Les Miserables* and *The Hunchback of Notre Dame*, Hugo also wrote drama, verse plays, and poetry. Important later works include *The Punishments* and an elegy for his drowned daughter, "Les Contemplations." Hugo was the most popular author in France for three decades. Born in Besancon, France, in 1802, Hugo began his literary career by founding *Conservateur Litteraire*, a literary journal, in 1819. Hugo was a giant figure in French letters and politics, becoming a vocal advocate of the republican cause. Hugo left France for 19 years after Napoleon III came to power. The creation of the Third French Republic in 1870 led to Hugo's triumphant return to Paris among adoring throngs. Hugo's revolutionary spirit can be seen in many of his works, particularly *Les Miserables* with its vivid depiction of the revolution. Hugo died in his beloved Paris in 1885.

Heinrich Heine

Heinrich Heine was perhaps the greatest poet of the German post-Romantic period. His first collection of poetry was published as *The Book of Songs* in 1827. His most controversial work was "Germany, A Winter's Tale," an epic satire on German politics. Heine wrote scores of impressive poems, and his works have been translated into most of the world's major languages. Heine's poetry was set to music by both Schubert and Schumann. Born in Dusseldorf, Germany, in 1797, Heine studied law in order to enter government service. He moved to Paris in 1831 and wrote articles on political, social, and economic issues of the day. Heine's works were banned in Germany in 1835, and he was forbidden to return to his homeland. His political views were considered radical for the time, and he was discriminated against for his Jewish heritage. Heine fell victim to a chronic illness that confined him to bed for the last years of his life. Despite this, he transcended his suffering in his last volume *Romanzero*. Heine died in Paris in 1856.

Honoré de Balzac

Balzac was a writer of prodigious output. He named his body of literature *The Human Comedy*. This French novelist wrote almost 100 works of fiction in his 51 years. His realistic description of 19th-century French society and manners provides a window to history. His first major success was *The Physiology of Marriage* in 1830. He followed this with *Lost Illusions*, an autobiographical novel of the corruption of a young poet in Paris, which is considered his greatest work. Later works include *The Black Sheep* and *Cousin Bette*, which were both successful. Balzac wrote in great detail and was an excellent plotter. His works were influential in the development of the novel. Balzac was born in Tours in 1799 and educated in Paris. He tried business and failed; he then gave his full attention to writing. Balzac was an obsessive worker, sometimes writing for days without rest. His tales could be melodramatic, but readers loved them, and his reputation soared. Balzac died in Paris in 1850 at age 51. His productivity in writing novels is unmatched.

Stendhal

Stendhal was the pen name of Marie Henri Beyle, a French novelist of great technical skill. His novels reflect deep and subtle psychological themes, using irony, cool, detached prose, and great realism. His greatest works include *The Red and the Black* (1830) and *The Charterhouse of Parma* (1839). Both books narrate the adventures of young men and their rise and fall. Later important novels include *The Life of Henry Brulard*, an autobiographical novel, and *Memoirs of an Egotist*. Stendhal also wrote several excellent biographies, including one on Rossini. Born in Grenoble, Stendhal joined the Ministry of War and later fought with Napoleon in his European and Russian campaigns. After the fall of Napoleon, he worked as a minor diplomat in Italy from 1831 until his death in 1842. Unappreciated in his own time, Stendhal's reputation has grown with the years. Modern novelists feel he is a major figure in the development of the genre.

Allen Ginsberg

Allen Ginsberg, American poet, was a major figure in the Beat Generation. He, Jack Kerouac, and William S. Burroughs led a group of artists in opposing the conformist society of America in the 1950s. Ginsberg's epic poem "Howl" (1956) became a rallying cry for the counterculture revolution. Ginsberg's poetry draws from traditions of free verse and symbolism in a probing voice demanding to be heard. Always socially and politically engaged, Ginsberg's later works include "Kaddish" (1961), *The Fall Of America: Poems of These States* (1973), and *Reality Sandwiches* (1966).

Born in New Jersey in 1926 to a working class family, Ginsberg was educated at Columbia University. He moved to San Francisco in the 1950s, where he found a flourishing counterculture of rebellion. Ginsberg and his friends lived bohemian lives and challenged all the accepted mores of society. Ginsberg died in 1997.

Eugene O'Neill

Eugene O'Neill, American playwright, was a pioneer in American drama. O'Neill was an innovator and experimented with aspects of realism and naturalism in his work. He was one of the most critically honored dramatists of his time, winning four Pulitzer prizes and the Nobel Prize for Literature in 1936. Financial success did not come with his critical acclaim, and O'Neill struggled for a long time. His most outstanding play, *Long Day's Journey Into Night,* was written in 1941 but not produced until after his death. O'Neill was born in New York to a show business family in 1888 and attended Princeton University. Suffering from tuberculosis, O'Neill turned his attention to drama and by 1920 had a play in production in New York. His later success was highlighted by *The Iceman Cometh* (1946) and *Strange Interlude* (1928), for which he would win a Pulitzer Prize. O'Neill remained an active writer until his death in 1953.

Voltaire

Voltaire was the pen name of Francois-Marie Arouet, French novelist, poet, playwright, and philosopher. Voltaire was a vocal and literate advocate for freedom of thought, political justice, and humanism in 18th-century France. Voltaire's fame is for his essays and letters defending human rights and arguing for reason and tolerance. Best known of his literary works are *Candide* and *Zadig,* fiction that blends philosophy and humanism. Nonfiction works include *Essays on the Manner and Spirit of Nations,* a seven-volume history, and a dictionary of philosophy. Voltaire was born in Paris in 1694 and educated by the Church. He soon abandoned the study of law for writing, philosophy, and advocating human rights. His sharp tongue and pen found ready targets in the Church, nobility, and government. A short stay in England exposed him to the ideas of John Locke and other liberal minds of the times. Many of his works were banned during his lifetime, which ended in Paris in 1778.

Alexander Pushkin

Pushkin was an immensely talented poet, playwright, and short-story writer. Possibly the most revered Russian writer, Pushkin began his literary career with narrative poetry, including "The Prisoner of Caucasus" and "The Gypsies." In 1831, he wrote his famous verse-tragedy "Boris Godunov." His verse novel "Eugene Onegin" (1833) became his most important work. Master of the short story, Pushkin produced many great ones, including "The Queen of Spades" (1834). Pushkin's later work is innovative and experiments with language, form, and characterization.

Born in Moscow in 1799, he was educated at the Imperial Lyceum and served in the Russian government until his exile for writing poetry critical of the Tsar. Allowed to return to Moscow by the new Tsar in 1826, Pushkin married and continued his literary career. Pushkin was killed in a duel with his wife's lover in 1837, only 37 years old. His impact on Russian literature is immeasurable.

George Sand

George Sand, the pen name of Amandine Aurore Lucile Dupin, was a French woman of letters who was an accomplished essayist, novelist, and playwright. Her novels often touch on themes of love, romance, and early feminist philosophy. Best known are *She and He* (1859), *Little Fadette* (1849), and *The Country Waif* (1850). Her four-volume autobiography *Story of My Life* chronicles her exciting life in detail. Sand's novels mix socialist and feminist ideas with erotic language and criticisms of society. Sand was born in Paris in 1804 and received a Catholic education. She married at 18 but began a series of love affairs that ended in her divorce. She was a striking figure, wearing men's clothes and having open affairs with Musset, Chopin, and others. She fascinated the public with her personal escapades and was an extremely popular writer in her day. Sand died in Nohant in 1876.

Ralph Waldo Emerson

Emerson was American essayist, poet, and transcendentalist philosopher. His first major work, *Nature*, was published in 1836. It proclaims the unity of nature and the universe and his belief that each man finds his way to the divine through individual apprehension. His two-volume *Essays* (1841–44) include his most famous essays, including "Love," "Friendship," and "The Oversoul." *Poems* (1847) and *May-Day* (1867) contain his best poetry. Emerson founded *The Dial*, a journal for transcendentalist writers, in 1840. Emerson was born in New England in 1803 and educated at Harvard University. Ordained as a Unitarian minister, he left the Church after being disillusioned with orthodox Christianity. Returning to America, he became a leading figure in the transcendentalist movement, joining such notables as Margaret Fuller, Henry David Thoreau, and Louisa May Alcott.

Henry David Thoreau

Thoreau was an American essayist and naturalist who published only two books in his life. His first book, *A Week on the Concord and Merrimac*, was a failure, and his prospects seemed dim. Then came *Walden* (1854), his masterpiece, which narrates Thoreau's experiment in simple living in a cabin on Walden Pond for two years. Initially unsuccessful, *Walden* became a classic and guide to a simpler, more natural life. Thoreau's *Journals* appeared in 1906. Thoreau was born in Concord, Massachusetts, in 1817 and graduated from Harvard in 1837. He was a teacher and major figure in the transcendentalist movement in New England. He wrote extensively on nature, society, and the spirit of individualism for many years. Often at odds with authorities, Thoreau spent a night in jail and defended his actions in a famous essay, "Civil Disobedience" (1849). He died in 1862 in his beloved Concord.

Nathaniel Hawthorne

Nathaniel Hawthorne was an American fiction writer. Hawthorne had a tragic vision of life, believing man is imperfect and a mixture of good and evil. His work reflects this view, starting with the publication of *Twice Told Tales* in 1837. Hawthorne gained public fame with *The Scarlet Letter* (1850), a novel of adultery in puritan New England. He followed this with the successful *House of the Seven Gables*, a novel tracing the history of a family hiding a dark secret. Hawthorne was born in Salem, Massachusetts, in 1804 to a prosperous family. He graduated from Bowdoin College in 1825 and vowed to devote his life to literature. Living in semi-seclusion in Salem for 12 years, Hawthorne produced his first stories. After briefly working in government, he joined a utopian community at Brook Farm, later satirized in his novel *The Blithedale Romance* (1852). Appointed American counsel in Liverpool, he lived in Europe for many years.

Henry Wadsworth Longfellow

Longfellow was one of the most popular American poets of his day. He gained lasting fame with his long narrative poems "Hiawatha" (1855) and "Evangeline" (1847). His *Tales of the Wayside Inn* (1863) contains "Paul Revere's Ride," a poem known and beloved by American schoolchildren. Among the best known of his shorter poems are "The Arsenal at Springfield," "The Wreck of the Hesperus," "A Psalm of Life," and "The Village Blacksmith." He also wrote essays and translated Dante's "Divine Comedy." Longfellow was born in Maine in 1807 to a wealthy family. He was educated at Bowdoin College and studied in Europe for several years before returning to Bowdoin to teach languages. He later became a faculty member at Harvard and was a well-respected professor. He died in New England in 1882.

Edgar Allen Poe

Poe was an American poet, novelist, and short-story writer of particular talent. His tales of terror and arresting poems have gained him lasting fame in American literature. Poe published a great anthology of short stories with *Tales of the Grotesque and Arabesque* in 1840. He cemented his fame with *The Raven and Other Poems* in 1845. Some of his greatest poems include "The Bells" (1849), "Annabel Lee" (1849), and "Ulaume" (1847). His best-known short stories include "The Pit and the Pendulum" (1843), "The Tell-Tale Heart" (1843), and "The Gold Bug" (1843). Poe was born in Boston and was orphaned at an early age. Raised by a wealthy Virginia businessman, he attended the University of Virginia and West Point. Poe's marriage to a young cousin would end with her early death. Poe would never recover from this loss and sank into a morass of drug addiction and alcohol abuse. He died in Baltimore in 1849.

Nikolai Gogol

Gogol was a Russian playwright, novelist, and short-story author who wrote sharp satirical prose in an innovative style. Two collections of his short stories, *Mirgorod* and *Arabesques*, were published in 1835. His best-known work, the novel *Dead Souls*, a biting satire on feudal Russia, appeared in 1842. The sequel to *Dead Souls* was to have been Gogol's crowning work, but he burned the manuscript in 1852, shortly before his death. Only fragments of the manuscript remain.

Gogol was born in 1809 in Ukraine. Moving to St. Petersburg, he worked in civil service and teaching as he began to write. Gogol began displaying symptoms of mental illness in the 1840s. He became obsessed with religion and fell under the influence of a fanatical priest who urged him to destroy the manuscript of the second part of *Dead Souls* to atone for the original book. Increasingly, Gogol became delusional. He destroyed the manuscript and then starved himself to death in 1852.

Alexandre Dumas

Known as Alexandre Dumas père (father), this great French novelist and playwright was the most popular literary figure in France in his time. Best remembered for his exciting historical novels *The Three Musketeers* (1844), and *The Count of Monte Cristo* (1845), Dumas published many other popular novels, including *The Man in the Iron Mask* (1850), as well as many dramas based on his stories. His forte was the historical novel, usually with heroic figures and imaginative plots that captured the fancy of the public. Dumas was born in Paris in 1802, the son of one of Napoleon's great generals. Dumas led a life worthy of his novels, having many mistresses and winning and losing fortunes regularly. He was a flamboyant character in the café society of Paris, living with the joy that seemed to permeate his fiction. Dumas left several volumes of his memoirs documenting his exciting adventures. He died in Dieppe in 1870.

Fyodor Dostoyevsky

Fyodor Dostoyevsky, Russian novelist, journalist, and short-story writer, was the master of the psychological character. He also had unusual skill as a prose writer and ranks as the greatest of Russian writers. His first major work was *Crime and Punishment* (1867), narrating a murder and its aftermath. This was followed quickly by a series of important works, including *The Idiot* (1874), *The Possessed* (1872), and *The Brothers Karamazov* (1880). All these works deal with the criminal mind and the struggles within the human psyche. Dostoyevsky was born in Moscow in 1821, the son of a physician who was murdered by serfs when Dostoyevsky was in his late teens. He suffered from epilepsy and was a chronic gambler, which left him in constant debt. Arrested for subversion, he spent eight years in Siberia before his release. With Tolstoy, he is considered the greatest Russian writer. He died in St. Petersburg in 1881.

Herman Melville

Melville was one of America's rare talents, excelling in short stories, poetry, and, above all, the novel. Melville wrote adventure stories, *Typee* (1846) and *Omoo* (1847), before writing his master novel, *Moby Dick* (1851). This novel was an allegory about men, life, and obsession. It is usually considered one of the greatest American novels. Unpopular at first, it was rediscovered in the 1920s and given the accolades it so richly deserved. Melville's later work includes *The Piazza Tales*, a collection of short stories, and the novels *The Confidence Man* (1857) and *Billy Budd* (1888).

Melville was born in New York in 1819 and went to sea as a teenager. In 1866, Melville became a customs inspector in New York. Stalked by tragedy with the death of two sons and his financial reverses, Melville persisted with his writing. He is now considered one of literature's finest novelists. Melville died in New York in 1891.

Harriet Beecher Stowe

Harriet Beecher Stowe, American novelist, rests her reputation on *Uncle Tom's Cabin* (1852), a polemic that brought the horrors of slavery to the world. The book became a bible for the abolitionist cause, and some credit it as a catalyst for the American Civil War. Three million copies were sold in the decade after it was published, and it was translated into more than 25 languages. Stowe's later works include *Oldtown Folks* (1869) and *The Minister's Wooing* (1859).

Stowe was born in Litchfield, Connecticut, in 1811. In her late teens, she moved to Cincinnati and married a clergyman. She became heavily involved in the abolitionist movement, which led her to write *Uncle Tom's Cabin*. Enriched and honored by her book, Stowe continued to campaign for social justice until her death in 1896.

Walt Whitman

Whitman, the American poet and journalist, sought to develop an American voice for poetry. His style mirrored the American ideal: democratic, idealistic, free-flowing, and panoramic in perspective. His life's work, *Leaves of Grass* (1855), embodied what Whitman conceived as the American spirit. Using free verse, Whitman produced an American original. Whitman was born on Long Island, in New York state, and was reared in nearby Brooklyn. He worked as a teacher, typesetter, and journalist, becoming editor of the *Brooklyn Eagle* in 1846. He lived most of his life in Brooklyn, until the publication of *Leaves of Grass*. During the Civil War, he traveled to Virginia to nurse his wounded brother. He stayed on as a hospital volunteer until the end of the war. Crippled by a stroke in 1873, he retired to New Jersey, where he died in 1892.

Charles Baudelaire

Baudelaire was a French essayist, poet, and critic. His reputation as one of the great French poets of his time was based on his seminal work, *The Flowers of Evil* (1857). *The Flowers of Evil* combines macabre imagery and a profane, cynical tone to produce a book of much power. Baudelaire was prosecuted and fined for obscenity following its publication, and a few of the poems were banned from future editions. Baudelaire was born in Paris in 1821 to a wealthy family. He turned to writing almost immediately and began friendships with Courbet, Delacroix, and Manet. After squandering a large inheritance, Baudelaire became addicted to opium and alcohol, and began to deteriorate. His later years were poverty stricken, and he was heavily in debt. The publication of *The Flowers of Evil* further alienated the public. His writing career was essentially over, and he died of syphilis in 1867 at the age of 46.

Gustave Flaubert

Flaubert was a French author of fiction, a master of the novel and adept at short stories. After an unsuccessful first manuscript, Flaubert spent five years writing his best-known work, *Madame Bovary*, published in 1857. This narrative of the adulterous affairs of a middle-class French woman shocked much of France, and Flaubert was prosecuted for the book's "immorality." His other novels include *Salaambo* (1862) and *A Sentimental Education* (1869). Flaubert is recognized as a pioneer in modern fiction writing. Flaubert was born in Rouen, France, in 1821 and began writing fiction as a child. He enrolled in law school but soon suffered a breakdown and abandoned his education. He committed himself to writing with great energy and gave up many of the distractions of Paris life to concentrate on his craft. Flaubert died suddenly of a cerebral hemorrhage at his home in Croisset, France, in 1880. He was 58 years old.

Emily Dickinson

Emily Dickinson is ranked as one of America's greatest poets. Dickinson's poetry is highly formal, her language both subtle and creative, and it reflects the quiet life she led. Dickinson's topics include death, art, love, pain, and betrayal, all couched in her wonderful poetic language. She wrote more than 1,800 poems, yet only ten are known to have been published in her lifetime. Her fame has grown through the generations, and she is at last recognized as a poetic genius. Born in Amherst, Massachusetts, in 1830, she was educated at Mt. Holyoke seminary. She returned to Amherst and went into virtual seclusion in her parents' home. She saw very few people socially and rarely left the house. Despite this isolation, Dickinson's work is vibrant and alive, reflecting her keen observation of the world. Dickinson is a true American literary voice, rivaling Walt Whitman. She died in Amherst in 1886.

Ivan Turgenev

Ivan Turgenev—Russian novelist, playwright, and short-story writer—wrote politically inflammatory stories criticizing Russian serfdom and government. His work managed to inflame both the tsarist generation and the young radicals of his time. Best known for his *Fathers and Sons*, published in 1862, he continued writing fiction for over 30 years. Some of his more successful novels include *On the Eve* (1860), *Smoke* (1867), and *The Virgin Soil* (1877), a controversial novel about Russia. His best-known play is *A Month in the Country,* first produced in 1855. Turgenev was born in Oryol in 1818 and educated in universities in Moscow and St. Petersburg before moving to Berlin. Here he became a Westerner for life. This was reflected in his work, which became increasingly critical of Russian society and economics. He left Russia in 1863 and lived in France and Germany for most of the rest of his life. Turgenev died in France in 1883.

Leo Tolstoy

Count Leo Tolstoy was Russia's leading novelist and moral philosopher. Tolstoy's two great masterpieces of fiction are *War and Peace* (1869) and *Anna Karenina* (1878). *War and Peace* is a love story set in the Napoleonic wars and provides a panoramic view of Russian life. *Anna Karenina* is the story of a woman who gives up everything for her love. Both are novels of great philosophical and psychological depth. Tolstoy described his spiritual crisis and its resolution in *Confessions* (1882). Tolstoy had a productive writing period in his later life, publishing novellas and a final novel, *The Resurrection* (1899). Tolstoy was born in Yasnaya Polyana in 1828 and educated at home by tutors. He served in the Russian army and fought in the Crimea and Caucasus campaigns. He returned to his estate in 1859, married, and taught the children of serfs while he wrote his great novels. Tolstoy retired to his estate and died in Astapovo in 1910.

Louisa May Alcott

Louisa May Alcott is one of America's beloved children's writers, novelists, and short-story writers. Alcott began her publishing career writing popular dime novels under pseudonyms to make a living. The publication of *Little Women* in 1868, and its huge popularity, allowed her to pursue serious fiction thereafter. *Little Women* is a fond narrative of family life based partially on her own family. It is a romantic yet realistic novel with strong and memorable characters. Alcott's later novels include *Little Men* (1871) and *Rose in Bloom* (1876), both written for young readers. Her best adult fiction includes *Moods* (1864), a novel of married life, and *Work* (1874), a story based on her financial problems. Alcott was born in Germantown, PA in 1832 and reared in nearby Concord. Her father was the famous transcendentalist thinker Bronson Alcott. She died in 1888.

Emile Zola

Emile Zola, French novelist, wrote finely detailed narratives with a realistic eye. Zola believed objective observation was necessary to maintain the integrity of his work. His first novel, *Therese Raquin* (1867), was written in this dispassionate style. His reputation rests on a mammoth 20-volume novel cycle, called *Les Rougon-Macquart*, narrating the fortunes of a 19th-century family over several generations. Topics in this series often involve the seamy side of life, including prostitution, labor unrest, and alcoholism. Zola was born in Paris in 1840 and raised in Provence. His education was mediocre, and he worked in a publishing house before becoming a journalist. He wrote for several French periodicals on a variety of topics as he honed his new style of writing. His mature novels were very successful and provided Zola with a comfortable life. He died in France in 1902.

Arthur Rimbaud

Arthur Rimbaud, French poet, was a literary figure unlike any other. A revolutionary in every sense, he pioneered the use of free verse in his poetry and lived a life of adventure and daring. At the age of 17, he wrote "The Drunken Boat" (1871), a surreal poem that would remain his greatest work. Rimbaud's "A Season in Hell" (1873) plumbed the depth of his despair, a cry of spiritual longing and the inability to love. His literary career was over at the age of 19, and he experimented with alcohol, drugs, and sensory deprivation. Rimbaud was born in northeastern France in 1854. His family was impoverished, and he left home at age 15 to live on his own. Rimbaud met and fell in love with Paul Verlaine, who served both as a mentor and lover. The relationship was a violent one, and Rimbaud left Paris to wander the world as a merchant, arms dealer, and vagabond. He returned to France and died in Marseille in 1891 at the age of 37.

Paul Verlaine

Paul Verlaine, French poet, was the leading light of the Symbolist movement, which stressed the importance of suggestion and shading rather than direct description. Symbolism intuited subtle connections between the spiritual and physical worlds. Verlaine's best work was reflected in his "Song Without Words" (1874) and "Fetes Galantes" (1869). His poetry in later life was influenced by his conversion to Catholicism when he embraced positive values and wrote "Wisdom" (1880), "Love" (1888), and "Happiness" (1891). Paul Verlaine was born in Metz in 1844. Educated in Paris, he joined the radical poets in the salons and cafés of literary Paris. He shocked society when he left his family for 17-year-old Arthur Rimbaud, with whom he carried on a tempestuous and violent affair. Verlaine embraced the Church in his forties, and achieved a peace that had eluded him. He died in Paris in 1896.

Henrik Ibsen

Henrik Ibsen, Norwegian poet and playwright, is known for his realistic descriptions of modern social problems and psychological dilemmas that haunt his characters. Perhaps his most popular work is *Peer Gynt*, published in 1876. His more mature work is composed of a number of plays written with marked realism. Those include *A Doll's House* (1879), *Hedda Gabler* (1891), *The Wild Duck* (1885), and his final play, *The Master Builder* (1893), perhaps his most autobiographical drama. Henrik Ibsen was born near Oslo in 1828 to a wealthy family. When he was a child, his father's business failed, and he was apprenticed to a pharmacist. Ibsen abandoned his apprenticeship and moved to Oslo to work in the theatre. He became a jack-of-all-trades, managing and directing groups of players. Ibsen died in Oslo in 1906 at the age of 78.

Mark Twain

Mark Twain, the pen name of Samuel Langhorne Clemens, was a true American voice in literature. Humorist, novelist, and travel writer, he is best known for *Tom Sawyer* (1876) and *The Adventures of Huckleberry Finn* (1884), beloved novels with memorable characters and undertones of social concern. *Life on the Mississippi* (1883) was an autobiographical account of his days on a riverboat. Twain's acid humor and stories of a fading rural America made him one of the most popular figures of his day. Born in 1835 in Florida, Missouri, Twain, who was self-educated, became a journalist and sometime printer. His literary success made him a popular lecturer in America and Europe. His travels abroad provided him with the material for the satirical *A Connecticut Yankee in King Arthur's Court* (1889) and *The Innocents Abroad* (1869). His later life was marred by tragedy, including the death of his wife and two daughters, as well as financial difficulty. He died in Connecticut in 1910.

Charlotte Perkins Gilman

Charlotte Perkins Gilman was an American writer of short stories, essays, and poetry. She was an early feminist and leader in the women's movement in the early part of the 20th century. She challenged gender stereotypes in her writing. Her most influential work was *The Yellow Wallpaper* (1892), a tale of the abuse of women, medical science, and madness. Other important works include *Women and Economics* (1898) and her utopian novel, *Herland*, published in 1915. Gilman was born in Hartford, Connecticut, in 1860 to a family that included Lyman Beecher and Harriet Beecher Stowe. An unhappy childhood and difficult first marriage contributed to her clinical depression. She divorced her husband and moved to California, where she did her best work. Gilman committed suicide in 1935 after a period of failing health. Her autobiography was published soon after her death.

Stephen Crane

American journalist, short-fiction writer, and novelist, Crane produced a number of memorable works in his 29 years. Best known for his unflinching evocation of a soldier in battle, *The Red Badge of Courage* (1895), Crane ironically never fought in a war. He published a collection of poetry, *The Black Rider and other Lines* (1895), which was a critical success. Crane traveled the world as a journalist, and his experiences provided him with ample material for his fiction.

Crane was born New Jersey in 1871 and became a journalist in New York City. He was what we now term an investigative reporter, writing grim and harshly realistic articles about the poor. Crane eventually settled in Sussex, England, and became an associate of the important literary figures of the day. His short stories are included in many anthologies and are the strength of his writing. He died in England in 1900.

Kate Chopin

Kate Chopin was an American novelist and short-fiction writer whose breakthrough work was the novel *The Awakening* (1899). This story of a woman's struggle to attain independence has become a landmark in feminist literature. The book was roundly condemned for its bold use of sexuality, particularly the heroine's illicit affairs. The criticism was so overwhelming it almost ended Chopin's writing career. Her later works are collections of stories of Creole and Cajun life. Kate Chopin was born in St. Louis in 1850. She married and moved to New Orleans in 1870. Chopin continued to live and write in St. Louis until her death in 1904. She is now regarded as an early victim of antifeminist opinion in literary circles. Her inquiries into the nature of female identity are remarkable for the period and prepared the ground for future feminist literature.

Theodore Dreiser

Theodore Dreiser was an American novelist and leader in the literary movement known as Naturalism. Naturalism sought a literary ideal based on an objective, dispassionate description of the world. Dreiser's first novel, *Sister Carrie* (1900), was so controversial the publisher refused to promote it. His magnum opus, *An American Tragedy* (1925), was based on a true story of the day. Dreiser later published three successful novels, *The Financier* (1912), *The Titan* (1914), and a late book, *The Stoic* (1947). Dreiser was born to a poor family in Indiana in 1871. He worked as a journalist for many years as he polished his writing skills. Besides his novels, Dreiser wrote short fiction, plays, and an autobiography. His work is understood to have had a major impact on novel writing in America by its rough portrayal of urban life. Dreiser died in 1945.

Anton Chekov

Anton Chekov, Russian playwright and short-story writer, is regarded as one of the greats in Russian literature. Known for his skillful blend of symbolism and naturalism, Chekov combines comedy, tragedy, and pathos into a heady brew. His greatest short stories include "The Black Monk" (1894), "A Dreary Story" (1889), and "Ward Number Six" (1892). His fame as a dramatist rests on his four later plays, *The Cherry Orchard* (1904), *Uncle Vanya* (1897), *The Three Sisters* (1901), and *The Seagull* (1897). Chekov was born in southern Russia and studied medicine at Moscow University. As a student, he wrote for periodicals to supplement his income. After his early successes, he concentrated on his writing and only occasionally practiced medicine. He suffered from tuberculosis and moved to the Crimea in hopes of a healthier environment. In this he was unsuccessful, and he died in 1904.

Henry James

American novelist, short-story writer, playwright, and essayist, Henry James is a founder of the modern American novel. His mature fiction includes *The American* (1877), *The Europeans* (1878), *Daisy Miller* (1879), and *Washington Square* (1880). James's middle period features novels of social concern and artists, such as *The Bostonians* (1886). James's mature works use the technique of presenting events through each character's limited perspective, as in *Turn of the Screw* (1898) and *Wings of the Dove* (1902). James was an excellent literary and art critic, writing for a number of newspapers and periodicals. James was born in New York City in 1843 but spent much of his time in Europe. From 1876 until his death, he lived in London, eventually becoming a British subject. Many of his works involve Americans living abroad, particularly in England. James died in London in 1916.

Jack London

Jack London was an American novelist, short-fiction writer, and essayist. London's first collection of short stories, *The Son of the Wolf,* was published in 1900. *The Call of the Wild* (1903), the story of a sled dog that becomes the leader of a wolf pack, was hugely successful, bringing the author both stature and riches. London's other well-known novels include *The Sea Wolf* (1904) and *White Fang* (1906), another tale of survival in the wild. His later works are more ideological, and the best known is *The People of the Abyss* (1903). London was born in Oakland, California, in 1876 into a poverty-stricken home. A vagabond who worked as a gold miner, cannery worker, and seaman, he went to the Klondike on a failed expedition to find gold. He was a passionate socialist, and he spoke and wrote often as an advocate. Destitute and alcoholic, he committed suicide in 1916.

Edith Wharton

Born Edith Newbold Jones, Wharton was a prolific American novelist, poet, short-fiction writer, and essayist. She was expert at narrating the foibles of Old New York society, of which she was a member. Wharton's first success was *The House of Mirth* (1905), a novel depicting an individual's struggles against society's mores. Writing in France, she published *Ethan Frome* (1911) and her most popular work, *The Age of Innocence* (1920), which won a Pulitzer Prize for Literature. *The Age of Innocence* chronicles a long and stormy love affair. Wharton was born in New York in 1862 and raised in elite society. Her marriage to Edward Wharton ended after he suffered a number of nervous breakdowns and was caught embezzling her accounts. She divorced Wharton, which presaged her most productive writing period. She moved to France in 1907, and her writing career became the focus of her life. Wharton, much honored and loved, died in 1937.

Upton Sinclair

Upton Sinclair was an American novelist, journalist, and essayist. He was the best known of the muckrakers, a socially-minded band of writers who decried and attacked perceived immoral conduct in business and government. His most popular novel, *The Jungle* (1906), attacked and exposed abuses in the Chicago meat packing industry. *The Jungle* was instrumental in forcing the passage of the Pure Food and Drug Act. Sinclair's later works include *King Coal* (1917) and a novel based on the Sacco-Vanzetti trial, *Boston* (1928). Born in Baltimore in 1878, Sinclair was an ardent socialist who ran (and lost) for the governorship of California in 1934. He remained a muckraker to the end, advocating socialism and attacking social ills. Upton Sinclair died in New Jersey in 1968.

Henry Adams

Adams was an American editor, biographer, and historian famed for his autobiography, *The Education of Henry Adams*, published in 1907. Adams produced two novels, *Democracy, an American Novel* (1880) and *Esther* (1884), both published anonymously. His life's work was the nine-volume *History of the United States of America During the Administrations of Thomas Jefferson and James Madison*, published in 1889–91. Adams was born in 1838 in Boston, the grandson of John Quincy Adams. Educated at Harvard, he chose a profession of scholarship rather than government service. Editor of the *North American Review* for six years, he then accepted an appointment as medieval history professor at Harvard. He remained there until he retired to write full time. Adams died in Washington D.C. in 1918.

Gertrude Stein

Gertrude Stein was an American poet, essayist, novelist, and short-story writer. Her major work is *Three Lives* (1909), a novel of working-class women. Her poetry collection, *Tender Buttons: Objects,*

Food, Rooms, published in 1914, was well received. Her autobiography, *The Autobiography of Alice B. Toklas*, published in 1937, has become an icon to millions of individuals. Born in America in 1874, Stein spent most of her childhood in Europe. She studied psychology with William James in Baltimore before moving to Paris for good. With her secretary and partner, Alice B. Toklas, Stein became the center of the Modernist literary scene in Paris and was a close friend of Picasso, Hemingway, and Ford Madox Ford. Stein was a flamboyant figure in Paris, famous for her acid tongue and repartee. Stein died in Paris in 1946.

Rabindranath Tagore

Tagore was an Indian poet, playwright, novelist, short-fiction writer, and songwriter. Best known for his spiritual poetry written in Bengali, his first collection was *The ideal One* (1890). Noted for his lyrical, spiritual poetry, also written in Bengali, Tagore dominated the Indian literary scene for decades. His most popular work, *Song Offerings* (1912), won him a Nobel Prize in literature in 1911. Tagore published a number of poetry anthologies, and his stories of Bengal village life were published as *The Hungry Stones* (1916) and *Broken Ties* (1925). His best novel, *The Home and the World*, (1916), was adapted for film by Satyagit Ray. Tagore was born in Calcutta in 1861 to a wealthy Hindu family. He studied law in London and traveled widely in the West before returning to India. He died in India in 1941.

Marcel Proust

Marcel Proust, French novelist, owes his reputation to his epic seven-part masterpiece, *Remembrance of Things Past*, published between 1913 and 1927. This monumental work examines the existential problem of finding meaning and value in the maelstrom of life. Using the device of interior monologue, Proust views the transient nature of life and the flux of consciousness, using observation of minute detail in a manner rarely done with such skill. Proust was forced to publish the first volume himself, but subsequent books were well received. The final three volumes were published after Proust's death. Proust was born in Paris in 1871 and educated at the Lycée Condorcet. As a young man, he was a favorite in the literary salons of Paris, a setting he used repeatedly in his novels. Suffering from chronic asthma and the early death of his mother, Proust withdrew into semi-seclusion, where he devoted himself to his life's work. He died in Paris in 1922.

T. S. Eliot

Thomas Stearns Eliot—American poet, playwright, and critic—was a major poet of the Modernist school of poetry. Eliot's first success was in 1915 with the publication of "The Love Song of J. Alfred Prufrock," originally appearing in *Poetry*, a small literary magazine. Eliot struggled with his own despair at the futility of life and the spiritual barrenness of modern life. He addressed these themes in "The Waste Land," a powerful and influential work in the history of modern poetry. Eliot wrote several dramas in verse including "Murder in the Cathedral" (1953) and "The Cocktail Party" (1950). Eliot was born in St. Louis in 1888 and educated at Harvard and Oxford University. He moved to London and worked as a banker before becoming an editor at Faber and Faber in 1925. In 1927, he became a British subject and converted to Anglicanism. He was a distinguished figure in literature until his death in 1965.

Robert Frost

Robert Frost, American poet, is remembered as a master of the technical aspects of poetry while remaining true to his New England heritage. Frost will always be remembered for his masterful simplicity in such poems as "Stopping By the Woods on a Snowy Evening" (1923) and "The Road Not Taken" (1916). While living in England before World War I, Frost published two collections of poetry. Returning to New England, he published a number of anthologies, including *Complete Poems* (1945), *West Running Brook* (1928), *A Witness Tree* (1942), and *In the Clearing* (1962). Frost was born in California in 1874 and was educated at Dartmouth College and Harvard. He received the Pulitzer Prize four times and capped his career by reading "The Gift Outright" at the inaugural of John Kennedy in 1961. Frost died in 1963.

Franz Kafka

Franz Kafka was a Prague-born and German-writing novelist and short-story writer. Using powerful symbolism and addressing the anxieties and chaos of modern society, Kafka wrote penetrating stories and novels during his lifetime, including the novella *The Metamorphosis* (1915), the short story "In the Penal Colony" (1919), and the collection *A Hunger Artist* (1924). Kafka instructed his executor and literary agent Max Brod to destroy his unpublished manuscripts after his death. Recognizing Kafka's genius, Brod published the works, including the great novels *The Trial* (1925), *The Castle* (1926), and *Amerika* (1927). Kafka was born in Prague to a middle-class Jewish family, with whom he lived most of his life. He attended law school but worked in an insurance firm for many years. His fiction was dark, wounding, and sometimes painful, but always arresting. Kafka died in 1924.

Edna St. Vincent Millay

Edna St. Vincent Millay was one of the best-known American poets of the 1920s. Millay won a poetry contest in 1902 with "Renascence," which became her best-known poem. Millay won the Pulitzer Prize for her poem "The Ballad of the Harp-Weaver" in 1923. She published a number of successful collections of poems, including *A Few Twigs from Thistles* (1920), *Fatal Interview* (1931), *Wine From These Grapes* (1934), *Conversation at Midnight* (1937), and *Make the Bright Arrows* (1940), as well as the posthumously published *Collected Poems* (1956). Millay infused traditional sonnets with the voice of an independent, modern woman. Millay was born in Rockland, Maine, in 1892. Educated in liberal arts at Vassar College, she worked as a reporter for *Vanity Fair* magazine in New York. Millay died in 1950 at the apex of her career.

Willa Cather

Willa Cather was an American novelist, short-story writer, and essayist. Her breakthrough came with the publication of her second novel, *O Pioneers!*, which narrated the story of an immigrant family's struggle in the new world. *My Antonia*, a story of a woman's struggle and eventual triumph on the prairie, met critical acclaim in 1918. Cather won the Pulitzer Prize in 1922 for *One of Ours*. Cather's later work bemoaned the loss of pioneering spirit in America, which was the theme for *Death Comes for the Archbishop* (1917). She published a successful essay collection, *Not under Forty*, in 1936. Other writing examines the topics of art, loss, and disillusionment, including a novel on the American Civil War, *Sapphira and the Slave Girl* (1940). Cather was born in Virginia in 1873 and moved to the Nebraska frontier as a child. Her experiences in Nebraska furnished much of the material on which she based her work. She died in 1947.

E. E. Cummings

Edward Estlin Cummings, American poet and novelist, was noted for his unique writing style, which used unconventional punctuation and typography, and innovative language and imagery, which made him a leading Modernist voice in poetry. His first book and only novel is *The Enormous Room* (1922). His verse is often light and joyful, but it contains a great depth of irony and complex feeling. His major works include *Tulips and Chimneys* (1923), *50 Poems* (1940), *95 Poems* (1958), and *73 Poems*, published after his death. Cummings also published works of nonfiction and prose.

- 61 -

Cummings was born in 1894, educated at Harvard, and served in France in World War I. He became a popular and important lecturer on the literary scene before his death in 1962.

Rainer Maria Rilke

Born René Maria Rilke, he was a German poet and a much beloved figure throughout the world, where his work is universally admired. Struggling with themes of life and death, Rilke explored man's relationship to the divine and particularly humanity's perception of the universal. His major works include *The Book of Images* (1906), *Duino Elegies* (1923), *Sonnets to Orpheus* (1923), and *New Plans*, his first volume published in 1908. Rilke is one of the most widely translated poets in the world, some of his translations done by well-known poets, such as Robert Bly and Randall Jarrell. Rilke was born in Prague in 1875. He lived across Europe, with sojourns in Germany, France, and Switzerland. Rilke visited Russia twice, which inspired his first book of poetry. Rilke died in Switzerland in 1926, a giant man of letters.

Thomas Mann

Thomas Mann, German novelist and essayist, was a writer of great importance in the early 20th century. His work usually focused on art and the struggle of the artist to flourish in European society. This conflict is the theme of the novels *Buddenbrooks* (1903) and *Death in Venice* (1912). Ultimately Mann turned to spirituality in his long allegorical novel *The Magic Mountain,* published in 1924. Later works include *Dr. Faustus* (1947) and *Joseph and His Brothers* (1933–43), a tetralogy of novels about the biblical character. Mann won the Nobel Prize for literature in 1929.

Thomas Mann was born in Germany in 1875 and fled Nazi Germany in the early 1930s after clashing with Hitler's policies. He became a United States citizen in 1944 but remained active in world affairs and visited Europe frequently after the war. He died in Switzerland in 1955.

Ezra Pound

Ezra Pound—American poet, critic, and editor—was a most controversial figure in world literature. He published his most important work of poetry, *The Cantos*, late in his career. His influence as a critic was formidable, and he fostered the work of Robert Frost, Ernest Hemingway, James Joyce, and T. S. Eliot. Pound was an important Imagist, advocating the use of free meter and the extravagant use of image. His first book of verse, *A Lume Spento*, was self-published in Europe.

Pound was born in Idaho in 1885, reared in Pennsylvania, and educated at Hamilton College and the University of Pennsylvania. He moved to Europe after college, where he became an influential critic and editor. Associated with Mussolini and his fascist regime, Pound was arrested for treasonable propaganda. Committed to an asylum in America for mental illness for 12 years, he returned to Italy until his death in 1972.

Ernest Hemingway

Ernest Hemingway, American novelist and short-story writer, was a Modernist master who became a legendary figure in his own lifetime. He achieved fame with his novels *The Sun Also Rises* (1926) and *A Farewell to Arms* (1929), based on his World War I experiences. Other important works include *For Whom the Bell Tolls* (1940), based on the Spanish Civil War, and *The Old Man and the Sea* (1952), a novel about a Cuban fisherman. Hemingway was awarded the Nobel Prize for Literature in 1954. Hemingway was born in the American Midwest in 1899 and worked as an ambulance driver in World War I. He joined a group of expatriate writers in Paris in the 1920s, a rich literary experience for a young man. Hemingway moved to Cuba in the 1940s and lived there for many years, where he became a local hero. Returning to America, he fell into a period of declining mental health, committing suicide in Idaho in 1961.

William Faulkner

William Faulkner, American novelist and short-story writer, wrote almost solely about Southern history in his fiction. After the publication of his first successful novel, *Sartoris* (1929), Faulkner reeled off a series of impressive novels, including *The Sound And the Fury* (1929), *As I Lay Dying* (1930), *Absalom, Absalom!* (1936), *Sanctuary* (1931), and *Go Down, Moses* (1942). Winner of the Nobel Prize for Literature in 1949, Faulkner also won two Pulitzer prizes. He is remembered as a giant in American literature. Faulkner was born in Mississippi in 1897 and spent most of his life there. His recurring themes include Southern aristocracy's attempt to survive in the modern world, racial inequality in the South, and the burdens of slavery carried by his characters. Much of his work is based on his own family history, both colorful and tragic.

Erich Maria Remarque

Erich Maria Remarque is the pen name of Erich Paul Remark, German novelist and literary figure. His experiences as a soldier in World War I formed the subject of his first and greatest novel, *All Quiet on the Western Front*, published in 1929. Detailing the experiences of ordinary German soldiers, the book became one of the more important literary works to emerge from the war.

Remarque was born in a small town in northern Germany in 1898. Drafted into the German army, he was gravely wounded and abandoned behind the French lines. He survived to write his fictional history of the conflagration that impacted millions of lives. Remarque never again achieved the fame following his first novel, but he remained active and lived in Europe until his death in 1970 at the age of 72.

John Dos Passos

John Dos Passos, American novelist, wrote sobering fiction and prose about the decline of the United States, both spiritually and socially. His literary reputation rests on a trilogy of novels published as *U.S.A.* in 1937. His jaundiced view of America is based on his observations of a country deeply divided by class and coarsened by commercialism. Early novels polished his stream-of-consciousness style he would employ so effectively in *U.S.A.* Dos Passos was born to a wealthy Chicago family in 1896. Educated at Harvard, he worked with Hemingway as an ambulance driver in France in World War I. Dos Passos's essentially negative view of American society is a recurring theme in his literary work. He worked as a journalist most of his life and published several works of biography and history before his death in 1970 at age 74.

Henry Miller

Henry Miller—American novelist, short-fiction writer, and essayist—is best known for two books that were banned initially in the United States, *Tropic of Cancer* (1961) and *Tropic of Capricorn* (1962), both of which were published in France first. These two autobiographical novels caused an uproar because of their controversial treatment of sex. The Supreme Court ruled in Miller's favor in 1964, and the books were then legal in America. Miller's later works include *The Rosy Crucifixion*, a trilogy based on Miller's life, along with anthologies of essays and stories. Henry Miller was born in Manhattan, New York, in 1891. He moved to Paris as a young man and celebrated his bohemian lifestyle. His works had a great influence on the Beat Generation of the 1950s. Miller returned to the United States and lived in Big Sur in Pacific Palisades until his death in 1980.

Lillian Hellman

Lillian Hellman was an American playwright and diarist who burst onto the literary scene in 1934 with *The Children's Hour*, a play about two schoolteachers who are accused of lesbianism. She followed this with *The Little Foxes*, a portrait of a ruthless Southern family. Other notable plays by Hellman include *Watch On The Rhine* (1941) and *Toys In The Attic* (1960). She published several volumes of her autobiography, which were lauded for their eloquence. Lillian Hellman was born in New Orleans in 1905 to a middle-class Jewish family. She grew up in New York and moved to Hollywood to work as a script reader. Blacklisted in the 1950s for her political activism, she fought a long battle to clear her name. Lillian Hellman grew to be a much-loved liberal icon until her death in 1984.

Clifford Odets

Clifford Odets, American playwright, was an important figure in the theatre of the 1930s. His forte was social protest theatre, in which he became a leader. Odets found his first success in *Waiting for Lefty* (1935) and *Awake and Sing* (1935), both powerful depictions of class struggle. Odets's other notable plays include *Golden Boy* (1937), *The Big Knife* (1949), and *The Country Girl* (1950).

Clifford Odets was born in Philadelphia in 1906 and raised in New York. He began his career as an actor with the Theatre Guild and later became a founding member of the famous Group Theatre. Odets remained active on Broadway as well, working in legitimate theatre. Clifford Odets died in Hollywood in 1963.

Anna Akhmatova

Anna Akhmatova is the pen name of Andreyevna Gorenko, Russian poet, whose work is set against repression in the Soviet Union. She was a leading light of the Acemist school of poetry, which valued accuracy, precision, and realistic clarity as a reaction to Symbolism. A collection of lyrical love poems, *Vecher* (1912), was her first book. Her epic poem "Requiem" (1940) was a response to her husband's execution by the Soviets. Regarded as her masterpiece, "Poem Without A Hero" (1965) narrates the difficulties of an artist working in a repressive regime. Akhmatova was born near Odessa in 1889. Stalinist officials banned her work for almost 20 years, judging it too concerned with love and God. Expelled from the Writer's Union in 1946, she was not published again until the late 1950s. She is now ranked as one of the great poets of the 20th century. She died in the Soviet Union in 1966.

Margaret Mitchell

Margaret Mitchell rests her reputation on one book, *Gone with the Wind,* published in 1936. The novel won Mitchell a Pulitzer Prize and was made into one of the most popular films of all time, starring Clark Gable and Vivian Leigh. The book narrates a Southern belle's rise and fall set against the panorama of the plantation South and the American Civil War. The protagonist, Scarlett O'Hara, suffers the end of her Southern society and her values before becoming a resilient and successful survivor. Margaret Mitchell was born in 1900 in Atlanta and lived all of her life there. She attended Smith College in Northampton, Massachusetts, and worked as a journalist in Atlanta. She wrote *Gone with the Wind* over a 10-year period, completing it in 1934. The unprecedented success of the book and film changed her life forever. She spoke, taught, and lectured over the next 10 years until her death in Atlanta in 1949.

John Steinbeck

John Steinbeck, American novelist and short-story writer, wrote with a realistic style about the lives of common people. Steinbeck's most important work describes the plight of itinerant workers set in rural and industrial California. His best-known works include *Of Mice and Men* (1937) and his Pulitzer-Prize-winning novel *The Grapes of Wrath* (1939). The latter evokes the depression-stricken Dust Bowl and a refugee family's travails. Other important books include *Cannery Row* (1945), *East Of Eden* (1952), and his whimsical *Travels with Charley* (1962). Steinbeck won the Nobel Prize for Literature in 1962. John Steinbeck was born in California in 1902. He was educated at Stanford University, where he studied marine biology. Most of his fiction is set in California, and the themes of the sea are evident in his early work. His writing exhibits a lyrical quality combined with a stark realism that was his trademark. Steinbeck died in New York City in 1968.

Robert Penn Warren

Robert Penn Warren was an influential American novelist, poet, and critic. His most famous work is the Pulitzer-Prize-winning novel *All The King's Men*, published in 1946. Based loosely on the life of Huey P. Long, it was adapted into an Oscar-winning motion picture in 1949. Other important fiction includes the novel *World Enough and Time* (1950) and the short story collection *The Circus in the Attic* (1947). Warren published 14 collections of poetry and won the Pulitzer Prize for *Now and Then* (1978). He was an influential literary critic, promoting the New Criticism in important textbooks. Robert Penn Warren was born in Kentucky and attended Vanderbilt University. He taught for many years at Louisiana State University, where he founded the *Southern Review*. He was named Poet Laureate of the United States in 1986. Warren died in 1989.

Richard Wright

Richard Wright, American novelist and short-fiction writer, was one of the most influential black voices in American literature. His first book, *Uncle Tom's Children* (1938), included four novellas and won critical acclaim. Wright's publication of the best-selling *Native Son* in 1940 ensured his place in literary history. In addition to *Native Son*, Wright's other important work includes *The Outsider* (1953) and his autobiography, *Black Boy*, published in 1945. Richard Wright was born in rural Mississippi in 1908, the grandson of slaves. Reared in Memphis, largely self-educated, he moved to Chicago at age 19 and entered the Federal Writers' Project. During the Depression, Wright joined the Communist Party and lived in Mexico before settling in Paris. Richard Wright died in Paris in 1960 at the age of 52.

Carson McCullers

Carson McCullers, born Lula Carson Smith, American novelist, set her fiction in the small Southern towns she grew up in as a child. Her themes were alienation, loneliness, and spiritual longing. Her best-known novel, *The Member of the Wedding*, narrates the story of a lonely adolescent girl in a Southern town who lives vicariously through her brother. Her literary reputation was established with the appearance of *The Heart Is a Lonely Hunter* in 1940. Other well-known works include *Reflections in a Golden Eye* (1941), *Clock Without Hands* (1961), and a posthumously published story collection, *The Mortgaged Heart* (1971). Carson McCullers was born in Georgia in 1917 and studied music at Julliard before attending Columbia to study writing. She was ill most of her life and a series of crippling strokes began in her twenties. She died in 1967 at age 50.

Eudora Welty

Eudora Welty—American novelist, short-fiction writer, critic, and essayist—was one of the great writers of the South. She mastered the Southern vernacular and the culture and customs of the South, and produced an impressive body of work. Her first collection, *A Curtain Of Green* (1941), contained many of her most popular stories. Her novel *The Ponder Heart* (1954) is a classic of absurdist humor. *The Optimist's Daughter* (1972) won her a Pulitzer Prize in 1972. She holds many honors, including the French Legion of Merit and the American Medal of Freedom. Welty was born in Jackson, Mississippi, in 1909, and attended Mississippi State University and the University of Wisconsin. She lived in New York until her father's early death caused her to return to Jackson, where she would live the rest of her life. She was a literary figure of great importance in the South until her death in 2001.

Bertolt Brecht

Bertolt Brecht, born Eugene Berthold Friedrich Brecht, was a German playwright and poet whose major contribution to drama was to utilize the stage as a platform for political and social commentary. Brecht believed that the stage was a forum for presenting patterns of human behavior, outlined in his theory of epic theatre. His success dated from the writing of *The Three Penney Opera* in 1928, a work of biting satire coauthored with composer Kurt Weill. Two other plays of interest are *Mother Courage and Her Children* (1941) and *The Life of Galileo* (1943). An anthology of English translations appeared in 1979. Brecht was born in Augsburg, Germany, in 1898. Brecht embraced Marxism and was forced to flee Germany in 1933 by the Nazis. He lived in Europe and the United States for many years until returning to East Germany in 1949. He died there in 1956.

Albert Camus

Albert Camus—French philosopher, poet, novelist, and playwright—explored the philosophy of the absurd through his work. He examined man's existence in an indifferent universe and stressed the need for humanistic and moral values in this situation. Success came with his novel *The Stranger* (1942) and his essay "The Myth Of Sisyphus" (1942), both arresting explorations of the absurd. Other significant works include the novels *The Plague* (1947) and *The Fall* (1956) and his influential essay "The Rebel" (1951). Camus was born in Algiers in 1913 to a middle-class family. He studied philosophy at the University of Algiers and later worked as a journalist. He was an intellectual leader of the French Resistance under Nazi occupation and served as the editor of the underground paper *Combat*. Camus was awarded the Nobel Prize for Literature in 1957. He died in an automobile accident in 1960.

Jorge Luis Borges

Jorge Luis Borges—Argentinean poet, novelist essayist, and short-story writer—combined fantasy, myth, and philosophy in the fabric of daily life. His work is highly original, and his collection of essays, *Other Inquisitions* (1952), explains the writer's philosophy of life and art. Other important works are a book blending poetry and prose, *The Book of Imaginary Beings* (1967), a collection of stories, *The Book of Sand*, and a collection of his poetry in English translation. Born in Argentina in 1899, Borges studied abroad and received his degree from College de Geneva in Switzerland before returning home. During the dictatorship of Juan Perón, Borges was a vocal critic of the government. After the fall of Perón, Borges was appointed director of the National Library of Argentina in Buenos Aires. Borges died in 1986.

Jean Genet

Jean Genet, French novelist and playwright, is the master of drama and fiction depicting criminal life and antisocial behavior. His absurdist dramas are existentialist nightmares that mix violence and erotic content in a powerful blend. Genet's breakthrough novel was *Our Lady Of The Flowers* (1943), written in prison while serving a life sentence. Sartre and Cocteau successfully argued for Genet's release, and he published his shocking autobiography *The Thief's Journal* in 1949. Genet then turned his attention to drama, writing several successful plays, including *The Maids* (1947), *The Balcony* (1956), and *The Blacks* (1948), all of which were influential in the development of avant-garde theatre. Genet was born in France in 1910, an illegitimate child abandoned by his mother. After spending his youth in unhappy foster homes and orphanages, he joined the Foreign Legion and promptly deserted. Genet died in France in 1986.

Tennessee Williams

Tennessee Williams, born Thomas Lanier Williams II, is regarded as one of the greatest American playwrights of the 20th century. His subject matter was drawn from the earthiest topics and treated with a lyrical touch in a romantic, yet realistic, view of America's South. His rise to fame was meteoric with *The Glass Menagerie* in 1945, followed by his Pulitzer-Prize-winning *A Streetcar Named Desire* in 1947. Other important plays followed, including *Cat on a Hot Tin Roof* in 1955, which earned Williams another Pulitzer, *Suddenly Last Summer* in 1958, *Sweet Bird of Youth* in 1959, and his last hit, *The Night of the Iguana*, in 1961. Williams was born in Mississippi in 1911 and educated at the universities of Washington and Iowa. After his dramatic success had slowed, he published a collection of poetry and his memoirs. Williams is generally regarded, along with Eugene O'Neill and Arthur Miller, as one of the greatest American dramatists. He died in 1983 at the age of 71.

William Carlos Williams

William Carlos Williams—American poet, novelist and short-story author—found inspiration for his work in the experiences of everyday life. He wrote 45 volumes of prose and poetry, typically American, using his realistic, or Objectivist, style. His best poetry was his five-volume *Paterson* (1946–58), based on the city near his home. His *Pictures From Brueghel* (1962), a three-volume work, won Williams a Pulitzer Prize in 1962. He also published numerous works of short fiction and the Stecher trilogy of novels. His prose includes a book of essays and an autobiography.

William Carlos Williams was born in Rutherford, New Jersey, in 1883 and studied medicine in college. He returned to his birthplace and practiced as a pediatrician for over 50 years while turning out a huge body of innovative and very American work. Williams was unusual in that he literally had two full-time careers his whole adult life. He is now regarded as a leading Modernist writer. He died in New Jersey in 1963.

Norman Mailer

Norman Mailer—American novelist, short-story writer, essayist, and journalist—won his initial success with *The Naked and the Dead*, his autobiographical novel of World War II, published in 1948. Blending gritty realism with a unique and arresting writing style, Mailer was granted instant celebrity. His later novels never approached the success of *The Naked and the Dead*, and his reputation today rests largely on his journalism. Mailer won the Pulitzer Prize for *Armies of the Night* and *The Executioner's Song*, both nonfiction books. Norman Mailer was born in New Jersey in 1923 and educated at Harvard University. After his initial success in fiction, he developed his own blend of journalism, political commentary, fictional allusions, and autobiography into a rich style with colorful language. Significant later works include *Ancient Evenings* and *Harlot's Ghost*. He died in 2007.

Arthur Miller

Arthur Miller, American playwright, described the pain of the common man in his stirring dramas. Perhaps his best-known play, *Death Of A Salesman* (1949) earned him a Pulitzer Prize. *The Crucible* (1953), a drama about the Salem witch trials, is regarded as an American classic. Miller was an extremely productive author, penning dramas over six decades. Some of his better early works include *A View From The Bridge* (1955), *The Price* (1968), and *The American Clock* (1980). Notable later works include *The Misfits and Other Stories* (1987) and a novella, *Homely Girl* (1995).

Arthur Miller was born in Harlem in 1915. Educated at the University of Michigan, he began writing plays in the 1940s. Haunted by his father's failure during the depression, Miller returned to the subject of failure in many of his plays. He had an extremely productive career, ending with his death in 2005.

Simone de Beauvoir

Simone de Beauvoir—French novelist, philosopher, and memoirist—was a powerful intellectual figure in post-World War II Europe. Perhaps her most important work is *The Second Sex* (1949), a ground-breaking feminist polemic about the secondary status of women in the world. Her best-known novel is *The Mandarins* (1954), which relates her struggles with the repressive regimes of Vichy, followed by Stalinist excesses. De Beauvoir wrote extensively about her life and published five volumes of memoirs that offered a window of history into her time. Born in Montparnasse in Paris in 1908, she met and formed the defining relationship of her life with Jean-Paul Sartre. This was a friendship, a love relationship, and a partnership of philosophy and art. She focused on the themes of individual freedom, particularly between the sexes. She died in Paris in 1986.

J. D. Salinger

Jerome David Salinger, American novelist and short-fiction writer, is one of the most enigmatic figures in 20th-century literary history. Salinger wrote one novel, *The Catcher In The Rye*, published in 1951, which has been a bible to coming-of-age youth ever since. His hero, Holden Caulfield, seeks meaning in a world he finds contrived and artificial. The book has been required reading in countless college courses over the years. Salinger also wrote several collections of short stories, including *Nine Stories* (1953) and *Franny and Zooey* (1961), which narrate young people's alienation from society. Salinger was born in New York in 1919 and little is known about his early life. After his success in the early 1950s, Salinger became a recluse in New England and withstood all attempts to interview or even meet him. He has published almost nothing since the early 1960s.

Ralph Ellison

Ralph Ellison, American novelist and essayist, published only one novel in his lifetime. His hugely successful *The Invisible Man*, published in 1952, was a candid and realistic examination of race relations in the United States. The unnamed protagonist, a black man, realizes his color makes him essentially invisible in American society. Winner of The National Book Award in 1952, *The Invisible Man* has become a classic in the study of race relations in modern America. Ellison remained a productive writer, publishing books of essays and short stories. Ralph Ellison was born in Oklahoma and originally trained as a musician. He joined the Federal Writers' Project in 1936 and met and befriended Richard Wright. He lived most of his adult life in New York City, where he held an endowed chair at New York University. Ellison died in New York in 1994.

Frank O'Hara

Frank O'Hara—American poet, playwright, and art critic—was a leader of a group of poets known as The New York School, which captured the spirit of New York in conventional and conversational verse. Drawing from expressionism and the sounds of jazz and cadences of New York, this school produced poetry that was truly American. O'Hara was known for his improvisational writing such as *Lunch Poems* (1964), *Meditations in an Emergency* (1956), and his tribute to Billie Holiday, "The Day Lady Died" (1955). Frank O'Hara was born in Baltimore in 1926 and raised in Massachusetts. Educated at Harvard and the University of Michigan, he migrated to New York and became editor of *Art News*, where much of his art criticism first appeared. Intimates such as Willem de Kooning and Jackson Pollock provided much of the inspiration for his improvisational work. O'Hara was killed in an accident at Fire Island in 1966, cutting short his career at age 40.

James Baldwin

James Baldwin—American novelist, playwright, and essayist—became the leading black author of his time. His autobiographical novel *Go Tell It On The Mountain* (1953) is the story of a teenage boy growing up in Harlem. His work almost exclusively deals with intolerance and the struggle for free expression. His own experience of racism in America resulted in his collection of essays, *Notes of a Native Son*, published to critical success in 1955. Several anthologies of his works have been published. James Baldwin was born in Harlem in 1924, the son of a popular clergyman. Depressed by race relations in the United States, Baldwin emigrated to Paris after World War II and remained in France the rest of his life. Baldwin was heavily involved in the Civil Rights movement in America and won praise for his activism. Baldwin died in Saint Paul de Venice in 1987.

Saul Bellow

Saul Bellow, Canadian-born American novelist, was noted for the ethical intensity of his work. He depicted the experiences of urban Jews in America in a new voice. Critical and popular success came to Bellow with the publication of *The Adventures Of Augie March* (1953) and *Henderson, the Rain King* (1959). A trio of his best work followed: *Herzog* (1954), winner of the National Book Award, *Mr. Sammler's Planet* (1970), and his Pulitzer-Prize-winning novel, *Humboldt's Gift* (1975). Bellow continued his productivity into the 21st century. Bellow was born in Montreal, Canada, in 1915. He grew up in Chicago, and like many young writers of this period, got his start with the WPA Writers' Project. He grew to be a grand figure in American fiction and is regarded as one of the great modern novelists. Bellow died in 2005.

Ray Bradbury

Ray Bradbury—American novelist, short-fiction writer, playwright, and poet—is known primarily as a writer of fantasy and science fiction. He is known for weaving social criticism into his work, and shows a constant wariness of the dangers of technology. Bradbury's best works include *Fahrenheit 451* (1953), *The Martian Chronicles* (1950), and *The Illustrated Man* (1951), all best sellers in the then-exploding field of science fiction. Bradbury, a prolific writer, has also published volumes of poetry, children's books, plays, and television and film screenplays. Bradbury was born in 1920 in the Midwest. He was an early contributor to pulp fiction and fantasy magazines. His early success gave him the freedom to experiment with different styles and genres. Bradbury has been a productive author for over 50 years and continues to develop fresh ideas and creative approaches to his craft.

Wallace Stevens

Wallace Stevens is one of the great Modernist poets. His verse covers a wide scope of themes but returns continually to the role of poetry in filling the emptiness created by the lack of God. Stevens did not publish his first book until he was 44. Through the 1930s, '40s, and '50s he produced a body of work that includes *The Man With The Blue Guitar* (1937), *Transport to Summer* (1947), and *Parts of a World* (1942), to name only a few. Stevens was ignored during his lifetime for the most part, and only in the last year of his life did he win a Pulitzer Prize and National Book Award.

Born in Reading, Pennsylvania, in 1879, he was educated at Harvard and studied law in New York City. He became an insurance attorney and worked for almost 40 years with The Hartford Accident And Indemnity Company. During this period, he turned out a body of work rarely excelled in modern poetry. Stevens died in 1955.

Vladimir Nabokov

Vladimir Nabokov—Russian-born American novelist, critic, and translator—was a skillful, imaginative, and creative writer who has earned a place in literary history. He published his first few novels under a pseudonym in Berlin. He will always be best known for *Lolita*, his landmark novel published in 1955. This highly controversial novel was about the affair of a middle-aged man and his young stepdaughter. Nabokov wrote other excellent novels, including *Pale Fire* (1962), *Pnin* (1957), and *Ada or Ardor* (1969). He was a translator of talent; his work with Pushkin's *Eugene Onegin* won him plaudits. Nabokov was born in Russia in 1899. He studied literature at Cambridge and then lived in Paris before emigrating to the United States in 1940. He taught at several excellent universities, completing *Lolita* when he was on the faculty at Cornell. He then devoted himself full-time to writing and died in 1977 at the age of 78.

Miguel de Cervantes

Miguel de Cervantes was an accomplished Spanish novelist, poet, and playwright. A giant in literary history, Cervantes is best known as the author of <u>Don Quixote</u>, an early masterpiece of prose fiction. Many view him as the originator of the novel, and it is agreed that Cervantes demonstrated the possibilities of satirical narrative and fictional realism. His work has inspired novelists for almost 400 years. Born into a poor family outside Madrid, Cervantes became a soldier and was captured and enslaved by Algerian pirates for five years. Ransomed by Trinitarian friars, he worked as a businessman in Andalusia until the success of <u>Don Quixote</u> allowed him the freedom to devote himself to writing. He was productive in later life, writing <u>Exemplary Stories</u>, a work of 12 diverse narratives. He authored at least 30 plays of which about half survive. Cervantes completed an epic romance, <u>The Trials of Persiles and Sigismunda</u>, only three days before his death in 1616.

Moilere

Jeb-Baptiste Poquelin, known as Moliere, was the greatest playwright of his time. Combining an acute ear for language, sharp character portraits, and the ability to evoke both profound and absurd moods, Moliere delighted his sophisticated Parisian audiences. His most popular plays include <u>La Tartuffe</u>, banned by the Church, <u>The Misanthrope</u>, and <u>The School for Wives</u>. Moliere's unique combinations of talents produced a new type of comedy—the comedy of manners—which brought him both fame and wealth. Moliere was born into a well-to-do Paris family in 1622. He eschewed a promising business career to devote himself to the theatre. He was active as an actor, writer, producer and director, and toured France for ten years. Moliere became a favorite of King Louis XIV who offered him a theatre in the Louvre. Here he flourished becoming a favorite of

French society. Moliere continued his dramatic work in Paris when during a performance of his last play, "The Imaginary Invalid", he collapsed and died in 1673.

Johan Strindberg

Johan Strindberg was a Swedish novelist, playwright, essayist, and short-fiction writer. His initial success was a novel of bohemian life in Sweden, The Red Room, published in 1879. His writing was noted for blending realism and naturalism together in a unique manner. His best novels include The Father (1887) and Miss Julie (1889). Strindberg later turned to Symbolism mixed with Expressionism for his Ghost Sonata (1908) and The Great Highway (1910), both autobiographical plays. Strindberg was born in Sweden in 1849. An unhappy childhood followed by three failed marriages influenced his work greatly. His public life was full of controversy and he flirted with debilitating mental illness all his life, describing a near-breakdown in Inferno (1897). He died in 1912.

F. Scott Fitzgerald

F. Scott Fitzgerald was an American novelist and short-story writer. Fitzgerald has transcended his early reputation as a period novelist, now being viewed as a great modern novelist. He launched his writing career with This Side of Paradise (1920), a novel of the jazz age. His masterpiece, The Great Gatsby (1925), chronicles the life of a bootlegger who reforms. Tender is the Night (1933) is a largely autobiographical novel about a psychiatrist's failing fight to save his wife from mental illness. Fitzgerald was born in St. Paul, Minnesota in 1896. Educated at Princeton University, he became a productive short-story writer after the success of his first novel. His marriage to the flamboyant Zelda Fitzgerald spiraled downward with alcoholism and her increasing mental illness. He worked in Hollywood as a screenwriter before his death in 1940.

Hart Crane

Hart Crane, an American poet, left behind one work on which his reputation rests. "The Bridge," Hart's 18-part epic poem based on the Brooklyn Bridge, celebrates America's muscular industrial strength in a manner that precedes Carl Sandburg. The poem, published in 1930, was a popular and critical success. Combining bold imagery with technical dexterity, the sweeping American themes captured the fancy of the public and critics alike. His complete works including a manuscript found after his death were published in 1966. Crane was born in Ohio in 1899, and was an industrial worker during World War I. Hart suffered from depression his entire life, and committed suicide when returning from a trip to Mexico by jumping off of the ship into the ocean. This bizarre death ended a promising talent in 1932 when Hart was only 32 years old.

Nelson Algren

Nelson Algren, born Nelson Ahlgren Abraham, was an American novelist and short-story writer. His work is noted by the stark reality with which he depicts the lives of the poor. Algren is best remembered for his novel The Man With The Golden Arm (1949) which brings the reality of drug addiction to the literary world. The book, which was later adapted into an award-winning film, earned him a National Book Award and gave him a national reputation. Later works include the story collection The Neon Wilderness (1947) and a novel about Bohemian life in New Orleans, entitled A Walk On The Wild Side. Algren was born in 1809 in Detroit and raised in Chicago. Educated at the University of Illinois, he set much of his fiction in the Midwest, where he explored the seamy side of urban life. Algren was always viewed as a radical personality and his work reflects a slice of American urban life largely unnoticed. He died in 1981.

Explanations of Medieval/Renaissance Christian allegory

The student should explain that in literature, authors of allegory use all of the literal plot elements of their writing as symbols to represent more abstract subjects. For example, in *The Divine Comedy*, Dante symbolizes the human soul's efforts to achieve moral beliefs and behaviors and become united with God by narrating his persona's literal adventures as he travels through the kingdoms of Hell, Purgatory, and Heaven (*Inferno, Purgatorio,* and *Paradiso*). What appear literal stories of fantasy experiences are allegorical references to the human spiritual quest. The student should provide textual evidence, for example, quoting the *Inferno*'s opening: "Midway on our life's journey, I found myself / In dark woods, the right road lost". The student could then explain that by the plural first-person possessive in "*our* life's journey", Dante connects his persona's story to all of humanity's universal experience, reinforcing this by referring to "the right road" of which he has lost track. The student should explain the "dark woods" as an allegorical symbol of a human being's sinful, unenlightened Earthly existence and the "right road" symbolizing the life of virtue that unites people with God.

Example student explanation of a poet using a quote from an earlier poet's work

In "The Love Song of J. Alfred Prufrock", Eliot's six-line epigraph is from Canto 27 of Dante's *Inferno.* Eliot quotes Dante's original Italian, spoken by Guido da Montefeltro: "*S'io credesse che mia risposta fosse / A persona che mai tornasse al mondo, / Questa fiamma staria senza piu scosse. /Ma perciocche giammai di questo fondo/Non torno vivo alcun, s'i'odo il vero, / Senza tema d'infamia ti rispondo.*" Eliot omits translation: "If I believed my answer would be to a person who could return to the world, this flame would stay without more motion; but because nobody has ever come back alive from this abyss, if what I hear is true, without fear of infamy I can reply." Guido, fearing worldly ill repute for evil Earthly deeds, believed he could confide these to Dante—also trapped in Hell, hence unable to repeat them. Guido's "flame" represents his disembodied form in Hell: if he believed Dante could return to Earth (which he ultimately did), he/it would move/speak no more. "Prufrock" echoes the hellish setting, depicting hypocrites pretending goodness. Prufrock's concern for his reputation echoes Guido's: *Prufrock*'s dramatic monologue is best safely addressed to nobody who would repeat it.

Interpretation of quotes and references in first section of T. S. Eliot's *The Waste Land*

In *The Waste Land*'s first section, "The Burial of the Dead", Eliot refers to Chaucer's *Canterbury* Tales opening about April—but twisting it from Chaucer's happy depiction of its "sweet showers" to "...the cruelest month, breeding / Lilacs out of the dead land, mixing / memory and desire..." He quotes Wagner's opera *Tristan and Isolde* retelling the Arthurian story of adulterous lovers and the loss experienced through their actions. Eliot used his extensive knowledge of literature to reinforce his depiction of the fragmented, decayed "waste land" of post-World War I twentieth-century society. Two major influences Eliot took were *From Ritual to Romance* by Jessie Weston and *The Golden Bough* by Sir James Frazier—both British contemporaries of Eliot (born in America but resettled in England). Both authors described ancient fertility rites reflected Arthurian legend and modern religion and thought—prominently, the Fisher King legend. His wounds, causing impotence, made his country a "waste land." The land's fertility could be reclaimed by healing the Fisher King. Eliot incorporates the Fisher King theme in *The Waste Land*—yet without healing potential, reinforcing the modern world's lack of mythological or religious narrative to unify it.

Example student explanation of extended metaphor of mechanical object as an animal

In her poem "I like to see it lap the Miles", Emily Dickinson describes a railroad train, a new invention during her time, via extended metaphor comparing it to a horse. She writes of seeing the train "lap the miles—/And lick the Valleys up—/And/...feed itself at Tanks..." She describes seeing it "...prodigious step / Around a Pile of Mountains...And then a Quarry pare / To fit its Ribs..." She describes the train's whistle as "...horrid—hooting stanza" and further characterizes it as a "neigh". She concludes the poem by describing how the train, like a horse, will "...punctual as a Star / Stop— docile and omnipotent / At its own stable door—", representing the train depot/station as a horse's "stable". Juxtaposing the opposites of docility and omnipotence, Dickinson alludes to the way horses are physically powerful, yet often gentle and obedient to much smaller, physically weaker humans. Through the extended metaphor, she moreover likens the train to a horse, for its great power harnessed and controlled by humans.

Student interpretation of imagery

In Act I, Scene V of *Romeo and Juliet,* Shakespeare writes dialogue wherein Romeo describes how beautiful Juliet is using visual imagery: "O, she doth teach the torches to burn bright! / It seems she hangs upon the cheek of night / Like a rich jewel in an Ethiope's ear..." By saying she "teaches" torches to burn brightly, Shakespeare makes the point that Juliet's radiance surpasses that of the flames, contrasting it with the darkness of night. Then, he compares night's darkness to an Ethiopian's skin, and Juliet's contrasting brilliance to a gem's glow in an earring against the dark skin. In "Ode to Autumn", Keats uses auditory imagery to bring the season's "music" alive: "...in a wailful choir the small gnats mourn /...Or sinking as the light wind lives or dies; / And full-grown lambs loud bleat from hilly bourn; / Hedge-crickets sing; and now with treble soft / The redbreast whistles from a garden-croft, / And gathering swallows twitter in the skies." He appeals to readers' hearing, describing intermittent wind; gnats mourning in a "wailful choir"; lambs bleating; crickets singing; a robin's soft treble whistling; and swallows twittering.

Rhetorical devices vs. figures of speech

Although figures of speech and rhetorical devices are very similar and overlap in many aspects of their definitions, one difference is that a figure of speech uses the effect of altering word meanings to express an idea more colorfully or vividly. For example, instead of saying a woman is strong-willed; free-spirited; feisty; attractive, yet unpredictable; and maybe dangerous, some people use the figure of speech, "She's a pistol." When the main purpose of a figure of speech becomes that of convincing or persuading the audience—the writer's readers or the speaker's listeners—of the writer's point or argument, then the figure of speech can be said to become a rhetorical device. One type of rhetorical device is anaphora: the repetition at regular intervals of the same word or phrase, used to create an effect. Walt Whitman used anaphora in his poems *Crossing Brooklyn Ferry:* "Flood-tide below me! I watch you, face to face; / Clouds of the west! sun there half an hour high! I see you also face to face." and *Song of Myself* (Part 51): "Do I contradict myself? / Very well then I contradict myself, / (I am large, I contain multitudes.)"

Both figures of speech and rhetorical devices are used to create calculated effects and communicate specific emphases. One main difference is that figures of speech change the meanings of words. For example, instead of writing, "She is brave", one writes "She is a tiger": this figure of speech employs a metaphor, conveying the same meaning but using a different word than the original. By contrast, one example of a rhetorical device is using repetition to create emphasis without changing word meanings: "I am never ever going to rob anyone for you and never, never ever give in to your sinful wish." In Book V of *Paradise Lost,* the great poet John Milton uses rhetoric: "...advise him of his happy state—/ Happiness in his power left free to will, / Left to his own free will, his will though free / Yet mutable…" Describing Adam, Milton emphasized humanity's free will by repeating the words "free" and "will". But he also created ambiguity by writing "though free / Yet mutable", i.e. free will was changeable: Adam could lose freedom by sinning/erring.

Use of rhetoric in poetry

In Holy Sonnet 10 – "Death, be not proud" – the great Metaphysical poet John Donne rhetorically berates Death. In the final sestet, Donne writes: "Thou art slave to fate, chance, kings, and desperate men, / And dost with poison, war, and sickness dwell, / And poppy or charms can make us sleep as well / And better than thy stroke; why swell'st thou then?" This illustrates the message stated in the first quatrain: "Death, be not proud, though some have called thee / Mighty and dreadful, for thou art not so; / For those whom thou think'st dost overthrow / Die not, poor Death, nor yet canst thou kill me." Donne opens denying Death is as powerful or horrible as some say, then adding that some whom Death thinks it kills do not die, and neither can Death kill him. He supports this argument by subsequently diminishing Death's reputed power, characterizing Death as a "slave"; associating it with the poor company of "poison, war, and sickness"; and ultimately asks the rhetorical question, "why swell'st thou then?" meaning Death has no reason to swell with pride—deflating Death's value and strength.

Rhetorical devices

Alliteration and hyperbole

Alliteration is both a literary and rhetorical device, using several words in sequence with the same initial sound. An example as literary device is in Wallace Stevens' (1922) poem "The Emperor of Ice Cream": "And bid him whip in kitchen cups concupiscent curds." Two examples of alliteration as rhetorical devices used by speakers for effect are Julius Caesar's "Veni, vidi, vici" ("I came, I saw, I conquered"), and John F. Kennedy's 1961 Inaugural Address: "Let us go forth to lead the land we love." Both repeated word-initial sounds to make their speeches more memorable. Hyperbole is extreme exaggeration for emphasis or effect. An example is in Andrew Marvell's famous (1650~1652) *carpe diem*-tradition poem "To His Coy Mistress": "My vegetable love should grow / Vaster than empires, and more slow; / An hundred years should go to praise / Thine eyes and on thine forehead gaze; / Two hundred to adore each breast, / But thirty thousand to the rest." Marvell exaggerates his love "Had we but world enough and time" as potentially growing longer than empires, hundreds and thousands of years.

Irony and oxymoron

Irony is the literary and rhetorical device of expressing one meaning by stating it using words that have the opposite meaning. In everyday speech it is also called sarcasm. An example of irony in literature in Shakespeare's tragedy *Julius Caesar* is in Act 3, Scene 2, in Marc Antony's famous eulogy speech at Caesar's funeral: "He was my friend, faithful and just to me. / But Brutus says he was ambitious, / And Brutus is an honorable man." Antony is using irony when he calls Brutus "honorable" to mean he is not. Four lines earlier, he also says "For Brutus is an honorable man; / So are they all, all honorable men…" ironically and indirectly indicting the many dishonorable men involved. Oxymoron juxtaposes apparently contradictory words; some everyday speech examples include "jumbo shrimp", "deafening silence", "conspicuous absence", etc. A literary example is in Shakespeare's *Hamlet,* Act 3, Scene 4: "I must be cruel only to be kind." Shakespeare's phrasing was so popular it has since been adopted into everyday expressions.

Literary irony

In literature, irony demonstrates the opposite of what is said or done. Three types are verbal irony, situational irony, and dramatic irony. Verbal irony uses words opposite to the meaning. Sarcasm may use verbal irony. An everyday example is describing something confusing as "clear as mud." In his 1986 movie *Hannah and Her Sisters,* author/director/actor Woody Allen says to his character's date, "I had a great evening; it was like the Nuremburg Trials." Notice these employ similes. In situational irony, what happens contrasts with what was expected. In dramatic irony, narrative informs audiences of more than its characters know. O. Henry's short story *The Gift of the Magi* uses situational irony: a husband and wife each sacrifice their most prized possession to buy each other a Christmas present. The irony is that she sells her long hair to buy him a watch fob, while he sells his heirloom pocket-watch to buy her the jeweled combs for her hair she had long wanted; in the end, neither of them can use their gifts.

Literal and figurative meaning

When language is used literally, the words mean exactly what they say and nothing more. When language is used figuratively, the words mean something more and/or other than what they say. For example, "The weeping willow tree has long, trailing branches and leaves" is a literal description. But "The weeping willow tree looks as if it is bending over and crying" is a figurative description—specifically, a simile or stated comparison. Another figurative language form is metaphor, or an implied comparison. A good example is the metaphor of a city, state, or city-state as a ship, and its governance as sailing that ship. Ancient Greek lyrical poet Alcaeus is credited with first using this metaphor, and ancient Greek tragedian Aeschylus then used it in *Seven Against Thebes,* and then Plato used it in the *Republic.* Henry Wadsworth Longfellow later famously referred to it in his poem, "O Ship of State" (1850), which has an extended metaphor with numerous nautical references throughout.

Drawing inferences

Inferences about literary text are logical conclusions that readers make based on their observations and previous knowledge. By inferring, readers construct meanings from text relevant to them personally. By combining their own schemas or concepts and their background information pertinent to the text with what they read, readers interpret it according to both what the author has conveyed and their own unique perspectives. Authors do not always explicitly spell out every meaning in what they write; many meanings are implicit. Through inference, readers can comprehend implied meanings in the text, and also derive personal significance from it, making the text meaningful and memorable to them. Inference is a natural process in everyday life. When readers infer, they can draw conclusions about what the author is saying, predict what may reasonably follow, amend these predictions as they continue to read, interpret the import of themes, and analyze the characters' feelings and motivations through their actions, and much more.

Textual evidence to analyze literature

Knowing about the historical background and social context of a literary work, as well as the identity of that work's author, can help to inform the reader about the author's concerns and intended meanings. For example, George Orwell published his novel *1984* in the year 1949, soon after the end of World War II. At that time, following the defeat of the Nazis, the Cold War began between the Western Allied nations and the Eastern Soviet Communists. People were therefore concerned about the conflict between the freedoms afforded by Western democracies versus the oppression represented by Communism. Author Orwell had also previously fought in the Spanish

Civil War against a Spanish regime that he and his fellows viewed as oppressive. From this information, readers can infer that Orwell was concerned about oppression by totalitarian governments. This informs *1984*'s story of Winston Smith's rebellion against the oppressive "Big Brother" government of the fictional dictatorial state of Oceania and his capture, torture, and ultimate conversion by that government.

Literary theme

When we read parables, their themes are the lessons they aim to teach. When we read fables, the moral of each story is its theme. When we read fictional works, the authors' perspectives regarding life and human behavior are their themes. Unlike in parables and fables, themes in literary fiction are not meant to preach or teach the readers a lesson. Hence themes in fiction are not as explicit as they are in parables or fables. Instead they are implicit, and the reader only infers them. By analyzing the fictional characters through thinking about their actions and behavior, and understanding the setting of the story and reflecting on how its plot develops, the reader comes to infer the main theme(s) of the work. When writers succeed, they communicate with their readers such that some common ground is established between author and audience. While a reader's individual experience may differ in its details from the author's written story, both may share universal underlying truths which allow author and audience to connect.

Determining theme

In well-crafted literature, theme, structure, and plot are interdependent and inextricable: each element informs and reflects the others. The structure of a work is how it is organized. The theme is the central idea or meaning found in it. The plot is what happens in the story. (Plots can be physical actions or mental processes—e.g., Marcel Proust.) Titles can also inform us of a work's theme. For instance, Edgar Allan Poe's title "The Tell-Tale Heart" informs us of its theme of guilt before we even read about the repeated heartbeat the protagonist begins hearing immediately before and constantly after committing and hiding a murder. Repetitive patterns of events or behaviors also give clues to themes. The same is true of symbols: in F. Scott Fitzgerald's *The Great Gatsby,* for Jay Gatsby the green light at the end of the dock symbolizes Daisy Buchanan and his own dreams for the future. More generally, it symbolizes the American Dream, and narrator Nick Carraway explicitly compares it to early settlers' sight of America rising from the ocean.

Thematic development in *The Great Gatsby*

In *The Great Gatsby*, F. Scott Fitzgerald portrayed 1920s America as greedy, cynical, and rife with moral decay. Jay Gatsby's lavish weekly parties symbolize the reckless excesses of the Jazz Age. The growth of bootlegging and organized crime in reaction to Prohibition is symbolized by the character of Meyer Wolfsheim and by Gatsby's own ill-gotten wealth. Fitzgerald symbolized social divisions using geography: the "old money" aristocrats like the Buchanans lived on East Egg, while the "new money" bourgeois like Gatsby lived on West Egg. Fitzgerald also used weather, as many authors have, to reinforce narrative and emotional tones in the novel. Just as in *Romeo and Juliet*, William Shakespeare set the confrontation of Tybalt and Mercutio and its deadly consequences on the hottest summer day under a burning sun, in *The Great Gatsby*, Fitzgerald did the same with Tom Wilson's deadly confrontation with Gatsby. Both works are ostensible love stories carrying socially critical themes about the destructiveness of pointless and misguided behaviors—family feuds in the former, pursuit of money in the latter.

Thematic development in *Les Misérables*

In Victor Hugo's novel *Les Misérables*, the overall metamorphosis of protagonist Jean Valjean from a cynical ex-convict into a noble benefactor demonstrates Hugo's theme of the importance of love and compassion for others. Hugo also reflects this in more specific plot events. For example, Valjean's love for Cosette sustains him through many difficult periods and trying events. Hugo illustrates how love and compassion for others beget the same in them: Bishop Myriel's kindness to Valjean eventually inspires him to become honest. Years later, Valjean, as M. Madeleine, has rescued Fauchelevent from under a fallen carriage, Fauchelevent returns the compassionate act by giving Valjean sanctuary in the convent. M. Myriel's kindness also ultimately enables Valjean to rescue Cosette from the Thénardiers. Receiving Valjean's father-like love enables Cosette to fall in love with and marry Marius. And the love between Cosette and Marius enables the couple to forgive Valjean for his past crimes when they are revealed.

Thematic development in "The Tell-Tale Heart"

In one of his shortest stories, Poe used economy of language to emphasize the murderer-narrator's obsessive focus on bare details like the victim's cataract-milky eye, the sound of a heartbeat, and insistence he is sane. The narrator begins by denying he is crazy, even citing his extreme agitation as proof of sanity. Contradiction is then extended: the narrator loves the old man, yet kills him. His motives are irrational—not greed or revenge, but to relieve the victim of his "evil eye." Because "eye" and "I" are homonyms, readers may infer that eye/I symbolizes the old man's identity, contradicting the killer's delusion that he can separate them. The narrator distances himself from the old man by perceiving his eye as separate, and dismembering his dead body. This backfires in another body part when he imagines the victim's heartbeat, which is really his own. Guilty and paranoid, he gives himself away. Poe predated Freud in exploring the paradox of killing those we love and the concept of projecting our own processes onto others.

Thematic development in A *Rose for Emily*

William Faulkner contrasts the traditions of the antebellum South with the rapid changes of post-Civil War industrialization in his short story *A Rose for Emily*. The central character, Emily Grierson, denies the reality of modern progress, living inside the isolated world of her house. Contradictorily, she is both a testament to time-honored history and a mysterious, eccentric, unfathomable burden. Faulkner portrays her with deathlike imagery even in life, comparing her to a drowned woman and referring to her skeleton. Emily symbolizes the Old South; as her social status is degraded, so is the antebellum social order. Like Miss Havisham in Charles Dickens' *Great Expectations,* Emily preserves her bridal bedroom, denying change and time's passage. Emily tries to control death through denial, shown in her necrophilia with her father's corpse and her killing Homer Barron to stop him from leaving her, then also denying his death. Faulkner uses the motif of dust throughout to represent not only the decay of Emily, her house, and Old Southern traditions, but also how her secrets are obscured from others.

Thematic development in *Moby-Dick*

The great White Whale in *Moby-Dick* plays various roles to different characters. In Captain Ahab's obsessive, monomaniacal quest to kill it, the whale represents all evil, and Ahab believes it his duty and destiny to rid the world of it. Ishmael attempts through multiple scientific disciplines to understand the whale objectively, but fails—it is hidden underwater and mysterious to humans—reinforcing Melville's theme that humans can never know everything; here the whale represents the unknowable and may be interpreted as symbolizing God. Melville reverses white's usual connotation of purity in Ishmael's dread of white, associated with crashing waves, polar animals, albinos—all frightening and unnatural. White is often viewed as an absence of color, yet white light is the sum total of all colors in the spectrum. In the same way, white can signify both absence of meaning, and totality of meaning incomprehensible to humans. As a creature of nature, the whale also symbolizes how 19th-century white men's exploitative expansionistic actions were destroying the natural environment.

Thematic development in *The Old Man and the Sea*

Because of the old fisherman Santiago's struggle to capture a giant marlin, some people characterize Ernest Hemingway's story as telling of man against nature. However, it can more properly be interpreted as telling of man's role as part of nature. Both man and fish are portrayed as brave, proud, and honorable. In Hemingway's world, all creatures, including humans, must either kill or be killed. Santiago reflects, "man can be destroyed but not defeated," following this principle in his life. As heroes are often created through their own deaths, Hemingway seems to believe that while being destroyed is inevitable, destruction enables living beings to transcend it by fighting bravely with honor and dignity. Hemingway echoes Romantic poet John Keats' contention that only immediately before death can we understand beauty as it is about to be destroyed. He also echoes ancient Greek and Roman myths and the Old Testament with the tragic flaw of overweening pride/overreaching. Like Icarus, Prometheus, and Adam and Eve, the old man "went out too far."

Universal theme in ancient religious texts

The Old Testament book Genesis, the Quran, and the Epic of Gilgamesh all contain flood stories. Versions differ somewhat: Genesis describes a worldwide flood, attributing it to God's decision that mankind, his creation, had become incontrovertibly wicked in spirit and must be destroyed for the world to start anew. The Quran describes the flood as regional, caused by Allah after sending Nuh (notice the similarity in name to Noah) as a messenger to his people to cease their evil. The Quran stipulates Allah only destroys those who deny or ignore messages from his messengers. Marked similarities also exist: in the Gilgamesh poems Utnapishtim, like Noah, is instructed to build a ship to survive the flood. Both men send out birds afterward as tests, and both include doves and a raven, though with different outcomes. Historians and archeologists believe a Middle Eastern tidal wave was a real basis for these stories. However, their universal themes remain the same: the flood was seen as God's way of wiping out humans whose behavior had become ungodly.

First-person narration

First-person narratives let narrators express inner feelings and thoughts, especially when the narrator is the protagonist as Lemuel Gulliver is in Jonathan Swift's *Gulliver's Travels*. The narrator may be a close friend of the protagonist, like Dr. Watson in Arthur Conan Doyle's *Sherlock Holmes*. Or the narrator can be less involved with the main characters and plot, like Nick Carraway in F. Scott Fitzgerald's *The Great Gatsby*. When a narrator reports others' narratives secondhand or more, s/he is a "frame narrator," like the nameless narrator of Joseph Conrad's *Heart of Darkness* or Mr. Lockwood in Emily Brontë's *Wuthering Heights*. First-person plural is unusual but can be effective, as in Isaac Asimov's *I, Robot*; William Faulkner's *A Rose for Emily*; Maxim Gorky's *Twenty-Six Men and a Girl*; or Jeffrey Eugenides' *The Virgin Suicides*. Author Kurt Vonnegut is the first-person narrator in his semi-autobiographical novel *Timequake*. Also unusual but effective is a first-person omniscient (rather than the more common third-person omniscient) narrator, like Death in Markus Zusak's *The Book Thief* and the dead girl's ghost in Alice Sebold's *The Lovely Bones*.

Second-person narration

While second-person address is very commonplace in popular song lyrics, it is the least used form of narrative voice in literary works. Popular serial books of the 1980s like *Fighting Fantasy* or *Choose Your Own Adventure* employed second-person narratives. In some cases, a narrative combines both second-person and first-person voices, speaking of "you" and "I." This can draw readers into the story, and it can also enable the authors to compare directly "your" and "my" feelings, thoughts, and actions. When the narrator is also a character in the story, as in Edgar Allan Poe's short story "The Tell-Tale Heart" or Jay McInerney's novel *Bright Lights, Big City*, the narrative is better defined as first-person despite its also addressing "you."

Third-person narration

Narration in the third person is the most often-used type, as it allows authors the most flexibility. It is so common that readers simply assume without needing to be informed that the narrator is not a character in, or involved in the story. Third-person singular is used more frequently than third-person plural, though some authors have also effectively used plural. However, both singular and plural are most often included in stories according to which character(s) is/are being described. The third-person narrator may be either objective or subjective, and either omniscient or limited. Objective third-person narration does not include what the characters described are thinking or feeling, while subjective third-person narration does. The third-person omniscient narrator knows everything about all characters, including their thoughts and emotions, and all related places, times, and events, whereas the third-person limited narrator may know everything about a particular character of focus, but is limited to that character; in other words, the narrator cannot speak about anything that character does not know.

Alternating-person narration

Although authors more commonly write stories from one point of view, there are also instances wherein they alternate the narrative voice within the same book. For example, they may sometimes use an omniscient third-person narrator and a more intimate first-person narrator at other times. In J. K. Rowling's series of *Harry Potter* novels, she often writes in a third-person limited narrative, but sometimes changes to narration by characters other than protagonist Harry Potter. George R. R. Martin's series *A Song of Ice and Fire* (the basis for the popular HBO TV series *Game of Thrones*) changes the point of view to coincide with divisions between chapters. The same technique is used by Erin Hunter (a pseudonym for several authors of the *Warriors, Seekers,* and *Survivors* book series). Authors using first-person narrative sometimes switch to third-person to describe significant action scenes, especially those where the narrator was absent or uninvolved, as Barbara Kingsolver does in her novel *The Poisonwood Bible*.

Classic analysis of plot structure

In *Poetics,* Aristotle defined plot as "the arrangement of the incidents." He meant not the story, but how it is structured for presentation. In tragedies, Aristotle found results driven by chains of cause-and-effect preferable to those driven by the protagonist's personality/character. He identified "unity of action" as necessary for a plot's wholeness; its events must be internally connected, not episodic or relying on *deus ex machina* or other external intervention. A plot must have a beginning, middle, and end. Gustav Freytag adapted Aristotle's ideas into his Triangle/Pyramid (1863). The beginning, today called the exposition/incentive/inciting moment, emphasizes causes and de-emphasizes effects. Aristotle called the ensuing cause-and-effect *desis*, or tying up, today called complication(s) which occur during the rising action. These culminate in a crisis/climax/reversal/turning point, Aristotle's *peripateia*. This occurs at the plot's middle, where cause and effect are both emphasized. The falling action, which Aristotle called the *lusis* or unraveling, is today called the dénouement. The resolution comes at the catastrophe/outcome or end, when causes are emphasized and effects de-emphasized.

Story vs. discourse

In terms of plot, "story" is the characters, places, and events originating in the author's mind, while "discourse" is how the author arranges and sequences events—which may be chronological or not. Story is imaginary; discourse is words on the page. Discourse allows story to be told in different ways. One element of plot structure is relating events differently from the order in which they occurred. This is easily done with cause-and-effect; for example, in the sentence, "He died following a long illness," we know the illness preceded the death, but the death precedes the illness in words. In Kate Chopin's short story "The Story of an Hour" (1894), she tells some of the events out of chronological order, which has the effect of amplifying the surprise of the ending for the reader. Another element of plot structure is selection. Chopin omits some details, such as Mr. Mallard's trip home; this allows readers to be as surprised at his arrival as Mrs. Mallard is.

Analysis of plot structures through recurring patterns in actions or events

Authors of fiction select characters, places, and events from their imaginations and arrange them in ways that will affect their readers. One way to analyze plot structure is to compare and contrast different events in a story. For example, in Kate Chopin's "The Story of an Hour," a very simple but key pattern of repetition is the husband's leaving and then returning. Such patterns fulfill the symmetrical aspect that Aristotle said was required of sound plot structure. In James Baldwin's short story, "Sonny's Blues," the narrator is Sonny's brother. In an encounter with one of Sonny's old friends early in the story, the brother initially disregards his communication. In a subsequent flashback, Baldwin informs us that this was the same way he had treated Sonny. In Nathaniel Hawthorne's "Young Goodman Brown," a pattern is created by the protagonist's recurrent efforts not to go farther into the wood; in Herman Melville's "Bartleby the Scrivener," by Bartleby's repeated refusals; and in William Faulkner's "Barn Burning," by the history of barn-burning episodes.

Conflict

A conflict is a problem to be solved. Literary plots typically include one conflict or more. Characters' attempts to resolve conflicts drive the narrative's forward movement. Conflict resolution is often the protagonist's primary occupation. Physical conflicts like exploring, wars, and/or escapes tend to make plots most suspenseful and exciting. Emotional, mental, and/or moral conflicts tend to make stories more personally gratifying or rewarding for many audiences. Conflicts can be external or internal. A major type of internal conflict is some inner personal battle, or "man against himself." Major types of external conflicts include "man against nature," "man against man," and "man against society." Readers can identify conflicts in literary plots by asking themselves who the protagonist is, who or what the antagonist is, why the antagonist is an antagonist, why the protagonist and antagonist conflict, what events develop the conflict, which event is the climax, what the outcome tells them about the protagonist, and whether they sympathized or identified with the protagonist or antagonist and why.

Mood and tone

Mood is a story's atmosphere, or the feelings the reader gets from reading it. The way authors set the mood in writing is comparable to the way filmmakers use music to set the mood in movies.

Instead of music, though, writers judiciously select evocative or descriptive words to evoke certain moods. The mood of a work may convey joy, anger, bitterness, hope, gloom, fear, an ominous feeling, or any other emotion the author wants the reader to feel. In addition to vocabulary choices, authors also use figurative expressions, particular sentence structures, and choices of diction that project and reinforce the moods they want to create. Whereas mood is the reader's emotions evoked by reading what is written, tone is the emotions and attitudes of the writer that s/he expresses in the writing. Authors use the same literary techniques to establish tone as they do to establish mood. An author may use a humorous tone, an angry or sad tone, a sentimental or unsentimental tone, or something else entirely.

Purposes of good dialogue

In literary fiction, effectively written dialogue serves at least one but usually several purposes. It advances the story and moves the plot. It develops the characters. It sheds light on the work's theme(s) or meaning(s). It can, often subtly, account for the passage of time not otherwise indicated. It can alter the direction that the plot is taking, typically by introducing some new conflict(s) or changing (an) existing one(s). Dialogue can establish a work's narrative voice and/or the characters' voices and set the tone of the story or of particular characters. When fictional characters display enlightenment or realization, dialogue can give readers an understanding of what those characters have discovered, and how. Dialogue can illuminate the motivations and wishes of the story's characters for its readers. By using consistent thoughts and syntax, dialogue can support character development. Skillfully created, it can also represent real-life speech rhythms in written form. Via conflicts and ensuing action, dialogue also provides drama.

In fictional literary works, effectively written dialogue should not have only the effect of breaking up or interrupting sections of narrative. Well-written dialogue does not reproduce verbatim things said in an author's real-life experiences. While dialogue may supply exposition for readers, it must nonetheless be believable. Dialogue should be dynamic, not static, and it should not resemble regular prose not representing conversation. Authors should not use dialogue as prose contexts for self-consciously "clever" similes or metaphors, which is unnatural and awkward. Dialogue should not slow down the movement of the plot or the story. When narrative would better establish a story's setting, authors should not substitute dialogue, which would be inappropriate. Authors should not express their own opinions in characters' dialogue. They should not try to imitate what real-life characters would say; dialogue must seem and sound natural, rather than actually duplicating natural speech. Dialogue should also not simply consist of conversations enclosed in quotation marks that do not serve the purpose of the story.

Effects of story events on works' meanings

Novelist E. M. Forster has made the distinction between story as relating a series of events, such as a king dying and then his queen dying, versus plot as establishing motivations for actions and causes for events, such as a king dying and then his queen dying from grief over his death. Thus plot fulfills the function of helping readers understand cause-and-effect in events and underlying motivations in characters' actions, which in turn helps them understand life. This affects a work's meaning by supporting its ability to explain why things happen, why people do things, and ultimately explain some of the meaning in life. Some authors find that while story events convey meaning, they do not tell readers there is any one meaning in life or way of living, but rather are mental experiments with various meanings and ways of life enabling readers to explore. Hence stories may not necessarily be constructed to impose one definitive meaning, but rather to find some shape, direction, and meaning within otherwise random events.

Analysis of character development

To understand the characters in a literary text, we can consider what kinds of observations the author makes about each character. We can look for contradictions in what a character thinks, says, and does. We can notice whether the author's observations about a character differ from what other characters in the story say about that character. We can note how the author describes each character. A character may be dynamic in that s/he changes in some significant way(s) during the story, or static in that s/he remains the same from the beginning of the story to the end. Characters may be perceived as "flat" or, in other words, not fully developed and/or without salient personality traits, or "round," as in more well developed, with characteristics that stand out vividly. Another thing to consider is whether characters in a story symbolize any universal properties. In addition, as readers we can think about whether we could compare and/or contrast the attributes of two characters in the same story to analyze how authors develop characters.

Figurative language

Figurative language is any language that extends past the literal meanings of the words. It serves the function of offering readers new insight into the people, things, events, and subjects covered in a work of literature. Figurative language also enables readers to feel they are sharing the authors' experiences. It can stimulate the reader's senses, make comparisons that readers find intriguing or even startling, and enable readers to view the world in different ways. Seven specific types of figurative language include: imagery, similes, metaphors, alliteration, personification, onomatopoeia, and hyperbole. Imagery is descriptive language that accesses the senses. Imagery can describe people, animals, or things. For example, the images T. S. Eliot uses in his poem "The Waste Land" of towers crumbling, wells dried up, and tombstones toppled over create mental images for the reader of the decay of a civilization.

Alliteration, personification, imagery, and simile

Alliteration is using a series of words containing the same sounds—assonance with vowels, and consonance with consonants. Personification is describing a thing or animal as a person. Imagery is description using sensory terms that create mental images for the reader of how people, animals, or things look, sound, feel, taste, and/or smell. This verse from Alfred Tennyson's poem "The Eagle" uses all of these types of figurative language: "He clasps the crag with crooked hands." Tennyson used alliteration, repeating /k/ and /kr/ sounds. These hard-sounding consonants reinforce the imagery giving visual and tactile impressions of the eagle. Tennyson also used personification, describing a bird as "he" and calling its talons "hands." Similes are stated comparisons using "like" or "as." William Wordsworth's poem about "Daffodils" begins, "I wandered lonely as a cloud." This simile compares his loneliness to that of a cloud. It is also personification, giving a cloud the human quality loneliness.

Metaphor and onomatopoeia

Metaphor is an implied comparison that does not use "like" or "as" the way a simile does. Henry Wadsworth Longfellow echoes the ancient Greeks in "O Ship of State": the metaphor compares the state and its government to a nautical ship and its sailing. Onomatopoeia uses words imitating the sounds of things they name/describe. For example, in his poem "Come Down, O Maid," Alfred Tennyson writes of "The moan of doves in immemorial elms, / And murmuring of innumerable bees." The word "moan" sounds like some sounds doves make, "murmuring" represents the sounds of bees buzzing, and "buzzing" is also an onomatopoetic word. And in his play *The Tempest*, in scene 2 of Act One, William Shakespeare's character Ariel says, "Hark, hark! / Bow-wow. / The watch-dogs bark! / Bow-wow. / Hark, hark! I hear/ The strain of strutting chanticleer / Cry, 'cock-a-

- 82 -

diddle-dow!'" Onomatopoetic words represent the sounds of a dog barking and a rooster crowing, respectively. ("Strain" is also imagery describing a rooster's crow as song; "strain" paired with "strutting" is alliteration.)

Hyperbole

Hyperbole is excessive exaggeration used for humor or emphasis rather than for literal meaning. For example, in *To Kill a Mockingbird*, Harper Lee narrated, "People moved slowly then. There was no hurry, for there was nowhere to go, nothing to buy and no money to buy it with, nothing to see outside the boundaries of Maycomb County." This was not literally true; Lee exaggerates the scarcity of these things for emphasis. In "Old Times on the Mississippi," Mark Twain wrote, "I... could have hung my hat on my eyes, they stuck out so far." This is not literal, but makes his description vivid and funny. In his poem "As I Walked Out One Evening", W. H. Auden wrote, "I'll love you, dear, I'll love you / Till China and Africa meet, / And the river jumps over the mountain / And the salmon sing in the street." He used things not literally possible to emphasize his meaning that he will love the person addressed forever.

Couplets and meter to enhance meaning in poetry

When a poet uses a couplet—a stanza of two lines, rhymed or unrhymed—it can function as the answer to a question asked earlier in the poem, or the solution to a problem or riddle. Couplets can also enhance the establishment of a poem's mood, or clarify the development of a poem's theme. Another device to enhance thematic development is irony, which also communicates the poet's tone and draws the reader's attention to a point the poet is making. The use of meter gives a poem a rhythmic context, contributes to the poem's flow, makes it more appealing to the reader, can represent natural speech rhythms, and produces specific effects. For example, in "The Song of Hiawatha," Henry Wadsworth Longfellow uses trochaic (/ ◡) tetrameter (four beats per line) to evoke for readers the rhythms of Native American chanting: "*By* the *shores* of *Gitche Gum*ee, / *By* the *shin*ing *Big*-Sea-*Wat*er / *Stood* the *wig*wam of No*kom*is." (Italicized syllables are stressed; non-italicized syllables are unstressed.)

Effects of figurative devices on meaning in poetry

Through exaggeration, hyperbole communicates the strength of a poet's or persona's feelings and enhances the mood of the poem. Imagery appeals to the reader's senses, creating vivid mental pictures, evoking reader emotions and responses, and helping to develop themes. Irony also aids thematic development by drawing the reader's attention to the poet's point and communicating the poem's tone. Thematic development is additionally supported by the comparisons of metaphors and similes, which emphasize similarities among things compared, affect readers' perceptions of images and enhance the imagery, and are more creative than writing in only literal terms. The use of mood communicates the atmosphere of a poem, can build a sense of tension, and evokes the reader's emotions. Onomatopoeia appeals to the reader's auditory sense and enhances sound imagery even when the poem is visual (read silently) rather than auditory (read aloud). Rhyme connects and unites verses, gives the rhyming words emphasis, and makes poems more fluent. Symbolism communicates themes, develops imagery, and evokes readers' emotional and other responses.

Poetic structure to enhance meaning in poetry

The opening stanza of Romantic English poet, artist and printmaker William Blake's famous poem "The Tyger" demonstrates how a poet can enhance the meaning of the work through creating tension by using line length and punctuation independently of one another: "Tyger! Tyger! burning bright / In the forests of the night, / What immortal hand or eye / Could frame thy fearful symmetry?" The first three lines of this stanza are trochaic (/ ͜), with "masculine" endings—that is, strongly stressed syllables at the ends of each of the lines. But Blake's punctuation contradicts this rhythmic regularity by not providing any divisions between the words "bright" and "In" or between "eye" and "Could." This irregular punctuation foreshadows how Blake disrupts the meter at the end of this first stanza by using a contrasting dactyl (/ ͜ ͜), with a "feminine" (unstressed) ending syllable in the last word, "symmetry." Thus Blake uses structural contrasts to heighten the intrigue of his work.

In enjambment, one sentence or clause in a poem does not end at the end of its line or verse, but runs over into the next line or verse. Clause endings coinciding with line endings give readers a feeling of completion, but enjambment influences readers to hurry to the next line to finish and understand the sentence. In his blank-verse epic religious poem "Paradise Lost," John Milton wrote: "Anon out of the earth a fabric huge / Rose like an exhalation, with the sound / Of dulcet symphonies and voices sweet, / Built like a temple, where pilasters round / Were set, and Doric pillars overlaid / With golden architrave." Only the third line is end-stopped. Milton, describing the palace of Pandemonium bursting from Hell up through the ground, reinforced this idea through phrases and clauses bursting through the boundaries of the lines. A caesura is a pause in mid-verse. Milton's commas in the third and fourth lines signal caesuras. They interrupt flow, making the narration jerky to imply that Satan's glorious-seeming palace has a shaky and unsound foundation.

Making predictions

When we read literature, making predictions about what will happen in the writing reinforces our purpose(s) for reading and prepares us mentally for beginning to read, and for continuing to read further. We can make predictions before we begin reading and during our reading. As we read on, we can test the accuracy of our predictions, revise them in light of additional reading, and confirm or refute our predictions. Some things that can help readers to make predictions about literary works include: thinking about the title of the book, poem, or play; looking at the illustrations when there are any; considering the structure of the text as we read; making use of our existing knowledge relative to the subject of the text; asking ourselves questions about the story, characters, and subject matter, particularly "why" and "who" questions; and then answering these questions for ourselves by referring to the text.

Making connections to enhance reading comprehension

Reading involves thinking. For good comprehension, readers make text-to-self, text-to-text, and text-to-world connections. Making connections helps readers understand text better and predict what might occur next based on what they already know, such as how characters in the story feel or what happened in another text. Text-to-self connections with the reader's life and experiences make literature more personally relevant and meaningful to readers. Readers can make connections before, during, and after reading—including whenever the text reminds them of something similar they have encountered in life or other texts. Knowing a work's genre (mystery, fantasy, or whatever it may be); common practices of a certain author; a story's geographical, historical, and social setting; characters that remind us of other people; familiar plot elements; literary structure and devices (such as flashbacks); themes encountered in other works; and similar use of language and tone to other works are all means for connections. Venn diagrams and other graphic organizers help visualize connections. Readers can also make double-entry notes: key content, ideas, events, words, and quotations on one side, and the connections with these on the other.

Summarizing literature to support comprehension

When reading literature, especially demanding works, summarizing helps readers identify important information and organize it in their minds; briefly monitor understanding; identify the main theme(s), problems and solutions; and sequence the story. Readers can summarize before, during, and after they read. They can refer to examples of other occasions in life for summarizing: giving others directions, generally describing our weekends or summers in limited time, and explaining news items/articles we read, to name a few. To summarize literary content, readers should use their own words. Previewing a text's organization before reading by examining the book cover, table of contents, and illustrations also aids summarizing. So does making notes of key words and ideas in a graphic organizer while reading. Graphic organizers can also be used after reading: readers skim the text, pick out the most important parts of three to five sentences, and determine what can be omitted with the aid of the organizer. Unimportant details should be omitted in summaries. Summaries of nonfiction can include description, problem-solution, comparison-contrast, sequence, main ideas, and cause-and-effect.

Evaluation of summaries of literary passages

A summary of a literary passage is a condensation in the reader's own words of the passage's main points. Some guidelines for evaluating a summary of a literary passage include: The summary should be complete yet concise. It should be accurate, balanced, fair, neutral, and objective, excluding the reader's own opinions or reactions. It should reflect in similar proportion how much each point summarized was covered in the original passage. Summary writers should include tags of attribution, like "Macaulay argues that" to reference the original author whose ideas are represented in the summary. Summary writers should not overuse quotations: they should only quote central concepts or phrases they cannot precisely convey in words other than those of the original author. Another aspect in evaluating a summary is whether it can stand alone as a coherent, unified composition, albeit a brief one. In addition, evaluation of a summary should include whether its writer has cited the original source of the passage so that readers of the summary can find it.

Textual evidence to evaluate predictions

Textual evidence to evaluate reader predictions about literature includes specific synopses of the work, paraphrases of the work or parts of it, and direct quotations from it. The best literary analysis shows special insight into a theme, character trait, or change. The best textual evidence supporting analysis is strong, relevant, and accurate. Analysis that is not best, but enough, shows reasonable understanding of theme, character trait, or change; contains supporting textual evidence that is relevant and accurate, if not strong; and shows a specific and clear response. Analysis that partially meets criteria also shows reasonable understanding, but the textual evidence is generalized, incomplete, only partly relevant or accurate, or connected only weakly. Or there may be only relevant, accurate textual evidence, but no analysis and a vague or unclear response. Analysis that is vague, too general or incorrect, with an unclear response and irrelevant or incomplete textual evidence; that only summarizes the plot; and/or that answers the wrong question, or answers no question, is not enough to be adequate.

Literary theories and criticism and interpretation

Literary theory gives a rationale for the literary subject matter of criticism, and also for the process of interpreting literature. For example, Aristotle's *Poetics'* requirement of unity underlies any discussion of unity in Sophocles' *Oedipus Rex*. Postcolonial theory, assuming historical racism and exploitation, informs Nigerian novelist and critic Chinua Achebe's contention that in *Heart of*

Darkness, Joseph Conrad does not portray Africans with complete humanity. Gender and feminist theories support critics' interpretation of Edna Pontellier's drowning at the climax of Kate Chopin's novel *The Awakening* (1899) as suicide. Until the 19th century, critics largely believed literature referenced objective reality, holding "a mirror up to nature" as William Shakespeare wrote. Twentieth-century Structuralism and New Historicism were predated and influenced by radical, non-traditional, historicized, cross-cultural comparative interpretations of biblical text in 19th-century German "higher criticism." Literary critic Charles Augustin Saint-Beuve maintained that biography could completely explain literature; contrarily, Marcel Proust demonstrated in narrative that art completely transformed biography. A profound 19th-century influence on literary theory was Friedrich Nietzsche's idea that facts must be interpreted to become facts.

Geoffrey Chaucer's "The Parlement of Foules"

In his dream-vision, Cicero views the universe with his famous grandfather, learning philosophical principles of virtue during earthly, illusory, and deathlike life, toward Heaven's rewards in the afterlife's true life. Geoffrey Chaucer uses less grand designs in his dream-vision: Hoping to learn something from Cicero's work and influenced by it, he also dreams of Scipio Africanus. However, instead of touring the universe and Stoic philosophy, Africanus takes Chaucer to the temple of Venus—connecting with Chaucer's preface statement that he writes about love. This poem is noteworthy for the first known reference to St. Valentine's Day as being for lovers. Leaving Venus's temple, Chaucer witnesses Nature's comic "parliament" wherein birds, symbolizing human suitors, select mates. He alludes to sexual maturity at two years for male predator birds contrasting with one year for females: Nature grants the female eagle's request to defer choice for another year, but lets other birds form couples. Chaucer's awakening by morning birdsong celebrates summer, and illustrates the phenomenon that dreams often retroactively incorporate real sounds heard just before waking.

Aristotle's criteria for tragedy in drama

In his *Poetics,* Aristotle defined five critical terms relative to tragedy. (1) *Anagnorisis:* Meaning tragic insight or recognition, this is a moment of realization by a tragic hero(ine) when s/he suddenly understands how s/he has enmeshed himself/herself in a "web of fate." (2) *Hamartia:* This is often called a "tragic flaw," but is better described as a tragic error. *Hamartia* is an archery term meaning a shot missing the bull's eye, used here as a metaphor for a mistake—often a simple one—which results in catastrophe. (3) *Hubris:* While often called "pride," this is actually translated as "violent transgression," and signifies an arrogant overstepping of moral or cultural bounds—the sin of the tragic hero who over-presumes or over-aspires. (4) *Nemesis:* translated as "retribution," this represents the cosmic punishment or payback that the tragic hero ultimately receives for committing hubristic acts. (5) *Peripateia:* Literally "turning," this is a plot reversal consisting of a tragic hero's pivotal action, which changes his/her status from safe to endangered.

Theory of tragedy proposed by Hegel

Georg Wilhelm Friedrich Hegel (1770-1831) proposed a different theory of tragedy than Aristotle (384-322 BCE) which was also very influential. Whereas Aristotle's criteria involved character and plot, Hegel defined tragedy as a dynamic conflict of opposite forces or rights. For example, if an individual believes in the moral philosophy of the conscientious objector, i.e., that fighting in wars is morally wrong, but is confronted with being drafted into military service, this conflict would fit Hegel's definition of a tragic plot premise. Hegel theorized that a tragedy must involve some circumstance in which two values, or two rights, are fatally at odds with one another and conflict directly. Hegel did not view this as good triumphing over evil, or evil winning out over good, but rather as one good fighting against another good unto death. He saw this conflict of two goods as truly tragic. In ancient Greek author Sophocles' tragedy *Antigone,* the main character experiences this tragic conflict, between her public duties and her family and religious responsibilities.

Revenge tragedy

Along with Aristotelian definitions of comedy and tragedy, ancient Greece was the origin of the revenge tragedy. This genre became highly popular in Renaissance England, and is still popular today in contemporary movies. In a revenge tragedy, the protagonist has been done some serious wrong, such as the assault and murder of a family member. However, the wrongdoer has not been punished. In contemporary plots, this often occurs when some legal technicality has interfered with the miscreant's conviction and sentencing, or when authorities are unable to locate and apprehend the criminal. The protagonist then faces the conflict of suffering this injustice, or exacting his or her own justice by seeking revenge. Greek revenge tragedies include *Agamemnon* and *Medea.* Playwright Thomas Kyd's *The Spanish Tragedy* (1582-1592) is credited with beginning the Elizabethan genre of revenge tragedies. Shakespearean revenge tragedies include *Hamlet* (1599-1602) and *Titus Andronicus* (1588-1593). A Jacobean example is Thomas Middleton's *The Revenger's Tragedy* (1606, 1607). The 1974 movie *Death Wish* is a contemporary example.

Hamlet's "tragic flaw"

Despite virtually limitless interpretations, one way to view Hamlet's tragic error generally is as indecision: He suffers the classic revenge tragedy's conflict of whether to suffer with his knowledge of his mother's and uncle's assassination of his father, or to exact his own revenge and justice against Claudius, who has assumed the throne after his crime went unknown and unpunished. Hamlet's famous soliloquy, "To be or not to be" reflects this dilemma. Hamlet muses "Whether 'tis nobler in the mind to suffer the slings and arrows of outrageous fortune, / Or to take arms against a sea of troubles, / And by opposing end them?" He sees the final sleep of death as "the rub; / For in that sleep of death what dreams may come... Must give us pause... that the dread of something after death... makes us rather bear those ills we have / Than fly to others that we know not of? / Thus conscience does make cowards of us all." Hamlet's excessive conscience leads to paralyzing indecision, at least temporarily.

For much of William Shakespeare's tragedy, Hamlet suffers anxiety over what to do about his uncle Claudius's murdering his (Hamlet's) father, Hamlet. During this time, Hamlet's tragic error might be considered a lack of action, as he seems paralyzed by his quandary. But making matters worse, Hamlet attempts to kill Claudius surreptitiously by stabbing him through a tapestry, accidentally killing Polonius instead. However, he eventually becomes inspired with a solution to avoid direct confrontation: "The play's the thing / Wherein I'll catch the conscience of the king." He presents a play depicting a similar murder. By observing his reaction, Hamlet can confirm or deny Claudius's guilt (reported by the late King Hamlet's ghost, which Hamlet was unsure was a true ghost or the devil) to inform his decision. During the presentation, Gertrude fatally drinks wine that Claudius poisoned and intended for Hamlet. Then Laertes kills Hamlet, to avenge Hamlet's accidental murder of Laertes' father Polonius, and his sister Ophelia's madness and eventual suicide in reaction to Hamlet's behavior. Hamlet's indecision delays action, but his actions have more tragic outcomes.

Theme of overreaching

A popular theme throughout literature is the human trait of reaching too far or presuming too much. In Greek mythology, Daedalus constructed wings of feathers and wax that men might fly like birds. He permitted his son Icarus to try them, but cautioned the boy not to fly too close to the sun.

The impetuous youth (in what psychologist David Elkind later named adolescence's myth of invincibility) ignored this, flying too close to the sun: the wax melted, the wings disintegrated, and Icarus fell into the sea and perished. In the Old Testament, God warned Adam and Eve not to eat fruit from the tree of knowledge of good and evil, that they might remain pure and innocent. Ignoring this banished them from Eden's eternal perfection, condemning them to mortality and suffering. The Romans were themselves examples of over-reachers in their conquest and assimilation of most of the then-known world and ultimate demise. In Christopher Marlowe's *Dr. Faustus* and Johann Wolfgang von Goethe's *Faust,* the protagonist sells his soul to the Devil for unlimited knowledge and success.

Carpe diem tradition in poetry

Carpe diem is Latin for "seize the day." A long poetic tradition, it advocates making the most of time because it passes swiftly and life is short. It is found in multiple languages, including Latin, Torquato Tasso's Italian, Pierre de Ronsard's French, and Edmund Spenser's English, and is often used in seduction to argue for indulging in earthly pleasures. Roman poet Horace's Ode 1.11 tells younger woman Leuconoe to enjoy the present, not worrying about inevitable aging. Two Renaissance Metaphysical Poets, Andrew Marvell and Robert Herrick, treated *carpe diem* more as a call to action. In "To His Coy Mistress," Marvell points out that time is fleeting, arguing for love, and concluding that because they cannot stop time, they may as well defy it, getting the most out of the short time they have. In "To the Virgins, to Make Much of Time," Herrick advises young women to take advantage of their good fortune in being young by getting married before they become too old to attract men and have babies.

"To His Coy Mistress" begins, "Had we but world enough, and time, / This coyness, lady, were no crime." Using imagery, Andrew Marvell describes leisure they could enjoy if time were unlimited. Arguing for seduction, he continues famously, "But at my back I always hear/Time's winged chariot hurrying near; / And yonder all before us lie / Deserts of vast eternity." He depicts time as turning beauty to death and decay. Contradictory images in "amorous birds of prey" and "tear our pleasures with rough strife / Thorough the iron gates of life" overshadow romance with impending death, linking present pleasure with mortality and spiritual values with moral considerations. Marvell's concluding couplet summarizes *carpe diem*: "Thus, though we cannot make our sun / Stand still, yet we will make him run." "To the Virgins, to Make Much of Time" begins with the famous "Gather ye rosebuds while ye may." Rather than seduction to live for the present, Robert Herrick's experienced persona advises young women's future planning: "Old time is still a-flying / And this same flower that smiles today, / Tomorrow will be dying."

Reflection of content through structure

Wallace Stevens' short yet profound poem "The Snow Man" is reductionist: the snow man is a figure without human biases or emotions. Stevens begins, "One must have a mind of winter," the criterion for realizing nature and life does not inherently possess subjective qualities; we only invest it with these. Things are not as we see them; they simply are. The entire poem is one long sentence of clauses connected by conjunctions and commas, and modified by relative clauses and phrases. The successive clauses and phrases lead readers continually to reconsider as they read. Stevens' construction of the poem mirrors the meaning he conveys. With a mind of winter, the snow man, Stevens concludes, "nothing himself, beholds nothing that is not there, and the nothing that is" (ultimate reductionism). Linguist and poetics expert Jay Keyser once remarked (NPR, 2005) that he wrote all the words of "The Snow Man" on white cards and made them into a mobile; it was "perfectly balanced, like an Alexander Calder creation." He said the mobile visually represented the poem's content.

Contrast of content and structure

Robert Frost's poem "Stopping by Woods on a Snowy Evening" (1923) is deceptively short and simple, with only four stanzas, each of only four lines, and short and simple words. Reinforcing this is Frost's use of regular rhyme and meter. The rhythm is iambic tetrameter throughout; the rhyme scheme is AABA in the first three stanzas and AAAA in the fourth. In an additional internal subtlety, B ending "here" in the first stanza is rhymed with A endings "queer," "near," and "year" of the second; B ending "lake" in the second is rhymed in A endings "shake", "mistake," and "flake" of the third. The final stanza's AAAA endings reinforce the ultimate darker theme. Though the first three stanzas seem to describe quietly watching snow fill the woods, the last stanza evokes the seductive pull of mysterious death: "The woods are lovely, dark and deep," countered by the obligations of living life: "But I have promises to keep, / And miles to go before I sleep, / And miles to go before I sleep." The last line's repetition strengthens Frost's message that despite death's temptation, life's course must precede it.

Aspects that combine to total effect in Theodore Roethke's "The Waking"

"The Waking" is a villanelle, with five tercets, one quatrain, and only two rhymes. Roethke alternately repeats two main lines: "I wake to sleep, and take my waking slow," and "I learn by going where I have to go" throughout, gradually revealing meaning. Continuous overall rhythm and revolving sound patterns of interconnected rhyming and assonance create perpetual motion, reflecting the life cycle. Roethke's use of villanelle form perfectly suits this cyclical effect: repetition, becoming hypnotically chant-like, reinforces the poem's mystical quality. Waking to sleep, learning by going, and "think[ing] by feeling" represent paradoxes: meaning, like form, becomes circular. These symbolize abandoning conscious rationalism to embrace spiritual vision. We wake from the vision to "Great Nature," and "take the lively air" in life's dance. "This shaking keeps me steady"—another paradox—juxtaposes and balances fear of mortality with ecstasy in embracing experience. The transcendent vision of all life's interrelationship demonstrates, "What falls away is always. And is near." Readers experience the poem holistically, like music, through Roethke's integration of theme, motion, and sound.

Sylvia Plath's use of villanelle form to convey meaning in "Mad Girl's Love Song"

Sylvia Plath wrote the poem "Mad Girl's Love Song" in college to exemplify young love. The two repeated lines, "I shut my eyes and all the world drops dead" and "(I think I made you up inside my head.)" reflect the existential viewpoint that nothing exists in any absolute reality outside of our own perceptions. In the first stanza, the middle line, "I lift my lids and all is born again," in its recreating the world, bridges between the repeated refrain statements—one of obliterating reality, the other of having constructed her lover's existence. Unlike other villanelles wherein key lines are subtly altered in their repetitions, Plath repeats these exactly each time. This reflects the young woman's love, also not changing throughout the poem. The final quatrain expresses some regret: "I should have loved a thunderbird instead; / At least when spring comes they roar back again." Plath contrasts the thunderbirds' rebirth with the unchanging love she depicts, and reinforces it. The unchanging repeated lines mirror the lack of progress in her love.

Ted Hughes' animal metaphors

Hughes frequently used animal metaphors, as in "Crow" and collected poems about the mythic creature-character Crow. In "The Thought Fox," a model of concise, structured beauty, Hughes characterizes the poet's creative process with succinct, striking imagery of an idea as a fox entering his head. Repeating "loneliness" in the first two stanzas emphasizes the poet's lonely work:

"Something else is alive / Beside the clock's loneliness." He treats an idea's arrival as separate from himself. Three stanzas detail in vivid images a fox's approach from the outside winter forest at starless midnight —its nose, "Cold, delicately" touching twigs and leaves; "neat" paw prints in snow; "bold" body; wide, deep, brilliant green eyes; and self-contained, focused progress—"Till, with a sudden sharp hot stink of fox," he metaphorically depicts poetic inspiration as the fox's physical entry into "the dark hole of the head." Hughes ends by summarizing his vision of poet as an interior, passive idea recipient, with the outside world unchanged: "The window is starless still; the clock ticks, / The page is printed."

Literary examples of metaphor

A metaphor is an implied comparison, i.e. it compares something to something else without using "like", "as", or other comparative words. For example, in "The Tyger" (1794), William Blake writes, "Tyger Tyger, burning bright, / In the forests of the night;" this is a metaphor as Blake compares the tiger to a flame not by saying it is like a fire, but by simply describing it as "burning." Henry Wadsworth Longfellow's poem "O Ship of State" (1850) uses an extended metaphor by referring consistently throughout the entire poem to the state, union, or republic as a seagoing vessel, referring to its keel, mast, sail, rope, anchors, and to its braving waves, rocks, gale, tempest, and "false lights on the shore". Within the extended metaphor, Wordsworth uses a specific metaphor: "...the anchors of thy hope!" This is a metaphor because, like Blake (above), Wordsworth does not say the state's hope is like a ship's anchors; he equates them without using comparative words.

Literary examples of similes

A simile is a directly stated comparison of one thing to another thing, often using "like" or "as". In his novel *Lord Jim* (1900), Joseph Conrad writes in Chapter 33, "I would have given anything for the power to soothe her frail soul, tormenting itself in its invincible ignorance like a small bird beating about the cruel wires of a cage." Conrad uses the word "like" to compare the girl's soul to a small bird. His description of the bird beating at the cage shows the similar helplessness of the girl's soul to gain freedom. In his poetic Scots song "A Red, Red Rose" (1794), Robert Burns writes, "O my Luve's like a red, red rose, / That's newly sprung in June: / O my Luve's like the melodie, / That's sweetly play'd in tune." Burns uses "like" to compare his beloved to a beautiful, freshly blooming flower. In a second simile, he compares her to a beautiful musical melody. In the poem *The Daffodils* (1888), Wordsworth writes, "I wandered lonely as a cloud / that floats on high o'er vales and hills," comparing his persona's loneliness to that of a single cloud in the sky.

When an author uses similes to compare one thing to another, this gets readers' attention; stimulates readers' imaginations; and appeals to readers' senses by describing sensations of sight, sound, touch, smell, and/or taste. Similes lend more lifelike characteristics to fictional and poetic characters. Readers can more easily relate emotions expressed by authors to their own personal experiences when they read similes authors use. Consequently, readers can better understand literary subject matter when authors compare things to other things using similes. Additionally, similes offer readers ways to introduce more variety into the way they think, and show them different/new perspectives for perceiving reality. In his "Sonnet 18" (1609), Shakespeare writes, "Shall I compare thee to a summer's day? / Thou art more lovely and more temperate". This simile does not use "like" or "as" the way many similes do, yet it does directly state a comparison by using the verb "compare".

Literary examples of personification

Personification is the device of attributing human qualities and/or behaviors/actions to something that is not human. While personification is the literary term for this, a synonym used in the social sciences is anthropomorphism. In his romantic tragedy *Romeo and Juliet* (1597), Shakespeare writes dialogue spoken by Capulet (Act 1, Scene 2): "When well-appareled April on the heel / Of limping winter treads..." This contains three instances of personification: (1) April is a month, not a lady, yet he describes April as being well-dressed and as (2) treading (walking); (3) winter is a season, does not have a physical heel, and cannot limp. In his poem "Loveliest of Trees" (1896), A. E. Housman describes the cherry tree as "Wearing white for Eastertide." He personifies the tree's white flowers as white clothing, as a human would wear for Easter. In her short story, "How Pearl Button Was Kidnapped" (1912), Katherine Mansfield describes "...little winds playing hide-and-seek..." She personifies breezes as playing children.

Personification, i.e. attributing human qualities and actions to inanimate objects, non-human living things, or abstract concepts, imbues text with more profound meanings. We humans tend to be anthrocentric; i.e., we view the world from our human perspective, seeing non-human entities in a human light as well. When authors and poets use personification, they bring inanimate objects to life and characterize plants, animals, and ideas with human traits. Readers can better understand the nature and behaviors of non-human things/creatures by reading about them through the lens of personification. We can more easily relate to human beings, qualities, traits, and behaviors than non-human ones. Moreover, author use of personification opens up new, divergent, varied, and creative perspectives for readers. As an example, in his poem "Ode: Intimations of Immortality from Recollections of Early Childhood" (1807), William Wordsworth writes, "The Moon doth with delight / Look round her when the heavens are bare". He personifies the inanimate object of the moon as a human female looking around "her", creating a vivid visual image and investing the scene with emotional mood and tone.

The Arts

Akhenaten Style

Although certainly notable for its exquisite realism, perhaps the most interesting aspect of the Akhenaten style is the shift from the rigidity of the past to a more relaxed expressiveness. This is particularly evident in the "Daughters of Akhenaten" mural from Tell el 'Amarna which depicts playful gesture and informal pose with complete indifference toward the royal dignity so evident in virtually all work from previous eras.

The limestone bust, "Queen Nofretete", is considered a masterpiece for its exquisite realism and beauty while, paradoxically, the limestone relief of Akhenaten himself appears almost comically exaggerated and ungainly.

Bust of Queen Nofretete

"Workmen Carrying a Beam" from the tomb of Horemheb in Saqqara depicts a realistic, manual labor struggle that is truly remarkable for its frank realism and freedom of expression.

The influence of Akhenaten style persisted for some time following his death despite a gradual regression to the religious rigidity of earlier times.

Minoan Style

One of the most notable finds is the statuette terracotta "Snake Goddess" from 1600 BC. "Snake culture" as it has come to be called is not believed to have been indigenous to the Minoan people due to a lack of snakes in the area. Likely imported, it's a solid indication that Minoan art was substantially influenced by outside cultures such as that of Mesopotamia during this time.

The flat forms and solid color of paintings such as the mural fragment "Cat Stalking a Pheasant" seem to belie an Egyptian influence although stylistically this find is much more unique for its playful, lyrical presentation.

Another notable find is the "Harvester Vase" from Hagia Triada which depicts an expressionistic scene of smiling workers engaged in the harvest of crops. The "Octopus Vase" from Palaikastro in Crete is an ornate and rather accurate rendition of swirling tentacles in the classic octopus form.

The Minoans also produced the Palace of Minos at Knossos. Its labyrinth like remains ultimately contributed to the Greek legend of the Minotaur.

Dorian and Ionian Influence

Around 2500 to 2000 BC various tribes began entering the Greek peninsula who contributed their own uniqueness to the indigenous culture that existed there. The Dorians and Ionians are two that deserve specific mention due to their close proximity to the Near East which added artistic influence from that sphere.

Eventually, the emerging civilization spread throughout the Aegean islands and Asia Minor, absorbing the minor cultures that existed in these areas.

Common language and beliefs among the disparate groups hastened a cultural cohesion that advanced much faster than its political counterpart, largely due to the difficulty in waging successful military campaigns within the rough geography of the region. It's believed that this retardation of civil advancement further contributed to a disparate richness of ideas and institutions.

The chronic necessity for military power must have certainly contributed to a consideration for physical excellence and health. The rise of the Olympic Games in 776 BC is another indication of a prevailing attitude which eventually gave rise to the Greek obsession with the human form in sculpture.

Archaic Greek Style

Archaic style emerged during the 7th century BC as a wider ranging enhancement of the previous Oriental influenced Geometric period. For the next three hundred years, the style infused every aspect of Greek art with a renewed freshness and freedom of expression.

In painting, figures were frequently silhouetted in black over red clay. Black areas would often be embellished in either purple or white to draw attention to certain details. The details themselves would be etched with a needle or similar pointed implement to emphasize delicacy. Painting was often on a circular surface with the design of elements incorporated accordingly.

Also appearing during this time is a new style of sculpting the human form. Marked by an almost awkward rigidity, surviving examples show free-standing, life-sized figures rendered entirely free of the stone from which they were carved.

Toward the end of the period, rendering of figures had become more stylistic. Beards and hair of male figures were sculpted with the appearance of textured, beaded embroidery while female figures exhibited conservative clothing that better hid the hint of rounded shapes beneath.

Coronation Gospels

With his coronation as Emperor of Rome in the year 800, Charlemagne expressed an interest in reviving Imperial artistic traditions. The portraits contained within the Coronation Gospels appear to demonstrate a style well-versed in Late Antique tradition. Many are painted on vellum stained purple in an impressionistic style that has been described as loose and free-flowing. It's nonetheless imperial in every respect, rivaling the splendor of similar Roman works from an earlier time. Figures are depicted within the manuscripts amidst landscapes rendered in an antique, naturalistic style that at least one critic has referred to as brooding and ominous.

It is believed that the author or at least one of the authors of the manuscript was Greek. The name Demetrius appears written in gold in the margin and the Empress Irene traveled from the region around the time the manuscript was created which lends support to the theory that a Greek artist may have traveled with her. The fact that Constantinople was under the prohibitive Iconoclast of the time is further circumstantial evidence that a deposed Greek artist may have accompanied her entourage north.

Famous Greek Sculptures

One of numerous so-called "victory monuments", the "Nike of Samothrace" depicts the Goddess Nike immediately upon her descent to the front of a ship. Still partially airborne with drapery flowing, her wings are spread majestically against the onrushing air. The image evokes a strong sense of accomplishment and is considered by some to be the greatest masterpiece of Hellenistic sculpture for the way it evokes raw emotion and beauty.

In contrast, The "Laocoon Group" of Agesander, Athenodorus and Polydorus of Rhodes was obviously sculpted to depict a strong sense of tragedy. The three are seen in the midst of divine punishment, ensnared by a serpent with no apparent means of escape. This sculpture held special significance for the Romans who apparently believed that the scene depicted the first of several events ultimately leading to its founding.

Roman Art

During the late 1st century BC reign of emperor Augustus, nobles and wealthy patrons began to demand sculpture and painting to commemorate individuals or public events. This demand gave rise to art which was purely Roman in inspiration. Nevertheless, much of it still bore the traditional influence of Greek style in the classical ideal. Art that has survived from the reign of Hadrian during the early to mid 2nd century typifies the pinnacle of classical influence within the Empire. Indeed, it was during this age that copies and adaptations of Greek art became so widely prolific. Shortly thereafter heavy classical influence fell out of favor and a new category, imperial art as it has come to be known, arose and quickly developed into three distinctly identifiable categories: relief structure adorning Roman architecture, painting and portrait sculpture.

Roman Portraiture

Detailed realism is, perhaps, the most striking aspect of late Roman portraiture. This appears to have been a direct inspiration both of Hellenistic work as well as the desire of those whose visage was being carved to appear in sculpture as favorably as possible. As a consequence, accuracy was likely of secondary importance. A notable example of the style of the period is the famous 14 AD statue of Emperor Augustus from the Villa of Livia at Prima Porta. The trend continued into the first and second centuries with portraitures of Vespasian, Trajan and Antinous as well as bearded vestiges of Hadrian.

Later work exhibited an expressionistic style that altered facial expression and features to emphasize the experience and character of the subject. This can be seen in the 3rd century sculptures of Decius and Diocletian.

Ultimately, style progressed to a more symbolic rendering of the subject matter, such as with the approximately 313 AD rendering of Constantine.

Roman Decorative Painting

Multi-colored marble slabs were often arranged to imitate the appearance of the masonry common to Hellenistic Greek buildings. This early style formed the basis for more sophisticated work emphasizing various landscapes and architecture during the Pompeian era of the 2nd century AD.

A rich assortment of motifs have been preserved including still-lifes, portraits, figures, landscapes with figures, panels and friezes.

Much of the landscape work appears to be from a relatively high, panoramic viewpoint showing considerable depth as well as use of linear and aerial perspective.

Other work appears to exhibit an impressionistic style with figures modeled in patches of shade, light and color, such as the 1st century AD rendering of the Trojan Horse of Troy found at Pompeii.

Roman artists were clearly concerned with the problems of rendering space and perspective in an artistically satisfying way.

Romanesque Style

Western and central Europe held strong artistic allegiance to what remained of Rome so Romanesque style took firm hold there whereas East and Southeast Europe remained under the influence of Byzantium.

Even so, regional traditions and earlier styles persisted in some locations much longer than others. In Germany and England, the trend began in the second half of the 11th century.

It's also interesting to note that the style emerged from a number of different locations rather than from a single starting point or area of the continent.

Romanesque painting and architecture largely arose from modifications of previous and varied traditions. Carolingian and Ottonian styles, as well as early Christian and Byzantine art are all considered influential to varying degrees.

Secular work is known to have existed, although most painting and architecture are religious in nature. Few paintings survive and those that do are usually found in churches. Murals long hidden under old whitewash are occasionally discovered. Large wall paintings are common in surviving Romanesque churches.

The Norman conquest of 1066 saw the introduction to England of Norman abbots and overseas monks whose illuminated initials consisted of foliage containing human and animal figures. The new style co-existed with the traditional one for almost a century, impacting architecture, sculpture and painting.

The Viking influence of transforming human and animal forms into abstract patterns can be seen during the work of this period as well.

A variety of active centers during this time produced numerous English Psalters and Bibles for both the pious and rich. Among these are Winchester, Canterbury, St. Albans and Bury St. Edmunds.

The secular artist Hugo produced the Bury Bible in 1145 for the abbey of Bury St. Edmunds. Considered one of the earliest known English books, it contains a number of Byzantine elements.

The St. Paul mural at Canterbury exhibits a similar style and it's thought to have originated from the same painter.

The Winchester Bible which took several years to complete is another notable work from the period due to its size and scope.

Christian Catacomb Paintings

It isn't known with certainty exactly when the first catacomb paintings were made, but it is generally agreed that one of the earliest tomb paintings is that of the Ampliatus crypt in the Domitilla catacomb on the Via Ardeatina inlay. The style of this work is distinctly latter Pompeian which dates it to the middle 2nd century.

The Urania cubicle paintings in the Praetextatus catacomb in Rome show various New Testament scenes and have been dated to the late 2nd century.

Paintings illustrating characteristic New Testament scenes such as the breaking of bread, the fish symbol and the Holy Eucharist can be seen in the Lucina and Callixtus catacombs in Rome. The Arenarium Madonna and child is a famous painting that can be seen in the Cappella Greca of the Priscilla catacomb in Rome. It's notable for being the earliest known rendition of the virgin mother.

Early Christian Sculpture

Most work discovered can be dated to the middle of the third century or later. The Ram Sarcophagus now on display at the Lateran Museum in Rome is considered by many to be one of the earliest (if not the earliest) examples of Christian sculpture. It features a carved ram on either end flanking a group which surrounds a female figure who is praying.

This work is particularly notable for the realistic evolution in style it represents. The figures exhibit realistic weighting and spacing with good proportion and balance which enhances the three-dimensional aspect so crucial to good sculpture.

Other examples from the period demonstrate realistic rendering such as the sarcophagus discovered at La Gayolle, France. It exhibits the same parentage as the Ram and appears to have been carved about 20 years later.

Other styles discovered include striated S shapes and bust portraits of the deceased surrounded by shells or medallions, as well as scenes of prayer, people reading from scrolls and the like.

Byzantine Art

The years from 867 through 1059 are particularly known for both the quality and beauty of the work produced. Though retrospective in style, the illustration of manuscripts created during this period are considered by many to be of exceptional quality. Notable examples include the "Paris Psalter" and "Homilies of St. Gregory Nazianzus" written for Basil I in the 9th century.

The trend-setting decoration of mosaics at a church in the Great Palace of Constantinople from about 843 show a figure of Christ looking down from the central dome as creator, presiding over panels depicting his life, with the Virgin in the apse and rows of saints on the lower level. This decorative system formed the basis for subsequent work such as the mosaics of the church of Hosios Lukas in Phocis, the Church of the Dormition, Daphni near Athens and the Nea Moni on Chios from the 11th century.

Byzantine Sculpture

With few exceptions, prolific work in sculpture that had so characterized the pre-Byzantine Christian movement had virtually disappeared by the 4th century. Work originating in the 4th and 5th centuries was mostly abstract in form, such as the stylized portraiture of Justinian's Empress, Theodora, or the consular diptych of Rufus Germadius Orestes, dated near 530.

Low relief ornamental sculpture took on heightened popularity during the Iconoclast prohibition. Tomb enclosure slabs decorated in fanciful geometric patterns and stylized animal reliefs were common.

Oriental influence is pervasive throughout Byzantine art and a substantial amount of work appears to have been inspired by imported textiles.

Christian sculpture once again became popular following the end of the Iconoclast. Various renditions of the Virgin, the apostles and Christ have remained. A 14th century slab depicting Christ in meticulous carving has been described by some as engraving for its delicate intricacy.

Gothic Sculpture

The rising popularity of Christianity in the latter part of the 13th century necessitated a more approachable and recognizable evolution of artistic style. The apparent intent of the Gothic sculptor was to embellish traditional Christian themes with greater emotional appeal for private devotees.

This new imagery, referred to in German as Andachtsbild, was often portrayed in Pieta which is a Latin term for "piety or pious".

It was during this time that certain elements entered popular notions of the Christian passion which cannot be supported specifically by Gospel accounts such as the 14th century painted wood carved Pieta of the grieving Virgin holding the departed Christ in her arms. Faces are stylized in over-accentuated grief and Christ's wounds are inflated for effect.

Realism, at least in some sense, was not entirely forsaken at the expense of maximizing emotional impact. The work of Claus Sluter is notable. His Portal of the Charteuse de Champmol and The Moses Well depict figures in lifelike emotional realism.

Awe and reverence are portrayed quite effectively.

Matthew Paris

Paris was a monk of St. Albans Abbey near London who, unlike many of his contemporaries, was keenly interested in the affairs of men. He compiled and kept an illustrated chronicle of the history of England which included a 1255 account of the presentation of an elephant to King Henry III from St. Louis. Paris claims to have been a witness.

Another major contribution of Paris was a "Lives of the Saints" series in full illustration targeted to the lay reader such as the "Martyrdom of St. Alban" from "The Life of St. Alban" thought to have been created around 1240.

Paris also created more romantic, illustrated versions of the Book of Revelation. One of these, the Douce Apocalypse on display in the Bodleian Library at Oxford, was painted for Henry III's son,

Edward. It is a balanced rendition of naturalistic realism and surface decoration. The style is evident in the surviving 1250 Apocalypse manuscript.

Giotto di Bondone

Prior to Giotto, the tradition of Western painting was mostly Byzantine in form. Primarily responsible for introducing the illusionary pictorial space, he was referred to by his contemporary Cennino Cennini as the individual most responsible for "translating the art of painting from Greek to Latin".

Although he was in great demand throughout Italy, few surviving works can be definitely attributed to him. It is believed by some that he painted the frescos on "The Life of St. Francis" in the Upper Church of S. Francesco at Assisi although this is a controversial view.

Most art historians agree that the 1313 frescos in the Arena Chapel in Padua can be attributed to him. The story of the Virgin and her parents along with the Life and Passion of Christ are depicted there.

It is also known that Giotto was the court painter to Robert of Anjou in Naples between 1329 and 1333 although very little survives from this time.

His panel painting, Ognissanti Madonna, is a masterful representation of his ability to render in the third dimension.

Jan Van Eyck

Van Eyck is credited as the inventor of modern oil painting. The development of various effects made possible by oil enabled Van Eyck and his contemporaries to achieve new levels of realism and detail.

"The Arnolfini Marriage" – one of the most famous paintings in all of Western art, wealthy merchant Giovanni Arnolfini is convincingly rendered in wool attire amidst the backdrop of a domestic interior. Giovanna, who appears to be pregnant, is painted in beautiful green attire. Fine details such as the mirror on the wall are very convincing.

"A Man in a Turban" – dated 1433, some have speculated that it's self-portrait. It's inscribed with Van Eyck's motto: "Als Ich Kan – As I can (but not as I would)".

"Cardinal Albergati" – two works exist here – the first is in silverpoint and it is believed to be a study for the later painting of the same name.

"The Madonna with Chancellor Rolin" – this work appears to be built up slowly in thin glazes intended to evoke subtle modeling and atmospheric luminosity.

Italian Renaissance Sculpture

The economic and social prosperity of Florence during this time translated into abundant patronage for the local artistic community. Wealthy merchants and guilds sought to reflect the pre-eminence of their city in art. At the same time, humanistic ideals and a clearer picture of past classical art began to emerge.

The result was a renewed fascination with rendering the human form in sculpture although with a decidedly stylistic flair consistent with the culture and religious beliefs of the day.

Luca Della Robbia's polychrome glazed terracotta roundel, "The Madonna and Child", is a colorful rendition in a style that remained popular through the next century. Other work such as Jacopo Della Qeurcia's "Great Door of S. Petronio" in Bologna and Nanni Di Banco's "Four Martyr Saints" at Orsanmichele aptly reflect the style of the period.

The church of Orsanmichele, once a granary, had 14 niches around its exterior that were allocated to leading guilds in 1414. Sculptors such as Lorenzo Ghiberti, Donatello and Andrea del Verrocchio competed with one another to produce the best work. Roman models and classical Roman styles are seen throughout.

"The Holy Trinity with the Virgin and St. John"

Believed to have been completed during the final year of Masaccio's short 27 year life through the patronage of the Lenzi family, the work depicts the crucifixion within a classical frame of Corinthian pilasters supported by a coffered vault. The outstretched arms of Christ are supported from behind by a majestic rendering of God the father and flanked by the Virgin, beckoning hand outstretched, on the left and St. John on the right. The Holy Spirit in the image of a dove hovers between the head of Christ and the Father.

The entire image is fully plotted in geometrically exact perspective designed with the intent to be viewed at eye-level. The painted architecture is quite convincing, owing to the exacting geometric precision of the entire work which could serve as an adequate model to reconstruct the scene in stone.

Though influenced to some extent by Donatello and Brunelleschi, use of directed lighting is all Masaccio.

Piero della Francesca

After beginning his career as an assistant in Florence, Piero worked primarily in the provincial centers of southern Tuscany.

He had a keen interest in mathematics from a young age and wrote treatises on it and perspective in his later years. His "Madonna della Misericordia" commissioned in 1445 for Borgo San Sepolcro shows a heavy influence of the rigid geometric characteristics of Masaccio.

"The Resurrection" and "The Victory over Khosroes" are both brilliantly colorful. "The Resurrection" is regarded as an accomplished study in foreshortening.

The major commission of his career began in 1452 at the Ducal Palace in Urbino with a fresco cycle on the theme "The History of the True Cross". It is a story taken from "The Golden Legend" which is a collection of the lives of the Saints divided into ten episodes, the first of which is "The Old Age and Death of Adam".

The "Flagellation of the Christ" and "Federigo and His Wife" are two notable works from Urbino. The latter is considered one of Piero's finest works.

Andrea Mantegna

Mantegna's love of classical antiquity is evident throughout much of his body of work and his enduring style became apparent with his first commission, frescos for the Ovetari Chapel of the Eremitani church in Padua, at the age of 17.

His most famous work is the "Camera degli Sposi" of 1474. The entire corner of a large room at the Ducal Palace, from floor through ceiling, is covered in fanciful frescos of the classic, secular world.

His fresco from Eremitani, "The Martyrdom of St. Christopher", is a depiction of two episodes divided by a foreshortened column. It's rich in color, ambitious in perspective and profuse in archaeological detail.

His nine large canvasses that comprise "The Triumph of Ceasar" are full of imagery from classic antiquity. The work, "St. Sebastian", depicts the tragic befalling of a Saint by many arrows and is innovative for its use of cut-off figures in the foreground.

Leonardo da Vinci

One of his earliest efforts was collaboration with his master of the time, Verrocchio. "The Baptism of the Christ" in 1472 is a graceful representation abundant in da Vinci style and Florentine influence. His "Adoration of the Magi" in 1481 introduced the sfumato borderless tonal blending technique and is a study in his preference to work from dark to light by successive layering in oils.

"The Virgin of the Rocks" completed in 1485 is a tonal-blending masterwork of light effects and quiet expression. "Mona Lisa", completed in 1506, has become one of the most recognizable oil paintings of all time.

His 1495 work, "The Last Supper", has unfortunately undergone substantial decay due to a failed experimentation in oil although enough of it remains to completely grasp the emotion and style it conveys. It has been said that da Vinci's painstaking obsession with perfection translated into more time spent pondering the work than in actually creating it.

Michelangelo

Although Michelangelo worked in drawing and paint, his most celebrated successes were his sculptures. Sculpture was his love and he considered it to be a vastly superior art form over paint and drawing.

Perhaps his most famous sculpture is the larger-than-life rendition of David completed in 1504. The 1499 Vatican Pieta, never fully completed, is considered a masterful union of Christian emotion with classical form. "Moses" completed in 1513, is a massive, muscle-bound, bearded figure of strange proportions thought by many to have been influenced by Donatello.

Michelangelo's Statue of David

The "Dying Slave", completed during the same period as Moses, is evocative of the torment many felt over the passing of Julius II.

"The Tomb of Giuliano de' Medici" in the Medici Chapel embodies the Active and Contemplative Principles of a popular Neoplatonic allegory of the day.

One of his last sculptural works began many years prior to his death but never completed was an expressionist rendition of mother and son titled, "The Rondanini Pieta".

Notable paintings include his famous and monumental Sistine Chapel ceiling work, "The Crucifixion of St. Peter" and "The Last Judgment".

Giovanni Bellini

Bellini was one of the artists instrumental in making Venice an artistic center to rival the more established Florence. His masterpiece was indisputably the S. Zaccaria altarpiece of 1505 – the last in a series of Madonna and Child renditions. Titled "The Virgin and Child with Saints", it is a truly monumental study in lighting and the depiction of a classical architectural frame. Evocative of the work of his more well-known contemporaries, its sheer quality and depiction of tender emotion have few rivals. The S. Giobbe altarpiece of 1490 is another work of the finest quality with a flawless rendering of figures and architecture.

Bellini's integration of figures and landscapes is considered another great strength. "The Madonna of the Meadow" is a depiction of the Virgin mother and child set in the foreground of a detailed agricultural scene.

He was also instrumental in his tutelage of promising young artists such as Giorgione and Titian. One of his last works, "Venus with a Mirror" in 1515, was influenced by the work of his former student, Giorgione.

Dutch Landscape Scenes

The Dutch were prolific landscape artists who worked on a variety of subjects. Among these were:

- Panoramas – featured vast plains stretching into the distance; characteristic of Dutch terrain
- Woods – representations of entire forests under a variety of interpretations

- Dunes and Country Roads – depictions of villages, trees, dunes, farms and roads
- Rivers and Canals – depictions of the vast waterways that traverse Holland
- Beaches – became a popular subject late in the 17th century; was a backdrop in much earlier work
- Winter – depictions of winter scenes, ice skating, fallen snow, etc.
- Sea – featured distant views of towns from sea, as well as nearby buildings and streets
- Nocturnal Views – allowed for experimentation with various effects regarding moonlight, fire and reflections; depicted normal activities of people at night – fishing, walking, etc.
- Views of Foreign Lands – Dutch painters were frequent travelers, particularly to Italy, Germany, Scandinavia, Brazil and Tyrol Imaginary Views – fanciful works intended to evoke a variety of moods including awe and melancholy; affirming the regularity and certainty of nature rather than its harsher, more violent aspects.

Jacques-Louis David

David was educated at the Ecole des Beaux-Arts school in Paris under the Rococo tradition.

His historically-based paintings, "The Oath of the Horatii", "The Death of Socrates" and "The Lictors Bringing to Brutus the Bodies of his Sons" depict qualities of virtue and valor in a style consistent with paintings from earlier eras. This ultimately served to influence public opinion regarding the civic failures of the ancients despite the fact that the people of the time were not unfamiliar with the characters and popular historical events of antiquity.

David accomplished this largely through artistic style. Figures are rendered in crisp relief against simplistic backgrounds. Their draperies are depicted in uniform hues such as greens, blues, reds and purples that enhance the intended dramatic effect.

His later works include the classics, "Marat Assassinated" and "Leonidas at Thermopylae". The latter is notable for its implausible assortment of nude figures surrounding a contemplative Leonidas with sword and shield in hand.

Francisco Goya

Francisco Jose' de Goya y Lucientes (1746 – 1828) is considered one of the greatest Romantic painters in history. He was forced to abandon his first love, theater and music, in 1792 when an inexplicable illness left him deaf. His interest in portraiture continued although the illness is thought to have affected his style toward a greater concern for character than appearance.

Goya was familiar with Rococo and knew many of the great European Baroque masters such as Rembrandt, Rubens and Titian.

He became a Spanish royal court painter in 1799. His 1800 oil on canvas, "Queen Maria Luisa of Spain" is thought to be, in some ways, a brutal but accurate rendition of a regal if plump, toothless woman who seems not completely comfortable in her position as a sitter.

Goya developed the technique of aquatint and, along with etching, published a set of eighty socially critical prints in 1799 titled, "Los caprichos".

His most enduring legacy is considered to be an extensive documentation of the atrocities committed by Napoleon's French occupation in the early 19th century.

Honore' Daumier

Daumier seemed fascinated by the various struggles and conditions of man. As a city dweller, much of his work depicts the discomforts, intellectual limitations, social pretensions and affections of the middle classes of the time. Daumier showed little concern for producing commentary on the impoverished and privileged extremes of the social spectrum.

His range of interest and sympathies was also revealed through painting and watercolor. "Six Months of Marriage", depicts a bored, yawning couple seated in a living room in parody-like style. His oil on canvas, "The Third Class Carriage", is a much more somber picture of discomfort and lonely endurance.

Following an 1832 imprisonment, he was barred from political commentary for the next 38 years. Among his last works are a series of commentary prints from 1870 – 1873 that show signs of his failing eyesight. These include "The Fall of the Empire", "The Birth of the Third Republic" and "The Commune".

Claude Monet

Monet spent much of his youth along the shores of Normandy immersed in the sea environment and its weather. He sold his first work, a series of caricatures, at the age of 15. During this time he also completed a number of sketches of sailing ships.

Monet's friendship with Eugene Boudin introduced him to the practice of open air painting which would be an enduring attribute of his work for the following 60 years.

Several significant paintings were completed prior to the development of his signature brush stroke beginning in the 1870's. These include the colorful, well-lighted "Women in the Garden" and "The Beach at St. Andresse".

Monet worked with Renoir in the late 1860's at a resort in Bougival where he produced the last of his pre-Impressionistic paintings.

His Impressionism, for which he is most well-known, began in earnest with "Poppies" and "Sunrise" during the early 1870's while living on the Seine near Paris.

He began to paint non-traditional Impressionist subjects during the late 1870's with works such as "Arrival of the Normandy Train".

In the 1890's he produced a number of paintings in series. "Stacks of Wheat" is a notable example from this period.

Claude Monet

- 103 -

Paul Cezanne

Paul Cezanne remained influenced by Impressionism perhaps more than any other Postimpressionist artist, largely through his relationships with Pissarro, Monet, Degas and Renoir. He initially drew significant attention with his painting, "The House of the Hanged Man at Auvers", which he displayed at the first Impressionist convention.

Unlike his predecessors, he had a reputation for painstaking observation of naturalistic subject matter prior to painting. "Mont Ste-Victoire with Viaduct" is a study in his painstaking observational style.

"The Basket of Apples" presents Cezanne's conception of space as being a product of the interrelation of objects contained within it.

Cezanne also completed a number of figure paintings although he had a reputation for slowness. The 1898 portrait of an unidentified male subject is said to have taken more than 100 sittings but is notable for its interest in conveying personality through clothing and posture as much as more traditional methods like facial expression.

Vincent Van Gogh

Following his altercation with Gauguin, Vincent entered the asylum of Saint-Remy near Arles. While there, he painted as his mental and physical health permitted. He produced a version of "Pieta" by Delacroix during this time, substituting his own features and hair for that of Christ.

After leaving the asylum, he moved north to Paris to be with his brother Theo. He believed this might help his mental and physical torment. One of his last works, "Crows Flying over a Cornfield", is an Impressionistic rendering of a symbolic scene believed to be consistent with his impending sense of doom.

His most prolific years were the decade immediately preceding his death. He shot himself on July 27, 1890, and died two days later.

Van Gogh's entire body of work consisted of more than 700 drawings and 800 oil paintings although he sold only one during his entire lifetime.

Starry Night

Pablo Picasso

Picasso's first caricatures of his friends were recognized by his father who was an academy professor in Barcelona.

The cubist style which would exemplify much of Picasso's best known work did not develop until a few years into his career. From 1900 to 1905 Picasso made frequent visits to Paris in what would later be known as a "Blue Period". During this time he painted the lower elements of humanity sunken in their despair. The oil "Boy with Pipe", completed in 1905, is characteristic of his first pre-Cubist style.

The period immediately following the "Blue" has been referred to Picasso's "Pink" in which he became interested in the circus, using it as subject matter for many of his pieces.

By the winter of 1906-07, Picasso began experimenting with angular figures and distorted proportions in "Les Demoiselles d'Avignon".

By 1909 he was working with fellow cubist Georges Braque. The two refined the cubist style and continued to experiment with different color palettes.

Cubism

Abstract Art

Also known as "nonrepresentational" or "nonobjective" art, its chief characteristic is its lack of specific references to natural objects and situations. French painter Maurice Denis noted that "a picture, before being a war horse, a nude woman, or some sort of anecdote, is essentially a surface covered with colors arranged in a certain order".

Russian Vasily Kandinsky divided his style into two categories – Improvisations and Compositions which were carefully planned prior to beginning work. In his Improvisations, Kandinsky claimed "automatic", instinctive inspiration. "Painting with White Form" is a notable Kandinsky oil composition in a myriad of colors, shades and hues bearing no real resemblance to anything recognizable.

Abstraction also had a substantial following in sculpture. Vladimir Tatlin's "Monument to the Third International" is a wood, glass and iron creation which, though interesting, also bears little resemblance to anything recognizable.

Surrealism

Surrealism began as an offspring of Dada and flourished, for a time, as a legitimate alternative to the more mainstream and formulistic Cubist movement.

Its chief proponent was Andre Breton who declared, in his 1924 Surrealist Manifesto, that Surrealism is a means of "reuniting the conscious with the unconscious realms of experience". Breton had studied Sigmund Freud and applied a dogmatic psychology to the movement, demanding absolute adherence to its doctrines.

The most notable Surrealist painters were Jean Arp, Max Ernst, André Masson, René Magritte, Yves Tanguy, Salvador Dalí, Pierre Roy, Paul Delvaux, and Joan Miró, although the work of each bore significant diversity from any one style as each explored their own avenues of expression.

Several artists employed techniques believed to evoke or promote psychic response. These included "frottage" which consisted of rubbing with graphite over wood or similar surfaces and "grattage" which was essentially a scraping of the canvas.

Short Lived Styles

- Futurism – the term originated from an early 20th century Italian group's optimism about the future; the artists rejected nostalgia and considered modernity to be more beautiful than Greek sculpture; content was stressed over form and the dynamic interaction of objects in motion and space was often articulated in "force lines"
- Vorticism – a brief phase in English art that combined the concerns of Futurism with many stylistic attributes of Cubism; the father of the movement was Wyndham Lewis
- Suprematism – this movement carried many elements of Futurism and Vorticism to an extreme by reducing color to pure black and white and form to basic geometric shapes
- Purism – proposed by Amedee Ozenfant and Le Corbusier as a disciplined, simplified form of art and architecture which rejected the decorative tendencies of Cubism
- Constructivism – the movement flourished in Russia from about 1914 to 1930; notable for its creation of sculpture that was constructed rather than chiseled or modeled; often machine-like in appearance.

Georgia O'Keeffe

American painter Georgia O'Keeffe studied at a number of art schools prior to her discovery by photographer Alfred Stieglitz who eventually became her husband. Inspired, perhaps, by precisionists such as Charles Sheeler and Charles Demuth, initially her style was mostly imitative and less original although by the early 1920's that changed. Common subjects in her repertoire included enlarged views of skulls and other animal bones, shells, rocks and natural land forms including mountains. O'Keeffe imparted her own style of rhythmic outlines and delicate color washes that inspired no shortage of interpretations. These ranged from symbolic to erotic and psychological.

"Cow's Skull", "Black Iris" and "Red, White and Blue" are considered among the most representative paintings embodying her style.

She completed most of her work in the 1920's through 1940's although she continued to paint well into her eighties.

Modern Primitives

These are terms used to describe art that is relatively primitive in appearance or that has been executed with obvious cues of naivety. Many such artists are self-taught.

To certain academics and critics, such art appears faulty or even crude. Conventions of perspective are either ignored or erroneously flaunted and figures are frequently rendered out-of-proportion. The overall effect is often highly unrealistic.

Others have discovered within such work important aesthetic accomplishment and fresh vitality. An obvious feeling for design is evident in many modern primitives.

Henri Rousseau is considered one of the foremost popular masters and, by many, a great artist in a general sense. His work prior to the turn of the 20th century proved influential in the development of modern art.

Rousseau, who was a Frenchman, nonetheless appears to have been influenced very little by the strong French artistic tradition. Likewise, American primitives appear to have not suffered from a weaker American tradition.

Well-known American primitives include John Kane, Edward Hicks and, more recently, Grandma Moses.

Tassili

Tassili is a region in the mid-western Sahara desert that has yielded notable finds for many years. However, it wasn't until Henri Lhote's 1956-57 expedition that the true volume of work at this location became evident. Just in terms of numbers, but also with respect to artistic quality and variety of styles, the collection at Tassili surpasses all others. It is believed that more than 30,000 paintings exist here.

Over 30 styles had been determined by the early 1970's which can be grouped into three basic divisions – cattle, horse and camel. The majority appear to be from an intermediate time between the Bubalus and Cattle (or Archaic) periods. Symbols and masks are depicted in much of the work from this later period.

By radiocarbon dating, it is believed that human occupation first began in Tassili around 5400 BC, + or – 300 years. Research at other sites in Tassili has indicated consistent occupation and painting through the first millennium BC. Attempts to date the paintings themselves have been largely unsuccessful.

Tassili Cave Painting

African Sculpture

Sculpture has been discovered mostly in the woodlands of the Congo basin and in West African forests. Due to deterioration, surviving wood carvings are rare if indeed much work was done in wood. The majority of finds have been either in terracotta or copper alloy castings of brass or bronze.

Although terracotta sculptures of various kinds have been discovered throughout the continent, these are on an individual basis and do not indicate any kind of continuous or evolving tradition. An exception appears to be in West Africa where two traditions are thought to have occurred over the course of 2500 years.

Large numbers of terracotta human and animal figures have been found in tin mines near the village of Nok in the North Central State of Nigeria. These were discovered along with remnants of an iron working industry that have allowed some radiocarbon dating to be performed. Effective dates have been established near approximately 4500 BC.

Assyrian Art

The Assyrians tended to work in more dramatic and symbolic themes than the Sumerians. Due to their dominance of the region, Assyrian kings lived in lavishly apportioned palaces full of paintings and relief sculpture.

The palace of Sargon II at Khorsabad is regarded as a centerpiece of Assyrian artistic accomplishment. The façade was decorated with multicolored tiles on an exterior surrounding its gateway entrance protected by powerfully expressive man-headed bulls on either side.

Decorating the entrances and gateways of brick structures with massive slabs of stone in low relief was a common method employed by the Assyrians. The painted Cretan "Torreador Fresco" dated from 1500 BC and the 650 BC limestone work "Dying Lioness" from Ninevah are significant examples of this kind of work.

In terms of subject matter, the culture knew no precedent with respect to historic storytelling so works which are historical in nature tend to depict scenes rather than time-based narratives. "The Sack of the City of Hamanu" from Ninevah is an example of this kind of style.

Indus Valley

It is believed that the Indus Valley civilization peaked between 2200 and 1800 BC in two principal cities – Mohenjo-Daro and Harappa. Studies of each indicate that a relatively high degree of social and political sophistication developed prior to the demise of the culture to invaders around 1500 BC.

The predominant art form of the period appears to be functional sculpture. Pieces recovered from the remains of the two cities tend to either be of a very formal or naturalistic nature. Works in sandstone, copper and limestone have been found which reveal a fairly intelligent study of the human body.

Notable examples include the naturalistic male "torso" in red sandstone from Harappa, a stylized, copper rendition of a nude negro-featured "dancing girl" from Mohenjo-daro and the bust of a man who appears to be a priest rendered in a style not dissimilar to early Sumerian figures recovered from Tello and Ur.

Buddha

The subject of the origin of the Buddha image has fostered no shortage of debate among scholars. One of the earliest researchers to publish an opinion on the subject was Frenchman A. Foucher in an early 20th century discussion of the art of Gandhara and the development of the Buddha image. He posits that the image originated in Gandhara and that it shows the influence of the Apollo visage common to Hellenistic art.

Another leading scholar during the height of the debate was Indian Ananda K. Coomaraswamy who argued that the image had a wholly Indian origin derived from that of the Yaksha.

Ultimately, historians concluded that both were right to some extent - the image clearly demonstrates Classical as well as Indian elements.

Regardless, perhaps the most significant fact is that its development occurred under a foreign dynasty – the Kushan.

Pre Shang Dynasty

The Neolithic, pre-Shang peoples of China appear to be relatively primitive by later standards although some interesting works in pottery have been discovered.

The Lung-Shan culture of Cheng Tzu Yai produced for functional purposes elegant, thin black pottery reminiscent of "egg shell" porcelain.

A slightly later culture, the Yang-Shao, is known to have produced painted and red pottery as well as jade sculpture. The work has been lauded for its beauty and similarity to the pottery of the Black Earth region of the Black Sea. Ancient trade routes existed throughout Asia and it has been speculated that potting techniques may have been imported from this area.

One of the most interesting finds from the area is a perfectly preserved, hard-fired earthenware funerary urn on display at the Seattle Art Museum which is believed to date to around 2200 BC. It depicts an intricate pattern of swirling geometric designs and symbols.

Chinese Jade

Although deposits of jadeite and nephrite are found throughout the world, no other culture is known to have worked jade for artistic purposes in such a consistent and unbroken tradition as the Chinese.

Nephrite recovered from the Ho-t'ien (Khotan) and Yarkland (now Sinkiang) supplied jade artisans with raw material for almost three millennia. Imported jadeite or jadestone began entering China during the 18th century from Myanmar through the Yunnan province.

The earliest jade objects recovered from China are tools and disks with central circular orifices but over the first 1000 years of carving the general artistic styles of the Shang and Chou dynasties effected an increased sophistication in style and subject matter.

With the advent of trade to the west during the last half of the previous millennium, Chinese jade work became world renowned for its quality and artistic merit.

Haniwa

Haniwa had their origin in the practical need to strengthen grave mounds against erosion and washouts. In its simplest form, Haniwa resembles a cylinder perhaps to the height of a picket fence around the mound. More often, Haniwa are objects of perhaps 24 to 26" in height such as armored warriors, coy ladies, human figures singing in chorus, animals, houses and birds tightly packed in a circle around the burial mound. Figurine Haniwa were produced from tubes, ribbons or slabs of clay in a manner that tends to emphasize the clay itself. Incidentally, this is in contrast to tomb figurines which demonstrate a greater emphasis on the style of the individual artist but is nonetheless a means of distinguishing between the two.

Terracotta Warriors

Primarily due to the extraordinary variance in subject matter, Haniwa art tells us much about early life in Japan and, due to their simplified, geometric styling, are considered by contemporary artists to be among the more interesting examples of ancient sculpture from a stylistic perspective.

Pre-Columbian Art

Pre-Columbian describes art produced by various civilizations that existed in the Americas prior to Spanish conquest and colonization in the sixteenth century. Much existing art was destroyed during this time. What is known has come through archaeological discovery.

The art primarily consists of masks, fabrics, vessels and similar artifacts that often depict animal and human forms. Snakes, condors and jaguars were frequent subjects and surviving renditions indicate that the artisans had a superior understanding of these creatures.

Mochica and Chimu ware are characterized by portrait-like faces of animals and human figures. Artifacts recovered from Nazca demonstrate stunning color and bold ornamentation while Maya vases often convey complex imagery.

The pre-Columbian artistic world has been divided into two principal parts based upon geography – Central and South America.

Mexico, Guatemala and Honduras have been excavated most extensively and works from these Central American civilizations are best known. Peru is regarded as the most important civilization in South America. It contains sites that have yielded artifacts from a variety of cultures.

There are three basic chronological periods into which materials recovered from these areas have been classified – pre-Classic (2000 BC to 300 AD), Classic (300 AD to 900 AD) and Post-Classic (900 AD to 1519 AD).

Giclee

"Giclee" is a French term meaning "fine spray". "Giclee" or "Iris" prints are created with high performance digital inkjet printers that produce more than four million water-based ink droplets per second through four tiny jets. The ink is deposited onto a canvas, "Somerset Velvet" or "Arches Cold Press" paper which spins on a drum at about 250 revolutions per second. The entire process is based upon complex, computer-controlled calculations that enable the production of over 500 shades of ink.

Precise duplications of scanned originals are possible using this process. The finished product has a vibrant, lush look and the velvety feel of a watercolor while retaining the clarity of an original. Such a result is impossible to achieve with offset printing.

Aside from superior results, Iris reproduction is technically simpler than offset printing because printing films and plates are simply not required.

"IRIS" is a Trade name of IRIS Graphics of Bedford, Massachusetts – a dominant manufacturer for many years of "Giclee" printing devices.

<u>Pottery and Clay Terms</u>
Bisque: the first firing of clay in a kiln and the point at which water can no longer be added

Ceramics: used to describe the shaping, finishing and firing of clay

Coil method in clay: the laying of long strands of clay on top of one another
Earthenware – a type of "low-fire" clay needing to be glazed; porous and non-water-proof

Firing: the process of heating clay at high temperatures to fuse its particles

Greenware: hardened but unfired clay; can be made wet and turned back into a useable material

Kiln: the oven or furnace used to fire ceramics; can be electric, of natural gas, wood, coal, fuel oil or propane he kiln is the furnace used to fire ceramics or metal

- 111 -

Pinch Pots – a process whereby an artist forms a pot by pinching the clay to create a center opening

Slab built: clay slabs are cut into shape, and joined together with scoring and wet clay called slip

Stoneware: sturdier then earthenware, stoneware is waterproof even without being glazed

Terra cotta: commonly used for ceramic sculpture, it is a brownish-orange earthenware clay
Wheel Thrown: the process of spinning clay on a potter's wheel

Texture

The term "texture" can be used to describe areas of a composition which have been treated in a decorative manner, such as where the area is covered by a formal arrangement of linear patterns and decorative symbols.

Throughout history, some artists have been known to incorporate actual materials in their compositions in order to mimic the real texture of an illustrated object. The qualities of silk, fabrics and fur, particularly in portraiture, were commonly recreated, such as with Peter Paul Ruben's "Self-portrait with Isabella Brant".

Aside from realism, there has also been an interest in preserving the texture of materials used in actual composition or, more specifically, texture resulting from technical processes of treatment. This is particularly true of work in metal, wood, stone and plastic where the marks left by tools and implements become incorporated features of the work. Brush and knife marks in virtually all types of painting have a long history of being purposeful design elements.

Shape

Shape can be manipulated to provide a clarification of facts not apparently visible or to alter the usual relationship of one shape to another. The following devices are commonly used:

- Voluminal shape – blocking figures to study essential volumes or characterize the mass and weight of an object such as the human body
- Linear shape – can be use to convey action or focus purely on narrative in a more simplistic manner than by literal rendition
- All-over patterns – can be used to fill space or for purely decorative purposes
- Conforming patterns – performed to fit subject matter into a particular space, such as what Greek painters did when painting a kylix (round plate)
- Varied patterns – employed to convey, for instance, a busy scene of many jumbled shapes or objects; also can be used to enhance contrast within adjacent, similarly-colored areas
- Geometric designs – can be employed to add a sense of vitality to a scene or to integrate an otherwise unimportant background into its overall artistic meaning
- Distortion for emotional effect – achieved by, for instance, altering the shape of the head, arms or shoulders of a figure to emphasize its emotional disposition or to point to its interest.

The Old Master Precept

Peter Paul Rubens combined exceptionally thin brushwork with thickly loaded lights to produce his masterpiece, "Landscape – Sunset". The blaze of the sun on the horizon is painted in an extraordinarily thick yellow – so much so that it stands out from the canvas in relief. The approach of twilight is sensitively conveyed by transparent shadowing.

Much of Rembrandt's work, particularly his later portraiture, involved a technique of working over a monochrome under-painting to obtain a richness of light and shade which was obtained by transparent glazes of a color darker than the areas to which they were applied. His technique included extra touches of heavy impastos for the lighter areas. The results were dramatic, as in his self-portrait, "Man with the Golden Helmet" and the work, "Flora".

Cezanne is renowned for his use of enamel-like translucency in his later works while an examination of Van Gogh reveals remarkable relief from his busy brushwork.

Abstraction

The preparatory phase consists of the artist narrowing his or her focus to exactly what is to be conveyed. Next, the artist carefully observes or studies the subject matter, sometimes employing tools and/or media for a documentary analysis in order to sharpen perceptions and become completely familiar with it prior to undertaking creative liberties.

In the exploratory phase, the artist seeks a unification of his or her response to the subject matter often experimenting with a selection/rejection process to arrive at the most ideal direction in which to proceed. This process often reveals additional details, patterns and rhythms and opens up yet additional paths of experimentation.

The terminal phase involves a resolution and final synthesis of previous exploration into a tangible course of action to resolve the work. All irrelevant details and paths are eliminated. The heart, mind and hand are finally brought into unity during this phase.

Composition

Composition is the summation of all means by which a painter arrives at unifying his or her intended overall effect. A general design or "marking out" is the usual first step. This can be in the form of a linear framework or geometric structure such as an arrangement of figures within a pyramid or triangle shape.

Raphael's "Madonna and St. John" is an excellent illustration of the triangle effect on overall form. Sometimes composition can take the form of angular divisions or curvaceous forms such as the diagonal division that occurs in Delacroix's "Death of Sardanapalus".

The manipulation of light and shade is another important aspect of composition that can be used to evoke emotion or provide a sense of depth.

Composition in color is another artistic technique that can be used to draw the viewer into a piece through, for instance, subtle (or not so subtle) gradations.

Asymmetrical composition or purposeful imbalance can 'force' the viewer to scan a work for its subject matter.

Two Dimensional Art

The following terms used to differentiate various forms of two-dimensional visual art:

- Portrait – a work that represents the likeness of a specific individual, group or animal; artists are frequently concerned with including some conveyance of emotion or painting the sitter in a manner that reveals some aspect of his or her personality; frequently performed in both two and three dimensions
- Portraiture – refers to the field of portrait making; also used as a general term referring to portraits
- Self-portrait – occurs when an artist represents himself or herself as the principal subject within a work; often accomplished using a reflection in a mirror or, in the modern era, a photograph
- Landscape – a work of art such as a painting or photograph that depicts natural scenery – valleys, mountains, trees, rivers, forests, etc.
- Still life – created by painting inanimate, common subjects such as food, flowers, vessels, books and clothing

Art vs. Natural Beauty

While both can be appreciated for their sensory appeal, unlike natural beauty, art cannot be fully experienced until it is fully understood. This is the prevailing opinion of many critics and philosophers who believe that a proper definition of art should be one in which knowledge far surpasses superficial aesthetics in importance.

Regardless, either deliberately or unintentionally, art can both express emotion and represent reality in a way that allows for the recognition of its meaning.

Art can also be thought of as having content that the artist wishes to be understood by his or her audience. Some also consider art as having symbolism in feelings, ideas, objects, or states of affair.

Another distinguishing characteristic of art is the mystique it often holds for a critical audience anxious to decipher its meaning since few artists have historically provided an analytical analysis with their work.

Artist vs. Cartoonist

This question has caused no shortage of controversy throughout the history of art criticism. Most have concluded that the answer has much to do with complexity. A good illustration is the difference between how a cartoonist might render motion or movement as opposed to the artist. The cartoonist frequently employs lines indicating motion, such as to rear of a figure.

In contrast, an artist might use more sophisticated techniques such as an afterimage, a particular pose on the part of a figure which would be quite unnatural if the figure were still, etc. Examples include Diego Velazquez's "The Spinners" in the case of the former, and Michelangelo's "Avenging Angel" in the case of the latter.

Another dimension has to do with intent. A cartoonist wishes to illustrate a narrative, typically with little intent for conveying any kind of message, emotion, thought or historical event through the illustration itself. His objective is to lend assistance to the primary vehicle – the narrative itself.

Art Appreciation

Individual variation is unavoidable whether one is properly schooled in the process of "art appreciation" or not. After all, the act of art appreciation is, by its very nature, a highly personal one.

Independence of judgment occurs when one maintains his own personal judgment despite the contrary opinion of fellows or when one resists adapting his or her opinion to that of others.

Tolerance of complexity requires a resignation that not every individual element or technique at its most elementary structure must be understood prior to engaging in an understanding or genuine appreciation of the work.

A sense of recreation or an ability to break from the normal rigors of adult life is necessary in order to engage one's appreciative faculties. This is simply a factor of engaging different parts of the brain for different purposes.

Craft

A craft, by definition, is a technique or skill considered apart from the aesthetic aspect of a creation often involving a constructive manual activity. The craftsman is rendering a finished product and is not engaging in an active process of aesthetic expression.

Over the last century, an attempt at such a sharp distinction has been recognized as largely futile – "craft" as it were – essentially the construction of practical objects with artistic embellishment (jewelry, kitchenware, etc.) has been found to evoke comparable aesthetic response on the part of the viewer.

Ancient processes continue to see widespread use by modern craftsmen. Many have leveraged them to produce works of impressive individuality.

Today, the term "Fine Art" is still frequently reserved for the classic modes of painting, architecture and sculpture.

Ultimately, defining and differentiating art is one of common opinion and subjectivity.

Signatures

The term "signed only" refers to an open edition print which has been signed by an artist but has not been numbered.

"Signed and numbered" is often abbreviated S/N and refers to a print which has been both signed and numbered by the artist. S/N prints are often also referred to as "limited edition".

An "artist's proof" is a "signed and numbered" print bearing the pencil-written initials A/P. "Artist proofs" are identical to "signed and numbered" works with the exception that there are far fewer A/Ps available. Generally, there is about 10 percent more A/Ps than S/Ns when paintings are reproduced as numbered editions.

A "limited edition" is a reproduction of an original painting that has been "signed and numbered" by an artist. True "limited edition" prints are considered collectible pieces of art and are usually produced on high quality, acid-free paper. "Limited edition" prints are sometimes referred to as lithographs.

Modeling

Early examples of modeling have been found in Egyptian tombs. Greeks fashioned dolls and figurines from wax while Romans made death masks of important individuals. The Chinese are known to have produced ceremonial bronze vessels during the Shang dynasty.

Numerous examples of clay modeling have been found from virtually every historical era throughout the world. Fire baking and sand were later discovered to add additional properties such as durability.

Terracotta modeling was used as early as the Greek, Roman and Etruscan eras and gained popularity during the Renaissance with such sculptors as Ghiberti and Donatello. Notable work has been discovered from the Pre-Columbian era as well, such as from Zacatenco and at Tlatilco.

Modeling continues in the modern era although mostly in interpretive form through the work of such sculptors as Marini, Matisse, Moore and, later, Clause Oldenburg, Edward Keinholz, Robert Graham and Charles Simonds.

Hardwoods

- Chestnut – a medium, light brown hard wood with a distinct grain. Durable and provides a good finish although possibly more prone to splitting.
- Ebony – an exceptionally hard wood with a distinct, fine grain and rich, dark brown to black color. It is not easily obtainable.
- Elm – yellow to reddish brown with a distinct grain, can be difficult to work.
- Holly – a white wood with a fine grain, smooth and easily workable.
- Mahogany – easily workable reddish, brown hardwood with a variable grain
- Maple – tight-grained, reddish-brown wood which finishes well.
- Oak – popular, very durable and easy to work with a variable appearance from yellow to dark brown, has a distinctive grain.
- Rosewood – valued for its even texture and color that varies from reddish-brown to purple and black
- Walnut – easily workable, provides a good finish, expensive, may be difficult to obtain, generally chocolate brown in color with a rich grain.

Wood Carving Tools

- Carving – Primary tools include the gouge and chisel. The gouge has a variable cutting edge which is curved in shape. Both tools are available in various sizes and shapes including bent and curved to provide access to inaccessible areas of a piece such as a hollow. Veiners and flutes or "V-shaped" gouges are used for fine work.
- Shaping – Basic shapers include rifflers, files and rasps. Files are finer than rasps while a riffler has a curved edge for rounded work. Surform shapers have a built-in space for shavings which prevents the tool from clogging.
- Carpentry – Half rip saws are the most popular due to the ability to cut with as well as across the grain. Bow saws are useful for curve-cutting while the fret saw is good for flat pieces. Wooden mallets are useful although selection is important as they tend to be heavy.

Foam Sculpting

Polystyrene – a relatively safe, non-toxic member of the thermoplastics group, it melts under heat and is soluble when exposed to certain solvents. Proper ventilation is important when working with these two methods and it should be noted that the material is highly flammable. It can be found in two basic varieties. The first, expanded, is used frequently in packaging and has an open cell texture. The second, known under the trade name Styrofoam, is a denser, closed-cell variety.

Polyurethane – a rigid, closed cell material with variable density which is not susceptible to melting although prone to release toxic fumes when heated.

Both plastics are generally cheap and conveniently available. They are relatively new as mediums due to their more recent advent.

Jean Dubuffet, a painter and sculptor, was a pioneer in the use of carved polystyrene while Louis Chavignier popularized foamed polyurethane.

More recently, they have gained popularity for use in large-scale carved molds of cement and concrete sculptures. These materials also prove useful as a lightweight core for sculptures comprised of heavy substances.

Diluents

Diluents, or thinners and solvents, are commonly used to alter the consistency of oils to achieve desired application. Turpentine, acetone and refined petroleum products such as benzol have found common use.

A thinner or solvent should be chosen for its ability to mix thoroughly, dry evenly and not react chemically with other constituents. It should disappear once dry and not leave behind noticeable odors or residue. Flammability is a common problem with these types of chemicals and manufacturers continue to research mixtures with more favorable characteristics for the artist.

Turpentine, which is a derivative of the pine tree, is by far the most common thinner and is available in a variety of grades. Rectified is considered the most suitable for artistic purposes. Pure gum spirits turpentine is a suitable grade as well and can be commonly found in hardware stores.

Mineral spirits and gasoline, once commonly found in the studio, have largely fallen out of favor as both produce unpleasant fumes and can be quite dangerous. Danger aside, modern additives make gasoline unfavorable from a chemical standpoint as well.

Canvas

Canvas, or stretched fabric, is the most common support for oil painting. Many materials have been used as canvas including linen and cotton in various weaves, unbleached calico, duck, twill, Hessian and man-made fibers. Linen is considered best and is available in a wide variety of weaves and forms. The finest, knot-free weaves are considered optimal although looser weaves with knots are sometimes preferred when a coarser surface is desired. Cotton is a relatively low cost alternative but can be inconsistent in quality and problematic when stretching.

Various weights are available for the different fabric types and are measured in ounces. Heavier weight fabrics tend to be more absorbent. Fabric color varies with material and level of bleaching.

The canvas is measured and cut to the desired size then later stretched over a wooden frame. It is generally affixed by a combination of stapling and gluing.

Paint

Paint itself is a compound of various constituents but the primary component is the pigment. Historically, artists had to be somewhat creative in finding suitable substances for pigment creation. Animals, plants and minerals were all tried with varying degrees of success. As pigment creation evolved into more of a science, paint began to be categorized by origin.

The first of these, organic paint, is carbon-based paint usually derived from animal sources. Two examples of these include the ink sac of a cuttlefish which is used to make sepia and the urine of an Indian cow which is used to make Indian yellow. Some organic paint is derived from vegetable sources such as madder from a plant root.

True organic paint has become increasingly rare as most colors can now be manufactured synthetically.

Inorganic paint is derived from natural mineral pigments such as raw sienna or yellow ochre. Additional tones such as umber are manufactured through burning minerals.

Synthetic paint is manufactured from man-made compounds. Examples include cadmium, viridian green and cobalt blue.

Two basic grades of paint are available – artist and student. The latter usually contains lower quality pigments which can produce less consistent and less permanent results. Types include watercolors, oils, gouache, tempera and acrylics.

Particularly in the case of oils and acrylics, paint has been supplied commercially via tubes for a number of years although some oil artists still prefer to purchase raw pigment for mixing at home or in the studio themselves.

Some common, commercially available pigment names include sepia, gamboge, carmine, sap green, indigo and Prussian blue.

The properties of most pigments are affected by heat, light, moisture, acidity, and alkalinity. Chemical interactions can be problematic as well. Permanence can vary although earth colors such as yellow, sienna, red and marines have good longevity. Carbon black, cobalt and viridian are relatively stable as well.

Excess oil is sometimes added to extend the shelf-life of many commercial paints. When using this type of paint, the artist will usually spread a portion onto an absorbent material such as cardboard to remove the excess oil prior to beginning work.

Acrylics

Acrylics are pigments bound in synthetic resin or polyvinyl acetate. Characteristically similar to watercolor and tempera, they are water soluble emulsions which dry to a matte finish and lend themselves quite well to layering.

Unfavorable weather conditions for exposed work such as murals in Mexico during the 1920's prompted the development of paint with quick drying and stability characteristics.

Early adopters of acrylics included Jose' Orozco, Diego Rivera and David Siqueiros. During the 1950's acrylics gained popularity in the United States and were used by such artists as Jackson Pollock, Mark Rothko, Robert Motherwell and Kenneth Noland in either abstract or popular form.

By the 1960's, acrylics became widely used in Great Britain. Notable British artists include Peter Blake, Tom Phillips, Bridget Riley and Leonard Rosoman.

Tempera Painting

Firm materials typically make the best surfaces. Chipboard, Masonite and hard board are suitable and relatively inexpensive. Best results are usually obtained when board surfaces are prepped with fine sand paper and methyl alcohol prior to applying paint. Cured hardwood works well but soft board and plywood should be avoided. Seasoned wood is best when it can be found for a reasonable price.

Canvas, provided it is of a sufficiently tight weave and stretched properly, works well. It is often useful to glue the canvas to a hardboard backing which has been properly sized to prevent buckling.

Sizing is best accomplished using rabbit skin glue although it can be expensive. It is often unnecessary to use the glue at full strength. Instead, it can be diluted with up to 10 parts water. The glue, whether diluted or not, should be warmed to approximately 100 degrees Fahrenheit prior to application with a brush. Gelatin makes a suitable alternative for size.

Gesso grounds should be applied when tempera painting. On canvas it is often useful to add zinc white to the gesso prior to application.

Watercolor Paper

Stretching prevents lighter weight papers from buckling when color washed. The cut-off weight of paper usually considered optimal for washing is about 140 lb. "Weight" is an important consideration when selecting paper and the term actually refers to the weight of a 480 sheet ream. Heavier papers need not be stretched although they are almost always clipped to a board or other suitable support prior to beginning work. Methodologies for stretching vary but a common method is to soak the paper in a water tray and then place it on a drawing board, tacking the corners down with tacks. The edges of the paper are then attached using gummed brown paper tape. As the paper dries, it can be repeatedly pulled smooth and taut.

Commercially available stretching frames allow edges to be crimped between an inner and outer framework.

Pre-prepared paper which has been mounted on cardboard does not need stretching and is a good commercial alternative to home or studio stretching as well.

It should be noted that washing often weakens paper, making it susceptible to accidental 'holing' by a brush.

Gouache Painting

Definitions of the technique vary among artists but most agree that gouache is opaque watercolor painting. It lacks the transparency of watercolor due to its covering power and opacity. It is applied similarly to brush oils but dries more quickly.

It is reflective by the power of the materials in the pigment itself rather than relying on grounds for such a property as in watercolor and tempera. Gouache is often used for color reproduction work.

The technique was first developed by a European monk around the fourteenth century who added zinc white to watercolor.

Albrecht Durer, a noted watercolor artist, was an early user of the gouache technique for his work on landscape and animals, as was English artist, Paul Sandby. Pablo Picasso also used the gouache technique occasionally, such as with his 1917 work, Pulcinella.

Pastel

Pastels cannot be mixed to obtain other colors. Fortunately, there are over 600 tints commercially available from a number of reputable suppliers. An artist might need, perhaps, 12 to 48 tints in total, depending upon the nature of the work planned. A beginner might need a basic set of just four colors. Typically these include black, white, red and brown. Outdoor sketching is a common use of pastels that typically requires a smaller quantity of them.

There are three basic qualities available – soft, medium and hard. Softs provide the widest range of colors and are generally easier to work. Colors are typically marketed on a scale from 0 to 8 which is an indication of the relative lightness or darkness of the tone. Some artists choose to make their own pastels. The process for doing so is relatively easy and inexpensive.

Oil pastels are a suitable alternative for sketching or for use by an oil artist interested in drawing an underlying initial design prior to beginning work.

Fixatives

Permanence is a direct factor of paper and pastel quality so the best materials should always be chosen when possible. Over time the pastel will "affix" to the paper lending a greater quality of durability. Nevertheless, many artists choose to frame their work under glass. When doing so, care should be taken to avoid contact with the glass surface itself and to properly seal out dust and other contaminants. If framing is not feasible, pastel work should be stored in a stack with paper tissue, greaseproof paper or cellophane interleaved between layers.

When affixing the paper to a mount, generally its best to glue the top edge only using a flour or starch paste.

Care should be taken when using fixatives with pastels as colors are particularly susceptible to dulling and distortion. Of the artists who do choose to use fixatives, some fix at various layers prior to completing the work while others will only fix the final product. Fast drying fixatives are generally best.

Pencils

- Graphite – available in a variety of hard and soft qualities on an 18 point scale which runs from the softest, 8B through the hardest, 8H, or, alternatively depending upon manufacturer, from a scale of 1 to 4, with 1 being the softest grade
- Charcoal and Carbon – notable for the high degree of blackness produced in the lines, like graphite pencils, also available in variable degrees of density and grades

- Colored – soft due to their constituent parts which include filler, binder, lubricant and coloring; available in a wide assortment of tints, typically not erasable with few exceptions although sometimes removable using a blade
- Clutch – a modified apparatus similar to a "mechanical" pencil with refillable 'lead' in a range of sizes and thicknesses.

Pen and Ink

Pen and ink is one of the least demanding art forms in terms of equipment requirements. Pen and ink artists simply need the addition of virtually any kind of paper to produce their work.

Historically, medieval monks employed pen and ink on prepared animal skins such as goat, sheep, calf, lamb or kid using the quills of goose feathers.

Pen use continued during the Renaissance and along with mixed media such as white highlighting, crayon and watercolors it flourished as an art form. It gained even more widespread use during the Post-Renaissance era by such artists as Rubens and Van Dyck. Hogarth is considered an exemplary penman of the 18th century while the advent of magazines and the mass production of books in the 19th century provided an outlet for notables such as Charles Keene and George du Maurier.

By the 20th century, pen and ink luminaries included Matisse, Pascin and Picasso.

Pen and Ink Technique

The primary pen and ink technique is 'line and dot' due to the ability to produce an almost limitless number of textures. Perhaps the most difficult to master aspect of pen and ink work is learning to use the correct amount of pressure to produce a proper ink flow. Pen and ink artists will routinely sketch their work with a pencil prior to beginning their drawing although some prefer a more freeform approach.

Arm movement is critical and often proper technique involves the use of the entire arm rather than just the hand and wrist. This is particularly true for brush work.

Shadow and tonal variations are achieved through various methods such as stippling, hatching and cross-hatching, toothbrush spattering and scribbling, among others.

Watercolors may be employed in combination with ink to produce various effects, as well as sponges, fabrics, fingerprints and wood.

Erasure can be accomplished to varying degrees of success through the use of blotting paper. India rubber often works well. For dry ink, glass fiber erasers and sharp blades work well, particularly when used in conjunction with a shield to protect the rest of the drawing.

Printmaking

The most basic form of printmaking, relief printing, has its origins in the Far East beginning approximately 1400 years ago in China. The process consists of removing specific areas of material from a block of wood or similar source in order to leave a raised image of what is intended to be printed. The raised surface is coated with ink or some form of paint and pressed onto a suitable surface.

An alternative form of relief printing is an opposite method whereby the paper is brought into contact with ink in the depressed, ink saturated areas of the printing block. The effect is successfully achieved by first removing the ink from the raised areas of the block.

Lithographic and planographic techniques involve printmaking from a flat surface such as a metal sheet through the use of a combination of ink suspended in a grease mixture and water.

Screenprinting involves printing through a stencil.

The various processes have increased in sophistication with the advent and refinement of printing press techniques.

Submerging

A work may need to be detached occasionally from a base such as card or wood if it has inadvertently become stuck to it. A work may need to be cleaned or stains may need to be removed.

Proper handling is crucial when submerging a work, particularly one in which a water-soluble paint or ink has been used. Take care not to touch any of the painted or inked surface. Never fold or bend a work at anytime prior to, during, or after submersion.

Using an underlying support such as glass, plastic or plywood can help add stability to the work during the submersion process.

An artist may want to submerge a work such as a watercolor in order to achieve a particular effect such as over-painting or rubbing and can usually do so with no damage provided the paper or card is of a sufficient quality and durability.

Fresco Technique

The first step in the fresco process is to ensure the wall is properly prepared to receive the work. There should be no evidence of moisture and the wall should be treated to avoid and potential seepage which might occur in the foreseeable future. Brick or tile walls work best but concrete should be avoided due to its inherent, destructive impurities.

The process of creating an acceptable quality fresco plaster is an intricate one. First, the artist should select only the highest quality, fired white quicklime and pure sand such as from a freshwater sand pit or clear stream bed. The mixture should be stored in a frost-protected pit, preferably lined with bricks. Over a two-year period, pure water is periodically flooded through the lime and mixed well.

The wall which is to receive the fresco must be washed and cleaned of any loose dust or brick. Plaster is applied in three successively thinner layers consisting of various proportions of the pre-prepared plaster and sand.

Paint selection is important – only certain pigments will react chemically as they should with lime.

Stone

- Soapstone – relatively soft and suitable for a beginner but susceptible to moisture.
- Sandstone – used for thousands of years; quality is dependent upon quartz content but generally quite porous and a poor performer for finishing.

- Slate – readily available and polishes to a nice finish although potentially difficult to work due to a tendency to split.
- Marble – available in a variety of colors, typically easy to carve and produces a nice finish.
- Limestone – available in a variety of densities and colors, Caen limestone from France is considered among the best for carving.
- Granite – a very hard stone requiring special tools to work successfully, polishes to an exceptionally high finish but is not suitable for detailed work.
- Alabaster – characteristically smooth and translucent, relatively soft and workable, best for smaller pieces which will be weather protected.

Perspective

Perspective is a system of creating the illusion of three dimensions on a two-dimensional surface. There are two basic categories of perspective – aerial and linear. Aerial perspective refers to atmospheric effects on objects in space and can be seen as diminishing tones for objects which are receding from view. Put simply, linear perspective describes a process of seeing lines on objects from various angles converge and diverge.

The position from which an object is seen and drawn is called the station point or point of sight. The horizon is represented by the eye level or horizon line. Ground plane refers to the horizontal plane where the artist is standing. The center of vision is the point on the horizon immediately opposite the eye. Vanishing points occur where parallel lines converge.

Grounds

The layer between the sizing or surface preparation coat and the paint is referred to as the ground. As this layer is not intended add to or alter the artistic paint layer, it is typically white in color.

Commercially available choices include oil and acrylic-based grounds although some artists prefer to prepare their own using a turpentine or white spirit and oil mixture.

Gesso, a traditional ground with a glue component, is suitable for hard surfaces but cracks into fine lines once dry rendering it less than ideal for canvas.

Emulsion grounds are oil-based mixtures that are both faster drying than purely oil solutions and more flexible than gesso.

Acrylic grounds are a more recent product that does not require size and, although fairly recent in their introduction, show promise as a reliable alternative to traditional solutions.

Transporting Sculptures

Other than consideration for local ordinances and regulations which may be present, there is no set methodology for transporting sculptures that will prevent damage from occurring. Such work is often best left to a professional moving company.

If professional help is not practical, adequate packing and preparation are essential. It is often necessary to disassemble large sculptures and number the pieces. When doing so, photographs and sketching a disassembly/reassembly plan can prove helpful.

Pieces should be protected by blankets and wood framing, including the use of struts and packing material within the container in which they are shipped.

For lifting, leather or canvas slings are often useful in conjunction with pulleys, levers, trolleys or, in the case of very large pieces, forklifts and cranes.

Paper Sculpting

Paper thickness is of primary consideration. Stiff drawing paper, card or cartridge paper is suitable for most work. Often artists will use wallpapers and metallic papers to produce favorable results. All of these are available in a variety of colors and are suitable for hand or spray painting.

The basic technique for working the paper involves cutting, curving, folding and bending. Free-standing work typically begins as a basic shape – pyramid, cube, cone, pleat, etc. Larger work can be supported by an inner wood frame.

Cutting is critical to good paper sculpting. The sharpest blades and knives available will produce the best effects, particularly when used in conjunction with metal rulers such as for cutting straight edges.

Folded edges are usually bonded with tape or fast drying adhesives.

Kinetics

A form of art involving time or motion or a combination of the two; water pumps, air currents, electro-mechanical and magnetic devices have all been used successfully as part of kinetic displays.

Notable displays by famous artists have included such disparate components as rotating glass discs and vibrating rods.

Hanging mobiles – paper, metal, mirror, plastic or fabric objects suspended from varying lengths of cotton, wire, string or nylon cord which are usually suspended from the ceiling using a wooden or metal strip.

Pendulum effects – a famous example is the ball-bearing model where metal balls are suspended next to one another on thin wire so that one or more of them can be pulled away and dropped against the remaining bunch to produce a kind of perpetual swing.

Other examples include electro-magnets and wire arrangements.

Casting

Casting is an ancient process in use continuously to the present day which was first developed in the Bronze Age to make tools and statuettes. The basic premise behind casting is to either copy an object using the same material as the original or to create a reproduction of an object in a different material. The latter objective is often for the purpose of improving an object's durability or appearance.

A cast is often created from materials such as clay, wax, plaster of Paris, rubber, concrete or plastics such as polyester resins. In its simplest form, the casting material is poured over the object and allowed to dry. Once dry, it is removed, usually in two pieces, to create a mold. The mold is then filled with the material chosen for the new object and allowed to cool, cure or dry. Finally, the cast is removed.

The process of casting metal from a wax positive, also known as cire perdue, is an intricate and potentially dangerous one generally only performed by a competent founder.

Modeling Material

Clay and terracotta are sensitive to fine detail and can be used in a variety of states from very firm to soft to achieve the desired result. Kitchen items such as knives, wooden spoons, rolling pins and purpose-made tools are commonly employed to work these materials. A water-sealed baseboard of thick ply makes for an ideal workspace.

Modeling wax is of the microcrystalline variety and is a synthetic product. It permits reshaping and alterations by remaining relatively pliable although as a consequence it is often preferred to be cast more permanently into a material such as bronze. Plaster modeling tools work well for wax, as do craft knives, dental instruments, nails and pencils.

Plaster is a water soluble material which hardens to shape. It is frequently built up on a wire netting or glass fiber matting. It is typically worked on a thick ply, water-proofed baseboard with tools such as old saws, cheese graters, axes and wood chisels.

Glass fiber reinforced plastics are resins worked similarly to plaster in terms of underlying form preparation although unlike plaster, the desired result is generally achieved using a layering process. Finishing is accomplished with files, rasps, and wet/dry carborundum paper or carborundum wheels on an electric drill with proper ventilation.

Storage Methods

Safety cans are special purpose containers designed to provide a rigid, spill-resistant vessel and usually provide a venting mechanism of some sort to alleviate the pressurized build-up of combustible fumes.

Flammable materials storage cabinets are specifically designed to protect the contents from outside fires.

Limit quantities on-hand to what will actually be needed in the near-term.

If a proper cabinet is not available, never store flammable materials near exits or windows.

Keep flammable materials away from direct sunlight and sources of heat.

Keep containers sealed when not in use.

Waste Disposal

Oily rags – should be placed in appropriate container such as oil rag can; the container should have a lid.

Solvents – should be considered hazardous waste; do not dump down the drain.

Paints – considered hazardous waste by the Environmental Protection Agency; do not dump down the drain; latex and water-based paint may be disposed of in regular trash.

Baby, linseed and lubricating oils – baby oil can be washed down the drain or disposed of in regular trash; linseed oil should be combined with solvents or oil-based paint for disposal; lubricating oils are recyclable and should be disposed of as such.

Ceramic glaze – glazes should be rinsed in special basins which catch the sediments prior to entering the drain.

Photographic chemicals – standard developers and rinses can be washed down the drain; fixers contain high quantities of silver and should be disposed of as hazardous waste; all other chemicals should be considered hazardous waste and disposed of accordingly.

Acids and bases – the general range for considering acids and bases as hazardous is between 2 and 12.5 on the pH scale.

Sharp implements – should be placed in a puncture proof container such as a glass jar and placed in regular trash.

Empty chemical containers – should be rinsed repeatedly and placed in regular trash.

Airbrushes, Spray Cans and Spray Guns

Due to the inherent danger involved, an artist should only spray paint when necessary. Spray mists often contain additional hazardous chemicals such as solvents. Aerosol sprays contain propellants such as propane or isobutene which are highly flammable. Airbrushing is particularly hazardous since artists are usually in close proximity to the fine mist it produces. The hazard is intensified when solvents are used in conjunction with the paint.

Water-based spraying of inks and paint is much safer than solvent based alternatives. If a spray booth or downdraft room is available, use it. If not, use of a respirator is highly recommended. At a minimum, only spray in a well-ventilated area – preferably outdoors or with windows open and air circulating by fan.

Protective Apparel

Protective apparel such as gloves, long sleeves, long pants and boots or shoes rather than sandals help prevent contact of chemicals with the skin. The garments should be dedicated for use in the studio or work area and washed frequently in a separate load from other laundry.

If skin contact does occur, flush immediately with soapy water or other suitable cleaners. Avoid the use of solvents or bleach to clean the skin as these will often absorb and enter the blood stream where they can accumulate in internal organs.

If splashes or flying debris are concerns, goggles should be worn in the work area. Ear protection is generally advised when working with noisy equipment for extended periods. Wear a properly fitted respirator or dust mask if vapors or dust are present.

Refrain from wearing jewelry when working and tie long hair back to prevent it from being caught in tools and equipment.

Do not work when fatigued and always wash hands before drinking, eating or smoking.

Sculpting Safety

A dust mask and goggles should be worn at all times when working with sculpting materials. Gloves or skin cream are advisable.

For body part casts, avoid using plaster directly on the skin. Instead, use plaster bandages.

Avoid working with stones that contain asbestos. Power tools should have portable exhaust systems and be properly grounded. When carving with hand tools, always carve away from you.

Keep solvents away from sources of heat and ignition and avoid the use of solutions which contain carbon tetrachloride, formaldehyde, methylene chloride, phosphate esters, DEHP and chlorinated synthetics.

Choose water or heptane-based adhesives.

Keep tools in good working order and replace any which have damaged handles or cutting surfaces. Take frequent breaks when using power tools.

ACMI

The Art and Creative Materials Institute (ACMI) is a non-profit association of art supply manufacturers concerned with the safe use of their products by the artistic community. The organization has 220 members and has evaluated and certified over 60,000 products in its history.

The institute provides a comprehensive toxicological analysis when appropriate and evaluates products based on based on several factors, including:

- Ingredients and their quantity
- Ingredient interaction with other ingredients and substances which may be in common use
- Potential acute and chronic harm to the human body including the potential for allergic reaction
- How a product is commonly used and misused
- Product size and packaging
- U. S. national and state labeling regulations

PPE

Personal protective equipment (PPE)refers to gloves, lab coats, safety glasses, chemical splash goggles, respirators, hard hats, safety shoes, disposable or cloth overalls and other protective gear designed to protect the wearer from various dangers. The gear must be compatible with chemical hazards, fit properly, provide proper dexterity, limit eyesight interference, and be comfortable. Artistic work is typically very precise in nature which can serve to discourage or limit the use of protective equipment. Nevertheless, there is no substitute for common sense when working with dangerous tools or chemicals. Always check the labeling of any substance you'll be using and request material product data safety sheets from the dealer whenever possible. If expense is a concern, check with other artists or organizations within your community who may be willing to loan safety equipment either for free or for a small fee.

Architecture and Art Education

The architecture of home construction is one obvious place. Although many newer areas around cities lack compelling diversity and creativity, there are almost always exceptions. This is particularly true of older areas with established traditions.

Churches are another excellent place to discover art. The relationship between religion and art is as old as most religions themselves. Christianity is certainly no exception. Modern churches frequently have collections of paintings and sculpture consistent with the beliefs of their own individual congregations.

For those fortunate enough live in Europe or in the Eastern United States, numerous older churches are accessible. Many of these are exemplary works of art in themselves.

A number of businesses, particularly large corporations, have substantial art collections in their common areas, many of which are accessible to visitors. Shopping centers, banks government buildings (particularly with respect to sculpture) are often rich resources for art seekers.

Early Civilizations

Civilizations such as Egypt, the Middle and Near East and Crete shared a commonality in their complexes of temples, tombs and palaces. Most of these structures appeared solid from the exterior although inside they sometimes contained vast open spaces of varying size.

The development of architecture was frequently dependent upon religious beliefs or practices such as those associated with "The Cult of the Dead" which heavily influenced designs in Egypt.

As might be expected, with few exceptions such as that of the Egyptians, architecture of earlier civilizations was rather simplistic by comparison to what would later be accomplished in Greece and Rome.

Still, early people left a remarkable if sporadic legacy of construction. The Assyrian "Palace of Sargon II" at Khorsabad and the monumental "Palace of Persepolis" in Persia bear convincing testament of their prowess.

The Forum

Noted for its strict adherence to space and mass, enough has been learned about the Forum to precisely reconstruct it. It consisted of a variety of structures mostly completed around the time of the Samnite ascendancy between the fourth and second centuries BC.

As a regular elongated rectangle, it measured 38 x 142 meters and was built with surrounding colonnades. The Temple of Zeus was situated precisely on axis at the northern end. Other buildings were gradually grouped around the forum.

Aside from The Temple of Zeus, the most significant building is the Basilica situated in the southwest corner of the forum. It was roofed around the first century BC creating a vast enclosed space.

The court represented a systematic concentration of stoas which were deliberately placed around the agora or marketplace.

Carolingian Period

The Carolingian period produced a lasting architectural heritage and revival throughout Europe. For the first time in many centuries, architects became concerned with matching the importance and grand style of Late Roman and Early Christian construction. This was largely the result of Charlemagne's desire to transform his growing French empire into something akin to that of the Eastern Roman Empire.

The "Gate-hall of the Monastery of Lorsch" is an example of his intended style. The application of Roman orders is evident and is an indication that the building was likely modeled on a Roman triumphal arch. It consists of three tunnel-vaulted passages framed by Corinthian half-columns. Its walls are covered by a variety of colored tiles and a row of Ionic pilasters sits above the frieze-band.

Charlemagne's Imperial Palace, Ingelheim, bears many hallmarks of classical tradition while the accompanying Palace Chapel is indicative of Early Christian Tradition.

San Giovanni Mosiac

The cupola contains a crown at the top with a chrismon or sacred monogram set in a star-filled sky. The work is divided into sections depicting various New Testament scenes as well as Evangelical symbols and figures of saints. Due to the different styles of the various sections, it's reasonable to assume that a number of artists from disparate traditions participated in the work. In one section the figures appear to be portrayed in a brightly colored, modeled fashion by workers trained in both the local and Roman traditions while in another the figures appear less defined, flatter and of a paler tone typical of contemporary Oriental art.

Although the church of San Giovanni was constructed much later, the mosaic work in the Baptistery appears to be from either the late 4th or early 5th century.

Northumbria

Most art work produced here came from a series of monasteries that include the Hiberno-Saxon of Lindisfarne, Monkwearmouth and Jarrow. Jarrow was the home of the Venerable Bede who is considered the most important historian of the Dark Ages.

The Mediterranean tradition was preserved and re-established in the illustration of manuscripts created at Lindisfarne. One example of this is the Book of Durrow from the 7th century depicting St. Matthew in a checkerboard cloak.

The origins of the important manuscript, Codex Amiatinus, were created at Monwearmouth. Accompanying illustrations employed artistic principles based upon northern barbaric, Hiberno-Saxon animal patterns and decorative forms, themselves a derivative of the 6th and 7th century metal work produced by Anglo-Saxon invaders, Irish-Celtic and Romano-Celtic people.

The Book of Kells was also produced here during the late 8th to early 9th century and is a varied synthesis of many styles first seen in earlier work here.

Gothic Style

Gothic style arose as part of an increased urbanization of northern France. Saint Louis was a prolific patron of the new style and bishops and popes became interested in raising the standard of living as well as serving the needs of more people, including laymen and clerics.

At this time, religion and daily affairs were inextricably linked through the local cathedral. The Notre Dame at Chartres was a cultural center whose cost was shared by virtually every member of the local society – nobility, royalty, and local townspeople.

Gothic cathedrals were lavishly constructed both inside and out. Rows of sculptures honoring various figures within Christendom and sculptured scenes illustrating the history and doctrine of the Christian faith were universal.

The relatively famous King and Queen of Judah column figures from the west façade of the Notre Dame Cathedral are typical of the sculptural style of the period.

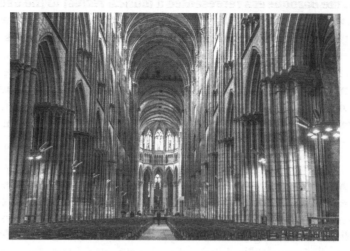

Music

Music as an artistic expression became documented during the Middle Ages. Prior to that time, music was used as an equally contributing part of worship, poetry, dance and served society by uniting a community to complete necessary labors, soothe mourners, express different emotions, and offer homage to a higher power. The older or ancient forms of musical expression set the foundation for the more disciplined arts of music since there was no musical notation for sharing these ideas until the Middle Ages. The Greeks with their love of the lyre established that musical foundation as surely as they did modern theories regarding culture and philosophy. Greek musical theory introduced intervals, or relationships between pitches, using a tightened string to show how the shortening of the string 3:2 or 4:3 could change the tone when plucked.

Polyphony

The music of the Middle Ages consisted of rhythm, melody, and words in a monophonic style. The ninth century saw the rise of music that consisted of multiple vocal parts and melodic lines, or polyphony, which moves in parallel intervals in the more hollow-sounding fourths or fifths. This style of singing is referred to as organum, which started the musical change still in existence today. The number of moving parts has increased, and the corresponding lines of music have increased in complexity and experimentation. The original melody of polyphony was selected from a chant and was extended and added to. Languages were combined for the multiple parts, so that French would be the first line and Latin the second. Pérotin with his Sederunt Principes in four parts pushed the musical society forward into fully notated music that combined consonance and dissonance.

Renaissance Dance Music

As music was shared aurally with little to no training involved, groups would gather together to enjoy the faster paced music used to inspire dances and merriment. This instrumental dance music was prolific in the Renaissance, and was composed and frequently improvised by different peoples of many diverse backgrounds. Much of the dance music of the Renaissance is attributed to certain collectors of those folk pieces, such as the dance music of Tielman Susato and the Terpsichore of Michael Praetorius. The work La Spagna is often attributed to Josquin Desprez and typifies the rhythm and sound of the Renaissance dance. The music was modified and improved upon by later composers, and much of the sprightly rhythms was rejuvenated in the Baroque style.

Baroque Period

Beginning about 1600, the Baroque era represented a musical retreat to the dependence on words for the meaning of the work and the idea that music should be used to illustrate the words. Opera, born in the Baroque era and based on a dependence on the text, was created as a model of Ancient Greek drama. The styles were classified as new music, or nuove musiche. The idea for a succinct and expressive kind of sound as a single melody with a harmonic accompaniment became the standard for Baroque music, and was first used by the Florentine Camerata. This new texture is referred to as homophony and is an offshoot and compliment to polyphony. With the combination of melody and harmony, the Baroque era serves as the beginning of the musical evolution.

Antonio Vivaldi

His best-known work which was rediscovered in the twentieth century and used most often as background music, The Four Seasons is a work made up of four programmatic concertos that follow the text of four separate sonnets. The music allows the sounds of the seasons to be heard, so the audience can hear birds, breezes, dogs, and other typical outdoor sounds. Vivaldi's genius in the Seasons is evident in how he creates the details of each season without allowing the piece to fall apart.

Vivaldi's 1712 L'Estro Armonico, or "the Harmonic Whip," opens with a concerto grosso that includes a concertino or solo group of violins and cello playing the first and last sections vigorously before the tutti ends the sections. The second section showcases the violin in a siciliano or lilting slow dance. The harpsichord plays throughout the D minor concerto and improvises the basso continuo.

Fugue

A fugue requires between 2 and 6 voices' the first voice is presented as a solo with a basso continuo and then answered or imitated by a second voice. The answering voice could be modified or exact per the composer's intentions with the piece. The third voice enters with the tonic, and the fourth voice enters with the dominant. This continues until all voices are represented. Each voice continues with a countersubject or free counterpoint and moves to a cadence. The exposition is followed by an episode or motivic subject suggested by the counterpoint, which contrasts the original subject and is achieved by harmonic sequencing. After significant contrast, the fugue subject reappears in the tonic or related key. The final section is an incomplete or complete exposition in the tonic with a pedal point in the bass.

Canon

As an imitation of an entire subject by different voices at fixed intervals of time or pitch, the canon allows the leading voice or dux to precede the following success voices or comes in every detail in a strict canon, while a free canon allows the comes to modify the dux with minor changes and accidentals. Canons can be independent pieces or parts of a larger work, as well as combined with independent lines or other canons. Canons can be classified on the time between each part's entry (e.g., canon ad minimam or at the half note, canon ad semibrevem or at the whole note) and on the interval between each entry (e.g., canon ad unisonum or at the unison, canon ad epidiapente or at the fifth above). Examples include Bach's Goldberg Variations and Canonic Variations on Vom Himmel hoch.

Franz Joseph Haydn

Regarded as the Father of the Symphony and the String Quartet, Franz Joseph Haydn did not create either style but earned such titles through his fatherly demeanor. As a young singer and violinist, Haydn attracted attention and was employed as a choirboy where he practiced voice, violin, and harpsichord. He continued to work as a tutor and composer and was commissioned to write a comic opera as well as other small pieces for string quartets and divertimenti, or background music for wealthy people of the time. Haydn knew how to perform as a servant, so that he could attract wealthy patrons and commissions, and he was eventually named music director for Count Morzin and composed over 100 symphonies in 30 years. Later he was employed by Hungarian Prince Anton Esterházy, where he composed magnificent pieces quickly and directed the opera house for the prince.

Symphony

As a work for an orchestra with multiple movements or multiple parts in one movement, the symphony contained three movements of fast-slow-fast and was named for the Italian opera Sinfonia. Performed with strings and winds, these musical pieces were enjoyed at private gatherings in palaces, monasteries, and residences, as well as civic functions and public concerts. The foundation for the symphony genre comes from Sammartini whose works used the three-part movement with both strings and winds. As the Classical Period developed, the symphonic format increased to four parts or movements with an even greater transition in the third movement. After being expertly worked by Haydn, the symphony became a more celebrated style of music that allowed for great freedom in composition and features.

Baroque Style vs. Classical Style

While the stylistic choices for music differ between Baroque and Classical, the integrity and depth of composition evident in both. Music requires a certain kind of simplicity for comprehension, and the simpler styles of the Classical Period did not take away that complexity. While Bach may create incredible musical feats on his polyphonic style, he incorporated a lucid design in his work. The surface sounds of works by Haydn and Mozart may appear simple but are in actuality incredibly organized and conceived, using a great amount of material and genius in that simplicity. The Baroque composers sought to express magnificence and grandeur in their music, while the Classical composers adopted an unpretentious format of hiding deep feelings. Baroque gave us the motet and opera, but from the Classical Period came the symphony, string quartet, and sonata.

Motet

As a major musical style between the thirteenth and eighteenth centuries, the motet has three major classifications. From 1200 to 1450, the motet referred to a tenor serving as the foundation for upper voices and a combination of those voices with the text. From 1450 to 1600, the motet referred to a genre of polyphony that set Latin texts to music. After 1600, the motet referred to a type of sacred music associated with church polyphony. The Renaissance motet focused on Biblical passages and was used as ornamentation for the liturgy. After 1600, the motet came to symbolize a sacred vocal work designed for liturgy or devotion. The Catholic and Protestant churches used the motet differently, and the style developed separately around the countries of Europe.

Mozart

With noted success in Idomeneo in Munich, Mozart married and moved to Vienna to be with other professional musicians and work at finding a rich aristocrat to pay for his room and board. He was able to make money as a freelancing soloist and his opera buffa, or comic opera, work. As the trend in Vienna went toward Turkish trappings, Mozart wrote The Abduction from the Seraglio, a piece that combined regular speech sections with arias in a form called Singspiel, which is similar to American musicals. The music, and his own performance in it, granted him great popularity and a hefty fee. However, his fortunes were at the mercy of the changing tastes in Vienna and other composers' competitiveness.

Ludwig van Beethoven

With a tyrant as a father, Ludwig van Beethoven was forcibly introduced into the world of music, so that he could achieve the notoriety of Mozart. Beethoven was instructed by Needed to play Bach fugues and preludes to learn the discipline and stamina of the period and to develop. Known for his improvisation, Beethoven was often hired to teach noblemen's children and became appreciated by the more sophisticated crowds. He studied music with Haydn, Italian vocal composition with Saltier, and counterpoint with Albrechtsberger. All the teachers saw the genius but the incomparable stubbornness and ego in the pupil. While his early pieces such as Symphony No. 1 were conservative, his middle works such as the Pathétique Sonata showed his developing fire. His later pieces showcased the more Classical sense of order.

Five piano and 1 violin concertos show his progression from the epitome of Classical music to the emotional whirlwind of the upcoming Romantic period. Sixteen string quartets were written during the course of his composing years as he progressed spiritually and emotionally through his music. His Symphony No.5 was refreshingly original at the time, and was seen as Beethoven's own realization of fate and a possible indication of madness. It has been redone and exaggerated since its premier so that it has lost some of its glamour with the dot-dot-dot-dash motive. The Sixth Symphony, or Pastoral, is a program piece along the lines of typical Romantic music as it suggests open countryside, evincing Beethoven's enjoyment of the outdoors.

Carl Maria von Weber

Opera was an Italian art until Carl Maria von Weber established it as a musical force in Germany by using aspects of his native country and heritage to establish the legitimacy of his work and the place for opera in Germany. Von Weber served as the unofficial first nationalist composer. He incorporated spoken dialogue in place of the recitative and drew heavily on the myths and legends of his home while emphasizing nature. Von Weber allowed the instruments to play important roles in developing the story in conjunction with voices, and his overtures, as shown in Der Freischütz, Oberon, and Euryanthe, represented a dramatic rendering of the story detailed in the opera. Von Weber inspired Richard Wagner, who changed the face of opera.

Handel

The London audiences enjoyed the more spectacular showcases of the Italian opera, but Handel was forced to conform his music to the specific rules and tastes of the time. The audience was not so interested in complex plot lines as in phenomenal singing and interesting set designs. The arias were formal and emotionally static, revealing only one aspect of the character, and written in da capo, or "from the beginning," style in an ABA standard outline. These pieces were often absurd though they did draw attendees' attentions. Audience members were also loyal to specific performers and could engage in fights with little provocation. His operatic works such as Julius Ceasar and Handel's Largo from Serse are some of his finest examples in this genre.

Handel saw the Royal Academy of Music fold financially, but he was able to attract more attention with his three oratorios, or extended musical dramas with religious themes, Esther, Deborah, and

Atalia. He went on to write 4 more magnificent oratorios: Saul, Israel in Egypt, Ode to Saint Cecilia, and L'Allegro, il Pensieroso ed il Moderato. These English oratorios helped reestablish Handel as a composer. The stories used in his works were usually well-known, and his command of the English language improved. While the stories reflected biblical themes, the presentation was never overly pious as they are productions for a concert hall with all the drama and color of an opera. Choruses rather than arias were his main focus in the style, and this choral style became a model for later composers.

Bach

Bach's work was kept on hand by his sons and other music teachers, including Beethoven's teacher who insisted on using Well-Tempered Clavier. It was Bach's mastery of counterpoint that greatly affected Mozart, and Haydn was also influenced by Bach's B minor Mass. Bach contributed to all genres of music in his day except for opera . He also exemplified his period's ability to fully convey a certain feeling in his music. Bach left music with such works as his 6 Brandenburg Concertos of 1721, his "Air on a G String," the 48 preludes and fugues of the Well-Tempered Clavier, the Toccata and Fugue in D Minor, the St. Matthew Passion, the B minor Mass, and others, giving audiences everywhere a taste of his genius and his incomparable technique.

Bach and Handel

Bach was well-known for his sacred music, and for his predictable and exciting fugues and canons. His church music was grand and often parochial. Handel began his enterprise with opera and then transitioned into oratorio with simpler melodies and more concise configurations of structure while minimizing counterpoint and asserting homophonic textures. Bach played to the church and upper crowds while Handel attracted the middle-class audience members who preferred a less traditional sound. Bach laid the groundwork for musical expression, and Handel filled the concert halls with average people just wanting to be entertained. Both appreciated the performance styles and regulations of the harpsichord, and both excelled at manipulating the audience while putting on an incredible show.

Sonata in E major K. 380

The main theme of the E major is played by itself at the beginning and then repeated in different registers. The theme is redone in an almost jazz-like way as the motive is repeated continuously in the right hand while the chords are played in an almost erratic progression in the left hand. The contrast part from the original theme occurs in a different key, and is then followed by an esoteric horn call. This call develops to the end of the section, and the whole first section is repeated. The second section starts with the horn call and transitions back to the original key of the first section. An invigorating music sweep carries the piece to its final cadence.

Johannes Brahms

Studying music while playing piano at bars and brothels to make money, Johannes Brahms created arrangements of lighter music that learned away from the Romantic Period. His success in sonatas, piano trios, and other works showed him that the utilization of the Classical form was a better way to proceed with his music career. His use of the tonality of the Classical Period allowed him to create music that celebrated the time of the Romantics. His music is often stirring, such as in the Four Serious Songs and the German Requiem. His Symphony No. 1 in C minor, Op. 68 is often referred to as Beethoven's Tenth, since the melodies are so similar to Beethoven's work.

Claude Debussy

Claude Debussy entered the Paris Conservatory at 11 and studied there for a decade, winning prizes and astounding his teachers with his beliefs on harmony. He joined the Symbolists in Montmarte and was encouraged to appeal to the senses with his art while learning about the art of the French Impressionists with the play of light on surfaces. Debussy focused on vocal and piano pieces, although he did compose the orchestral tone poem Prelude to the Afternoon of a Faun. His music increased in popularity in 1902 with his only opera Pelléas et Mélisande and later with his symphony-like work La Mer. Debussy's greatest writing involved his 2 books of preludes for the piano.

Jazz

Influencing different types of music, jazz started as an African-American creation of principally instrumental music combined with elements of the church, storytelling, vocal inflections, and the call-and-response technique. Jazz combined the strong tonality, instrumentation, and rhythms of the American marching band music, ragtime, piano music of Debussy, American popular music, and Latin-American dance music. As technology played a bigger part in music creation, jazz also incorporated the electronic innovations of rock and soul. New Orleans was the birthplace of jazz, where all the cultural icons converged between 1890 and 1910. Jazz offered many opportunities for improvisation and development, and the different wind, brass, and percussion instruments allowed for different combinations and rhythms. Jazz gave rise to swing in the 1930s and 1940s.

Aaron Copland

After gaining technical background and understanding of the orchestra from his teacher Nadia Boulanger, Aaron Copland worked as a composer, performer, and new-music advocate, writing music that was heavily influenced by jazz. Years later, Copland turned to avant-garde music as shown by his Piano Variations of 1930 and his 1939 book What to Listen for in Music. Focusing on making his sound more mainstream and American, he composed El Salón México in 1936 with great success. In the 1930s and 1940s, Copland composed several ballets based on folk style such as Billy the Kid, Rodeo, and Appalachian Spring, which would be his most successful. His dissonance involved familiar chordal progressions, so they were deemed acceptable rather than avant-garde. His "Fanfare for the Common Man" in 1942 was part of his Third Symphony, and "Lincoln Portrait" accompanied texts from Lincoln's writings. Copland music helped form the accepted Americana style.

Duke Ellington

Edward Kennedy "Duke" Ellington worked to improve the perceptions of jazz as a lesser art form, so that more people could appreciate the musical genius and glory of exploration with jazz music. After organizing a 10-piece group in 1923, Ellington headed the ensemble for the next 50 years. His body of work completed with that small group was astounding in its complexity, quality, and originality. He and his group helped form jazz into what audience members hear today. Ellington created musical forms, melodies, harmonies, textures, and colors in a different way than any other jazz musician and composer had up to that point. He combined folk music with jazz without comprising the quality of the musicality, as in his "East St. Louis Toodle-oo" and the "Black and Tan Fantasy." His popular songs include "Don't Get Around Much Anymore" and "It Don't Mean a Thing if it Ain't Got that Swing."

Rock 'n' Roll

Popular music of the 1950s, Rock 'n' Roll was founded on the tenets of African-American music and rhythm. Rock pieces by such artists as Bill Haley and the Comets, Elvis Presley, Jerry Lee Lewis, Chuck Berry, Little Richard, and Fats Domino were disseminated worldwide with great success. The appeal of rock transcended racial and cultural lines and attracted lovers of the music of Tin Pan Alley, country and western, and black popular music. As a form of rhythmic blues, rock pieces are written in some variation of the 12-bar blues form with instrumentation of electric guitars, saxophones, and a rhythm section of piano, drums, and bass. With a fast-paced tempo, rock music lyrics are usually about sex while the dynamic level is high with rough and raucous musical stylings. The genre originally was splintered to include rhythm and blues while the writing and arranging followed the same pattern.

Minor, Diminished, and Augmented

Intervals

A major interval reduced by a half step creates a minor interval. A chromatic half step or semitone refers to the same note but with different accidentals, such as the C and C#. The diatonic half step refers to the half step between 2 different notes, such as C# to D. These notes may appear to be written identically on the staff but represent two different intervals based on the relationship of each note to the other. Augmented, or increased in size, and diminished, or reduced in size, major and perfect intervals rely on the half step to change the quality of the interval. Augmentation refers to the raising of the upper note or lowering of the bottom note by a half step in major and perfect intervals, such as with the C major 6th of C A being augmented to C A#.

Interval Abbreviations

Indicating intervals on staff paper can become a space issue so that abbreviations are often used to facilitate better reading of the composition. Perfect and major intervals are shown by the number, such as 5 for P5 or perfect fifth or 7 for M7 or major seventh. The word "sharp" or the "#" demonstrates augmentation, as well as "aug." The word "flat" or "b" demonstrates diminution, as well as "min" or "m." The diminution of a major interval can be written with 2 flats or texts, such as "bb" or dim7 or d7. The use of symbols or no descriptive text can indicate the presence of augmentation or diminution, but musicians should still be familiar with the shorthand to understand that b3 is minor while b5 is diminished.

Consonant Intervals

There are three types of consonant intervals: perfect consonance (e.g., Perfect Octave or P8, Perfect Fifth or P5), imperfect consonance (e.g., Major Third or M3, Minor Third or m3, Major Sixth or M6, Minor Sixth or m6), and variable consonance (e.g., Perfect Fourth or P4). All other intervals are classified as dissonant. Since context determines the classification of intervals, enharmonic equivalents should not be given the same classification as their counterparts. For example, a minor third is consonant, but an augmented second is dissonant. The perfect fourth interval can be consonant or dissonant depending on the context, since fourths at the roof of a key center are dissonant, while fourths are consonant when in any other part of the chord.

Triad Inversions

The major triad is referred to as the common chord, while the tonic, fourth, and fifth triads are referred to as primary triads. Triads can also be inverted, so that the root note is played at the top or at the middle of the chord. The lowest note of the inverted triad is referred to as the bass. Though the root is the foundation for the triad, it is accepted that the bass as the bottom of the inverted triad cannot be the root. The sonority of the chord changes when the bass changes. For example, the C Major triad of C E G can be inverted to E G C and then again to G C E. The same rules of construction apply for minor, augmented, diminished, and suspended.

Upper Structure

Upper structures usually refer to triads played in the upper register . They have a different root than the triads played in the lower register where the upper structure is often a major or minor triad. This extended chord is referred to as the polychord and is very common over the dominant seventh chords. Polychords can, however, compliment other chordal structures. With the top 3 notes as B E G# in the E major triad, the G# acts as the diminished ninth and E is the thirteenth of the G7 chord. The specific notes maintain their own harmonic function within the G7 but are heard as 1 sound, which is really 2 keys at the same time. This combined sound of E and G major is polytonality. This format is often shown as one key over another, such as E7.

Minor Chords

The natural minor contains half steps between the scale degrees 2 and 3 and between 5 and 6. The notes of the natural minor scale, in essence, begin on the sixth degree so that the C minor scale is played as the E b major scale but starting on C.

The harmonic minor contains half steps between scale degrees 2 and 3, 5 and 6, and 7 and 8. The augmented second, or whole step plus half step, occurring between the 6 and 7 degrees gives this minor its characteristic sound.

The melodic minor is either ascending or descending with no augmented second between 6 and 7. The ascending melodic minor is a natural minor with augmented 6 and 7 with half steps between 2 and 3 and between 7 and 8. The descending melodic minor refers to the natural minor scale.

The 7 Modes

Chord I, or first chord, is the major chord and is referred to as Ionian. Chord ii, or second chord, is minor and is referred to as Dorian. Chord iii, or third chord, is minor and is referred to as Phyrgian. Chord IV, or fourth chord, is major and is referred to as Lydian. Chord V, or fifth chord, is dominant and is referred to as Mixolydian. Chord vi, or sixth chord, is minor and is referred to as Aeolian. The Aeolian chord is the natural minor. Chord vii, or seventh chord, is minor diminished fifth and is referred to as Locrian. The modal system is based on the Greek study of sounds.

Pentatonic Scales

Similar in origin to the modes, pentatonic scales are constructed from the Greek penta- for five and consist of five specific notes. Though any five notes could be referred to loosely as a pentatonic scale, there are accepted versions or scales. The pentatonic scale, a musical line with no half steps, is used in different styles of folk music, since it occurs worldwide. Pentatonic scales have been featured in works by Ravel and Debussy as well as in other Western music. The types of pentatonic scales are major and minor. A C major pentatonic scale is spelled C D E G A and includes scale degrees 1 2 3 5 6. The corresponding C minor pentatonic scale is spelled C E b F G B b and includes scale degrees 1 b3 4 5 b7.

Harmonic Analysis

The study of music through harmonic analysis provides an understanding of the harmonic and melodic structure of a work. Chord progressions can be composed to sound logical and smooth if the composer has studied and is knowledgeable about the harmonic principles that determine chord motion. This familiarity with musical composition enables composers, as well as improvising performers, to reharmonize existing melodies to provide for increases in tension and an individual interpretation of a piece. This reharmonization, or chord substitution, is widely used in jazz and can be employed to keep the performer's personality in the chordal progression. Roman numerals are used to show how different chords function in the key centers, and other markings are employed to direct the musician.

Dominant Functions and Structural Divisions

Dominant functions can cross structural divisions; the descending fifth still occurs to resolve the chord. Structural divisions do, however, upset the ii-V7 motion since the motion cannot maintain its characteristics as it crosses the structural division. The Am7, for example, would sound like an extension of the Fmaj7, since it acts as the diatonic chord with the tonic function. In this case, the subsequent D7 would not be bracketed to the Am7 chord in the chordal progression Fmaj7 Am7 D7 Gm7. A full arrow would connect the D7 to the Gm7 in its interpretation.

The minor seventh chord should occur on the strong beat of the harmonic motion to qualify as a ii-V7 progression. The ii chords would usually occur on odd-numbered measures, while the V7s would occur on even-numbered measures. Any minor seventh chords on the second half of the measure are usually not part of the ii-V7 sequence.

Tempo

The tempo or speed of the piece of music can be designated by specific tempo marks as well as certain Italian words that describe the speed and also the character of the piece. The words used include grave for very slow and serious, largo for broad, lento for slow, adagio for slow and with ease, andante for steadily moving, moderato for moderate, allegretto for fast, allegro for fast and cheerful, vivace for lively, presto for very fast, and prestissimo for as fast as possible. Other relative changes in tempo can be described with the words ritardando, or rit., for slowing, as well as accelerando for quickening and più mosso for faster. The tempo marking are a guide for the performance and can be interpreted differently by different conductors.

Written Music Structure

The clef shows the location of a pitch, and the lines and spaces of the staff combine with the clef to show the diatonic scale. Ledger lines provide the pitches that are located either just above or just below the particular staff. The scale is laid out in the white keys of the piano, so that the seven letters of the alphabet repeat from octave to octave. The pitches that follow the black keys of the piano are named according to their relationship to the surrounding white keys and the type of scale with its corresponding accidentals. The lines of the staff specify the name of the note, such as A or D, and any pitch is shown on the staff with a # or b placed by the note on the particular line.

Rhythm Classifications

As rhythm can refer to many different focuses in musical analysis, rhythm can be described in many different ways as it relates to pitch and the texture of the work. Different analyses can focus on the durational rhythm, accentual rhythm, timbral rhythm, textural rhythm, melodic rhythm, and harmonic rhythm as each relates to the discussion. The four dimensions of rhythm should be determined independently of each other. The musical work should have definite duration, pulse, rhythm, and meter, all of which could be present in any combination. Accentual rhythm is the most prominent in Western music, and the even spacing of pulses arranged in regularly occurring stress patterns can be regarded as basic rhythmic material.

Arpeggio

Usually played as a chord, the arpeggio sound out the 1, 3, and 5 degrees of the scale and played in ascending or descending order. Occasionally, the arpeggio played initially as a full chord and then the notes spelled out individually from lowest to highest pitch. Full arpeggio chords written with wavy lines running alongside both staves indicate that the performer should play each note individually in succession as the arpeggio and not as one full chord. This shorthand allows composers to condense the writing, especially since the arpeggio would be played within a particular time but without taking up a lot of room. Diagonal strokes on the shaft of the note also indicate the arpeggio to be played from extreme to extreme, and the curved line between two notes combined with the diagonal stroke is another kind of shorthand for composers.

Brass Instruments

The particular bore of the medium-length instruments also determines the kind of sound. Trumpets and trombones are narrow, while the flugelhorns and euphoniums are wide. The sound produced by the brass instrument family is forceful, ranging in texture from bright and piercing sounds in the smaller instruments to dark and mellow sounds in the larger instruments. The brass instrument family can produce more notes when fitted with valves or a slide, which extends the tubes to create additional series of tones and subsequent fundaments on several groups of half steps lower than the previous group. The bugle, used primarily in the military, is not fitted with valves or tubes, but is played entirely by the performer's ability to compress the lips and create forceful sounds at a designated pitch.

Stringed Instruments

Stringed instruments have a stretched cord attached to a resonant chamber and held with tension. The cord can be plucked, bowed, or struck to create resonance in the chamber, and can be manipulated to produce a specific kind of sound based on the pressure of the fingers against the cord at different locations along the neck of the instrument. The strings can be made of lamb gut, silk, wire, horsehair, nylon, and other synthetic materials. As the creation of strings became more commercial, the range of the stringed instruments and the subsequent performance of the family improved. The clarity of sound and brightness are influenced by the tightness of the twisting of the strings. The number of strings used on the various instruments also allows a greater range of sound and color.

Keyboard Instruments

Keyboard instruments include any instrument with an entire set of levers that will actuate the tone-producing component of the instrument, such as the piano, organ, harpsichord, clavichord, and other comparable instruments. Each instrument has seven natural tones and five chromatic tones arranged in chromatic order and repeating along the width of the instrument. The C major scale consists of all natural tones or white keys, and the accidentals used in other scales are often shown as the black keys or raised notes. There is no black key between the E and F and between the B and C as these notes are natural semitones similar to the relationship between C and C#/Db.

Other Instruments

A *slapstick* is made of 2 flat and narrow pieces of wood about 30 cm long that are hinged together, so that they can be slapped for a whip-cracking sound. *Maracas* are round or oval Latin American rattles filled with seeds or small particles that are shaken by the handle and played in pairs. A *güiro* is a Latin American scraper made from a hollowed-out gourd with repeating ridges that are rubbed across with a stick. *Claves* are a pair of Cuban clappers about 20 cm long, and are played by one hand holding one bar and acting as the resonator when the second bar is clapped against it. *Castanets* are 2 shell-shaped structures that are clapped together. *Timbales* are tuned single-headed drums played with sticks. *Bongos* are 2 small single-headed drums of differing sizes that are played with the hands. *Congas* are tall single-headed drums played with the hands.

Vocal Registers

There are six accepted designations of vocal registers with three for men and three for women. The malevocal registers include the bass, baritone, and tenor, and the female vocal registers include contralto or alto, mezzo soprano, and soprano. Most untrained voices can be classified as baritone or mezzo soprano, since some training is needed to accurately hit the range for the tenor or soprano parts. Basses can sing in the range of D2 to C4 or Middle C. Baritones can sing between G2 and F4 with Tenors at B2 to G4. Contraltos sing between D3 and D5 with mezzo sopranos singing between A3 and F5 and sopranos between C4 and C6 or High C.

Register Breaks

Different types of singers are best defined by their ability to maintain vocal quality before completing a register break. The coloratura soprano traditionally has light registration with high tessitura and vocal agility, and the comparable tenor is referred to as tenore robusto. Young tenors and sopranos employ the light registration and are often referred to as lyric voices. When a heavier registration is employed by singers to create a more powerful sound, the lyric quality is said to push the voice more fully. This type of tenor is referred to as tenore di forza. Basses and altos sing mostly in chest voice, though basses may employ falsetto for comic relief. The basso profondo enjoys a rich, low tessitura, while the basso cantante has a higher tessitura, lighter register, and more vocal flexibility.

Solfège

Used as a textless vocal exercise for technique, solfège originated with seventeenth century Italians and was later used by the French. Scales, intervals, and melodic exercises were completed in solfège since this style was preferred in the instruction of basic aural and tonal skills of vocalists. The adaptation for solfège for the musical instruction of children was developed by Zoltán Kodály. The revised Guidonian syllables of do, re, mi, fa, sol, la, and ti are associated with notes in fixed and movable formats. In the fixed do format, the syllables each correspond to the note of the scale in which do equals C, re equals D, and so on. The fixed do format does not regard accidentals. Movable do format corresponds the syllable with the note in the scale so that do equals D, re equals E, and mi equals F#.

Sight-Reading

Performing a musical piece when seeing it for the first time is sight-reading or sight-singing depending on the instruments involved. A musician can only sing or play the note correctly at first viewing of the piece if he or she is familiar with how the note should sound when it is sung or played. The ability to accurately sight-read or sight-sing is improved with practice and familiarity with the notes and their corresponding sounds. Ear-training allows the musician to have some kind of recognition of how notes will sound and to be able to reproduce those notes more accurately. Solfège and solmization are effective techniques to help musicians improve their sight-reading abilities. An understanding of the notation used in the music and other cues usually given by the conductor allows musicians to feel more comfortable and confident in their sight-singing abilities.

Computers in Music Production

The use of computers in sound and music production is most significant in the ability to synthesize sound waves. The sound waves, which are stored as numbers, are converted into voltages that are connected to loudspeakers which transmit the sound that is heard. Direct digital synthesis is the most intriguing aspect of computerized music, since the composer can modify, record, and rearrange sounds easier than an ensemble could be redirected with the music rearranged. Because of the time required to translate the musical ideas and patterns into a language that is understandable and replicable to the computer, most composers do not utilize the computer programming option for music creation and production.

Conductor

As the music began to focus more on dynamics and timbre, the conductor became more important in the overall production. As orchestras grew in size, there was a need for some direction when several of the sections were playing similarly written patterns, playing against each other, or engaged in back-and-forth musical statements and responses. Composers were the conductors in the Classical and Romantic periods since they usually were able to lead the smaller ensembles from the harpsichord which was loud enough that the other members could verify the tempo and meter. When visiting composers began to refer to the keyboardist's score to conduct a particular piece, the ensemble recognized the need for a central conductor to direct the performance.

Score Notation

The first page of the score may list the required instruments and appropriate voicing, such as first, second, and third horn. The larger groups of instruments such as woodwinds or brass may have the section of staves linked together by a bracket at the beginning of the system. Within these sections, any instruments encompassing four parts or requiring the use of two staves, such as the organ or harp, would also have these staves connected by curved braces. Choir music can be available in part format or partbooks instead of the entire score format since the score format was preferred for the keyboard. Score format is not beneficial for individual performers but would greatly assist in the musical study of the interrelationships of instruments, musical families, and keyboard performance.

Complex Sounds

Any complex pattern or tone can be displayed as a total number of pure tones at different frequencies and different amplitudes or strengths. These components that create the complex sounds are called partials and have corresponding partial frequencies. A decaying or continuously sounding musical tone shows the changes in frequencies and amplitudes and has partial frequencies that equal an integer times the single frequency. This mathematical equation is called the fundamental. Partial fundaments can be 440, 880, 1320, and so on and register as 1f, 2f, 3f etc. where f 1(frequency) is 440 cps; the frequency of the nth partial corresponds to n times the frequency of the fundamental. A harmonic set of partial frequencies characterizes the musical tones continuously produced.

Sound Envelope

More than timbre or tonal quality, the number of frequencies and amplitudes of the partials is an important consideration of the sound. The number of partials that make up the tone is an important facet of the timbre. The basic sound associated with certain instruments results from the related intensities of the partials. The ear and brain perceive the specific frequencies and amplitudes to identify the sound of the instrument, and the association with the start and end of the particular phrasing also defines an instrument and its characteristic sound. As a tone begins and completes a steady creation of sound, it forms the attack; as a tone dies away or ends, it forms the decay. The sounds of the attack and decay together create the sound envelope.

Orchestra Seating

The standard orchestra with strings includes four first violins, four second violins, four violas, four cellos, and three basses in addition to the non-stringed instruments. Stringed instruments produce sound that radiates, therefore the lower voices should be behind the higher voices. The first tier should include first violins, violas, first cellos; second tier second violins, first and second flute, first and second oboe, first and second clarinet, second cellos; third tier up to three trumpets, up to two trombones, four French horns, possibly a tuba, and basses. The tympani should be at the right back with the percussion at the left back and any harp or keyboard instrument in the center back. Orchestras with stringed instruments generally do not require full instrumentation for non-stringed instruments, since the other instruments could very well overpower the strings.

Music Sequencing

Random musical sequences are not as easily remembered as tonal melodic and harmonic sequences, and nondiatonic components in sequences are often confused with the diatonic components. Tonal functions with an established foundation define the relationship between tones and chords, and the ear is more adverse to processing modulations and transpositions to distant keys than to related keys. Music sequencing is similar to linguistic structuring as it relates to the audience member: patterns of melody, harmony, and rhythm work together better with appropriately defined tone, key, and chord structures. Infants are able to approximate a tone and distinguish between transposed phrasings, and young children can reproduce short or limited contours with some discrepancy in pitch. Early childhood musical education provides opportunities for children to learn to produce pitches accurately and distinguish between scale and key structure.

Rhythmic Stresses

Western music shows the recurrent accent on the first beat of the phrase by being louder than succeeding beats, softer than succeeding beats, or fuller than succeeding beats. The cadence in a traditional sequence of intervallic harmonies strongly shows how metric accent can be defined by the texture and progression of pitches or chords. This progresses from the consonant preparation to the dissonant suspension before moving to a consonant resolution. When the harmonic interval of the consonant resolution can transcend to a perfect consonance, the cadential closure is possible. This succession as defined by preparation, suspension, resolution, and cadence can be simplified to weak-strong-weak accents. The change of harmony provides the unaccented pulse of harmonic rhythm. The tonic harmony moves toward a strong accented harmony of a predominant class before going to a weak accented harmony and ends with the strong accented tonic or tonic substitute.

Trumpet

The trumpet is a soprano brass instrument with 4 1/2 feet in tube length folded twice over. The mouthpiece extends at one end while the expanded bell extends at the other. At the center is the 3-valve structure with the extra tubing for increases in range. The bore is mostly cylindrical and expands just before the bell. Trumpets are available in different sizes based on the corresponding pitch of the fundamental. While the Bb is the most common trumpet for school and community performances, the trumpet also comes in C, D, Eb, F and piccolo Bb or A with the C trumpet as more favored in professional performances. Piccolo trumpets, or Bach trumpets, are smaller with less tubing and have 4 valves. American trumpets usually have Périnet piston valves for the right hand, and some are equipped with rotary valves.

Flugelhorn and Bugle

The flugelhorn was originally a hunting horn in eighteenth-century Germany but progressed to a valved horn similar to the bugle. The transition of the flugelhorn to becoming a valved instrument led to the proliferation of other valved brass instruments that are commonly used in brass bands. Soprano flugelhorns have comparable ranges as the cornet and are used in jazz and popular music.

The bugle is a soprano brass instrument with a very large bore. Originally used as a signaling instrument, the bugle was later given valves and keys for amore complete chromatic performance and became the solo instrument for early brass bands. The instrument used in the military is without valves and is pitched from Bb to F similar to the modern trumpet and plays pitches 2 through 6 of the harmonic series.

Recorder

A duct flute with a fipple mouthpiece, the recorder has 2 principal types: Renaissance and Baroque. The Renaissance recorder is made of a single section with 9 holes and a thumb hole in back. The recorder has a conical bore that is usually larger at the top while the exterior is smooth and wider at top and bottom. The Baroque recorder is more ornate and usually consists of 3 sections without a ninth hole. Modern recorders are pitched in C despite the individual tones of each instrument. The sopranino, soprano, alto, tenor, bass, great bass, and contrabass recorders have a range of 2 octaves and a whole step which can be increased with more accomplished musicians. The lowest recorders have curved mouth pipes similar to the bassoon, while the highest records are written an octave below where they play.

Oboe

A double-reed woodwind instrument with a conical bore, the oboe has a flared bell while other members of the oboe family such as the English horn and baritone or bass oboe have a hollow, bulb-shaped bell. Oboes are usually made of grenadilla or African blackwood. Cross keys for the G# and F were added in the early nineteenth century though the development of the oboe progressed at a much slower pace than the flute due to its lack of popularity. Additional keys for the C, B, Bb, and a cross key for the upper C were added later. The 13-key instrument perfected in 1825 is the same Viennese oboe still used today. The term oboe is often used generically to refer to a double-reeded instrument.

Double Bass

As the lowest pitched stringed instrument, the double bass is a hybrid of the viol and violin families and is also referred to as bass viol, contrabass, string bass, and bass. Its 4 strings are tuned to E, A,

D, and G an octave lower than the cello while some music calls for a fifth string tuned to C. The orchestral instrument has levers to allow the double bass to reach the C without an additional string. The double bass is tuned in fourths rather than fifths and can use either the French bow where the palm is held downward or the German bow where the palm is held upward. Many double bass solo pieces have been composed since the eighteenth century, though the instrument was popular in chamber music written by Mozart, Beethoven, and Schubert. The double bass played pizzicato has been greatly used in jazz performances.

Organ

The organ is made up of a keyboard attached to 1 or more sets of pipes. The sets of pipes or stops combine with the action of the organ to allow the musician to combine the sounds produced by the different sets of pipes during the performance. The organ's pipe work is properly voiced and scaled with wind supply and wind chests for projection, and the organ includes the keys, stop actions, and case. The pipes are made of metal or wood and are either classified as flue or reed depending on the type of sound created. Flue pipes can be divided into stopped flute, chimney flute, gemshorn, and principal. Reed pipes can be divided into 2 types of trumpet pipes.

Tonic Sol-fa

Tonic Sol-fa is a nineteenth century English type of sight-singing method and musical notation similar to the German Tonika-Do system and the Hungary Kodály system. Developed by Rev. John Curwen in 1841, tonic sol-fa was intended to help beginning vocalists sing more accurately. Curwen used the solmization syllables of doh, ray, me, fah, soh, lah, and te as the ascending pitches of the major scale. The key would be established by doh in the major scale while lah would be the tonic in a minor scale. Sharp notes would add an –e to the syllable, and flat notes would add an –a to the syllable. Punctuation was added to show rhythm, but modern users of Tonic Sol-fa use a Modulator with corresponding hand signals to indicate the syllables.

Rhythm, Beat and Tempo

Rhythm is the pattern of long and short sounds. Music educators could begin a discussion about beat by taking a simple song like "Mary Had a Little Lamb" and clapping each syllable. The rhythm associated with the syllables will be more obvious when children can focus on the clapping instead of the words.

Beat is the pulse of the music which might speed up or slow down during the course of the music. Music educators should have students practice grouping beats together so that the first of 3 or 4 beats receives the emphasis. While chanting out the specific beat pattern, the students could march. This exercise will demonstrate more fully how music is grouped together in musical notation.

Tempo is the speed of the music. Music educators should help students learn the distinction between slow, moderate, and fast tempos by speeding up or slowing down their students' recitation.

The Music Publishers' Association

As an organization founded in 1895, the Music Publishers' Association facilitates communication between publishers, dealers, music educators, and all music enthusiasts. This non-profit association emphasizes the proper use of print music for both performance and educational purposes and works with the America Choral Directors Association, the American Music Center, the American Music Conference, and other groups by establishing guidelines for proper duplication and distribution for copyrighted and published musical work. The Association argues for the protection of intellectual property rights in both legal and legislative areas and maintains an awareness of new laws and regulations that involve the music publishing industry. As a forum for publishers, the Association resolves to speak to the issues of the industry while providing solutions for the music community.

Counterpoint

As a combination of 2 or more melodic lines, counterpoint can also be defined as the technical considerations involved in combining those melodic lines and their resultant sounds. The two lines may be written parallel in thirds but may include fourths for the sake of the key of the piece. The intervals of the work are measured and discerned by the ear, so more movement could be perceived than is actually occurring. Counterpoint as a property of polyphony is defined by its relationship to melody, since the melody must have a perceived continuity independent of the rest of the work. The two lines must balance each other so that the audience may focus on one line, then the other, and then perceive the combined sound as one line. While counterpoint has a linear emphasis, harmony has a more vertical emphasis.

Monteverdi

Monteverdi attended the 1600 production of Euridice, an opera by Jacopo Peri, and was introduced to this greater exploration of opera as a scenery play with characters and plot for his madrigals. His madrigals of 1605 incorporated a more monodic, or homophony created by solo and accompaniment style, in which more soloists would be accompanied by a basso continuo, or continuing bass line not written out but understood to follow the chords. These madrigals were more like arias than normal madrigals, and Monteverdi produced his first opera L'Orfeo in Mantua in 1607. It has been touted as the first operatic masterpiece. His orchestras were broadened to include the violin and other strings, records, organ, harpsichord, recorders, cornets, sackbuts, guitars, lutes, and 11 soloists. He also wrote Vespers of the Blessed Virgin and was later accepted as maestro di cappella of the Basilica of St. Mark in Venice.

Romantic Period

Whereas the Classical Period appealed to a sense of order and imagination, the Romantic Period, stretching between 1825 and 1900, appealed to emotion and focused on music that was subjective and yet astounding. There was a social awareness of self that was greatly analyzed. The visual arts were at their peak in the late 1800s, and many influential people expressed their emotional state through poetry and other philosophical exploits. The emerging modern music was frequently compared to the more familiar Classical music, and the Romantic musicians sought a way to define themselves separately from the past. Composers felt they had to work harder to overcome the past musical successes, so there was a movement to study and preserve the music of past generations.

Romantic Symphony Composition

Much of the Romantic symphony composition was based on the program music concept, and the symphony style of the time played to all extravagances of emotion and subjectivity with the more advanced and larger growing orchestration. Hector Berlioz studied the instrumentation of the musical instruments and wrote his Treatise on Orchestration, a document still in use for composers and arrangers. His Symphonie Fantastique and Rakoczy March were criticized for their excessive ornamentation and technique. Gustav Mahler also utilized the singing voice in his symphonic work similar to Beethoven, and Mahler's idea of the symphony as a separate entity with the possibility of greatness or just presence coalesced into his Symphony No. 8 "Symphony of 1000."

Romantic Composers

The early part of the Romantic Period saw many of the famous Romantic composers born within a few years of the each other: the German composers Robert Schumann and Felix Mendelssohn, the Polish pianist Frédéric Chopin, the French composer Hector Berlioz, and the Hungarian piano showman Franz Liszt. Early nineteenth century opera composers included Carl Maria von Weber, who referred to German folktales for his operatic works, and Gioacchino Rossini, who referred to current literature to create the Bel canto, or beautiful singing, opera. German opera would later come under the influence of Richard Wagner, while Italian opera became the feature work for Giuseppe Verdi. Non-Germantic composers such as Nicolai Rimsky-Korsakov and Modest Mussorgsky looked to their own history and culture for operatic plots and to the folk music of their own peoples as inspiration for new symphonies and instrumental pieces.

Technology

With different inventions and increases in technology, the music of the twentieth century and modern music can be shared on a grander scale and in more different formats than at any time before 1900. Whereas the music of the previous centuries was expressed from one person or ensemble to another person or audience, the twentieth century saw music disseminated to larger groups of people through radio and television broadcasts, as well as through pre-recorded sessions on other media. There has also been developments in the field of electronically-produced music.

Atonality

As the absence of tone, atonality refers to a weakening or suppressing of the characteristics most closely associated with tone. This removes the need for the central tonic triad with all its resultant harmonies. By relaxing the restrictions on the key, this style allows composers to use chromatic runs or arpeggios without conforming to the key signature. The tones are equally balanced so as to prevent any unwanted dissonance. The Classical and Romantic periods both saw chords that would modulate to correct the tones, while atonal music introduces a new approach to musical composition with a unique format to displace the more traditional modes of tonality. Schoenberg's Three Piano Pieces op.11 and Webern's works from op. 3 showcase this chromaticism, complex chordal structures of several intervallic types, and a moving away from the more established tonality in modern music.

Chord Families

In the seven major keys, all of the diatonic chords can be grouped into three segments or families relating to the harmonic function of each and the shared connection with other notes that can suggest certain emotional effects. The three families are the Tonic, Subdominant, and Dominant. The Tonic is comprised of I, iii, and vi; the Subdominant is comprised of ii and IV, and the Dominant is comprised of V and vii.

The VI chord in minor keys is often considered part of the subdominant family. The resultant grouping for minor is as follows: Tonic includes i and III; Subdominant includes ii, iv, and VI; and Dominant includes v (or V) and VII.

The ii-V-I Cadence

With a certain degree of refinement, the ii-V-I cadence starts on a subdominant in lieu of the tonic, which can make the initial key features more ambiguous. The motion of the root is still up by a perfect fourth or down by a perfect fifth, as is evidenced in jazz, Classical, and Romantic musical styles. The cadence itself provides a certain texture to the contours of the piece, since the ii-V-I cadence allows the melodic lines to be formed by the harmony notes created when the chords themselves change. As an important part of jazz composition and improvisation, the ii-V-I cadence should be verified immediately when reviewing the chord progressions of a piece, so that the performer can anticipate the necessary changes as they relate to the tonal structure.

Diminished Chords as Dominants

The diminished seventh chord can occur naturally on the seventh step of the harmonic minor sequence, and as such, can also function as a secondary dominant chord. Diminished seventh chords can also work as 7 b9 chords that are rootless. For the diminished seventh chord to be classified as a functioning secondary dominant, it must precede an intended target or harmonic progression, such as a diatonic chord that is a half step higher than any of its tones. Any tone that occurs in a dim7 chord can be considered the root of the chord. Since diminished seventh chords can resolve in different ways, they are best employed as the pivot chords in any changing of theme or modulation.

Modulation Types

As changes in the key, modulations can be subtle or abrupt, suggesting a new tonal center or establishing a different key. Modulations are categorized into four types: direct, prepared, pivot chord, and transitional. Direct modulation, also called unprepared or abrupt, changes the key between chords with no indication of an eminent change. Prepared modulation uses the V7 to set up for the key change, since the diminished seventh chord resolves to the key one half step up. Pivot chord modulation uses a diatonic common chord for both keys, so that the work can pivot between the two areas. Transitional modulation occurs when the music ends at a different key from the start, moving through cyclic chromatic ii-V progressions.

Trill

The trill is an ornamentation completed by rapidly moving between two pitches that are sequential within the key of the particular piece. The trill can be shown in the music by the abbreviation tr above the note to be trilled, and performers can often determine if the notes to be trilled should start with the note as it is written, a step just above or below the written note, or a beat just before or after the time shown. Vocal trills are more common for pieces that would benefit from vibrato, while organ or keyboard trills usually hold the main note, and the upper tone is reiterated. Trills are also expected to be interjected by the performer and are not necessarily written out by the composer.

As the trill or tremolo is an ornamentation, it is not the focus of the piece and usually carries little importance to the overall work. Therefore, the performer must be cognizant of how to end the trill or tremolo. Sometimes the music will show that the ornament is suddenly stopped or snapped off at the main note. If the ornament is for a shorter duration, the sound could be held to the early part of the beat; if the ornament is for a greater duration, the sound could be held a little longer. For shorter notes, the trilling can be combined to transition to the next phrase. A suffix, or descent to the lower auxiliary before the main note, may also be used and may be separated from the remainder of the music by a small rest.

Frequency and Pitch Change

The basilar membrane vibrates in response to each frequency in a position that is related to the type of frequency. The smallest frequency difference between any tones produced at the same time,

- 147 -

or the limit of discrimination, defines when the ear barely perceives two distinct pitches. Below this, any pitch occurring between the two is combined with the sound of the two pitches or pulses. When a tone changes pitch, the ear can differentiate the differences in frequency. The frequency range and tonal duration also determine the resolution of sound. The roughness caused by two disagreeing sounds created at the same time or the canceling out of a sound by another is called critical band. The more advanced neurons will change over time in the firing rate and detect certain patterns in dissonances and poorly configured consonances.

Guillaume de Machaut

Guillaume de Machaut brought the polyphonic style of music to its full maturity in the fourteenth century with his new art style. Acting as both secretary and court composer for wealthy men, de Machaut composed music that was touted as the premier style and even produced the La Messe de Notre Dame, one of the early polyphonic works for the Ordinary of the Catholic Mass. This Mass combines the tonality of the traditional church modes with a more then-modern minstrel flair. Interestingly, de Machaut embodied the courtly love ideology in his personal life and his more secular music. His works created subtle relationships between the theme and the sound of words, and he brought polyphony to more mainstream musical audiences.

Jean Jacques Rousseau

In his 1762 work Emile, Jean Jacques Rousseau hypothesized that children should learn the simple joy of true vocal sound to understand about harmony and vocal resonance. The music created and exercised with children should be simple and within a narrower range than that for an adult or older child who would have a broader range of flexibility. Rousseau argued that real words should not be used in the exercises and songs, since children will focus on the word and its meaning more than the sound created. Musical notation should not be pushed on to children who are striving to learn to read ,since music learned by feel first is better understood in notation learned later. He recommended that children be encouraged to compose their own simple songs about their interests and with some dance steps included.

Maria Montessori

As the founder of the Montessori school format, Maria Montessori argued that children learned best through a combination of sensory experiences and hands-on work. She believed that any scholastic environment should be designed to match a child's degree or level of growth and development. Believing that children learn differently from adults, Montessori collaborated with pianist Maria Maccheroni to create a music program that involved children's ability to listen, play instruments, and dance. All participation was at will, and children were encouraged to explore sounds created by instruments and voices and to differentiate between sound and noise. The Montessori principle focused on the child learning how to create music and recognize rhythm before learning how to read music and musical notation.

Jerome Bruner

Bruner believed that the education and instruction of children should include four separate features. First, children should be encouraged to explore and learn about their world, and teachers should seek out how to foster that curiosity. Second, information should be easily accessible and comprehensible, so teachers should research the most effective way to present new information. Third, the order or sequence should be logical and orderly, so that children can follow along with the development of an idea or way of thinking. Fourth, a method of reward should be installed, so that children can be encouraged and feel that their participation and responses are good. Verbal

- 148 -

praise is an extrinsic reward, while the child's pride in figuring out the concept or puzzle is an intrinsic reward.

National Music Education Standards

Standards as outlined for music educators instructing children in grades K-4 as they perform when singing alone or with others involve the following tasks:

- Ability of each child to sing independently, in rhythm and on pitch, while following the appropriate directions for diction, timbre, and posture and maintaining a consistent tempo
- Ability of each child to incorporate expressiveness into singing and use appropriate dynamics, phrasing and interpretation as directed or as indicated in the literature
- Ability of each child to sing from memory songs comparable for education levels
- Ability of each child to sing rounds, partner songs, and ostinatos correctly
- Ability of each child to sing in groups and blend vocal timbres and dynamics while following the conductor

Standards as outlined for music educators instructing students in grades K-4 as they listen to, analyze, and describe music involve the following tasks:

- Ability of each child to identify basic musical forms upon hearing them
- Ability of each child to exemplify perceptive listening skills through movement and by answering questions or describing aural examples of the different styles of music showcasing great diversity
- Ability of each child to incorporate correct terminology while explaining music, musical notation, musical instruments and voices, and performances
- Ability of each child to identify sounds of specific various instruments, such as orchestral and band instruments, and different voices, such as male and female
- Ability of each child to respond through deliberate movement to specific musical selections

Standards as outlined for music educators instructing students in grades K-4 as they learn about how music relates to history and culture involve the following tasks:

- Ability of each child to identify aural examples of the different genre or style of music as shown throughout historical periods and cultures
- Ability of each child to describe the use of the elements of music as shown in various selected pieces from different cultures
- Ability of each child to verify how music is used in his or her culture and daily activities as well as the different types of music
- Ability of each child to describe the roles of musicians in different cultures and at different historical times
- Ability of each child exemplify the audience behavior as appropriate for the style of music performed and its context

Rhythm Instruments

Rhythm instruments such as shakers, cowbells, tambourines, and drums are the easiest to work with when instructing children about rhythm, beat, and tempo since they are small, and children can easily be taught to use them correctly. Before using these instruments to indicate each syllable or to set up a tempo for the singing of a song, such as "Hot Cross Buns" or "Twinkle, Twinkle, Little Star," children should be introduced to these instruments and how they work and produce sound.

- 149 -

Otherwise, the children will focus entirely on how the instrument works and not use it in the way the music educator directs. This will prohibit any kind of attentive listening to the structure of the music and possibly create noisy pandemonium. Once students are familiar with how sounds are produced, they can be instructed to incorporate those sounds in their exercises.

Introducing Musical Instruments

Music educators should not just hand rhythm or simple instruments to young children and expect them to figure out on their own the required technique or style to create a certain sound. The music educator should give instruction in how to use the instrument and then allow the child to replicate that instruction and eventually to improvise. Music educators should respond to a child's production of sound with positive and supportive comments, asking the child to make a louder or softer sound or to change the beat from fast to slow. By educating the child on how to make different sounds on the instrument with different mallets or ways of playing, the music educator can keep the exercise fresh and challenging for the child.

Movement

Movements that are associated with music and performed as dance or exercise by young children are classified as either creative movement or synchronized movement. Creative movement gives children a freer avenue for expression and allows them to improvise and enjoy the physical act itself. Synchronized movement follows an established routine and is choreographed to the rhythm and beat of the selected music. Synchronized movement helps children work as a group and realize the importance of teamwork, while creative movement allows them to freely express themselves to song. Both types of movement allow children to develop their listening skills and focus on what they are hearing. Focused listening is also considered perceptive or active listening.

Teaching Creative Movement

Children can move creatively to music if they are encouraged to do so by the teacher, and if they have a repertoire of movements they are comfortable using. Music educators can show children how to move faster through the faster pieces of music or slower through slower pieces. Children can also be introduced to musical dynamics when the music educator combines such movements as loud marching through the louder music and tiptoeing through the softer music. This kind of exercise also helps students actively listen and focus on the type of music being played. The music educator can also teach children about changes in the phrasing of sections by changing the direction of movement at the end of the phrase.

High School Music Software

Aside from the computer centers and workstations, the technological music classroom for high school should contain at least different software programs that deal with listening, analyzing, reading, and describing various types of music. Other software programs should be dedicated to the discussion of music and its interconnectivity with history and culture as well as the other arts. Creation, improvisation, and composition software should also be available for students, and Internet access should be available with supervision. Students should be encouraged to utilize the technology for practice and performance, while music educators can access different programs for such things as grading and instrument inventory. Other software programs should be considered for students to use in researching music styles and changes over time or by region. These software tools should be updated as required.

Song Teaching

One of the easiest ways to teach a song to students is through repetition. Children have the ability to build on what is learned, so the same song taught to first graders will be well remembered by those children when they are fifth graders if that song has been practiced each year. A listing of several songs, such as the National Anthem or other patriotic or seasonal songs, can be displayed at the front of the music center. As each song is learned and mastered, the music educator can check off that song from the list. Young children feel a sense of accomplishment as more songs are checked off the list. Music educators should encourage students to teach any new or modified song to their parents, who can help students with their pronunciation of words and support their children's enjoyment of music.

Increased Focus

Music currently stands as a sideline to the major focus of science, math, and language regardless of the studies that show how music education can improve students' whole educational experience. An increased focus on music and the arts could motivate students to learn more in other areas, and all educational encouragement avenues should be considered for the changing student body. More researchers and educators are beginning to recognize music as a form of intellectual development along the same lines as Howard Gardner's multiple intelligence theory that encompasses linguistic, spatial, intra-personal, bodily-kinesthetic, logical-mathematical, inter-personal, naturalistic, musical, and possibly existential intelligences. These theoretical systems support the inclusion of music in the basic curriculum and argue that teaching music is only the first step to teaching all other subjects students must learn. Any learning that occurs can be fortified in other areas.

Music Aptitude

Edwin Gordon works as a researcher in music and music psychology and has postulated that all children have a natural inclination toward and appreciation for music. As with all personality types, some children may be more or less inclined to excel at music than others. Without the continued stimulation and exposure to music, young children may lose their affinity for it, or experience a diminishing ability or performance. Gordon's research shows that a child has a greater increase or decrease in aptitude for music between ages five and six, regardless of whether the child's environment included musical stimulation or not. As the child progresses over the next three years, that aptitude decreases or increases at a lesser degree than during that specific year. After age nine, the child's musical aptitude is established and remains at the same level.

Assimilation

The third type of preparatory audiation, assimilation involves the two stages of introspection and coordination. Between three and six, a child may develop the ability to coordinate the movements involved in moving while singing. During the introspection stage, the child should discover, with no assistance from the parent or teacher ,how the body movements coordinate with the rhythmic pulse of the chanting or singing. Once this awareness takes place, the child can then progress to the final stage of coordination. The coordination stage involves the child actively participating in timing the movements with the musical or rhythmic pattern of the song or chant. As this stage occurs about the time children start school, the music educator at the school should be able to help students with any aspect of this process.

Vocal Exploration

Most children are not comfortable making the transition from speaking voice to singing voice and require some time to experiment on how to make that change. This experimentation is referred to as vocal exploration. The singing voice of young children is usually light and airy without much volume. The music educator should make a point to differentiate between singing loud and shouting, since these sounds do not produce the same desired result and should not be confused. Any shouting done by children can strain their voices and further hamper them from finding their singing voice. When they do sing, young children have a limited range of about an octave, from middle C or D to A or the next D.

Self-Listening

Singing involves children listening to themselves and others sing and is considered a self-listening activity. This activity allows children to define their own projection of voice and to find their most comfortable singing voice. Children can sing in tune when they can hear the song, and the information is transmitted to their brain for them to audiate. Once children can audiate or think the musical sound, they are better able to reproduce that sound. The audiated sound is transmitted to the larynx and projected. Children must be able to hear themselves in order to sing in tune, and so in order to sing a song, they must listen to themselves. Music educators should encourage parents to allow children to sing by themselves into a tape recorder and then play that recording back, so that they can hear what they sound like. Music educators should model good singing techniques and allow children to sing often.

Listening With No Movement

Children should be involved in activities that incorporate no movement while listening to music, because the absence of movement will force the child to concentrate on the music. The musical mind of the child is dependent on learning how to match movements to music while maintaining an observance of the beat and also on listening to the music as an activity in itself. Nap time can be an excellent opportunity for children to listen to music without combining any physical movements with the beat. Playing slow, soothing music can also help direct children toward a restful state of mind. This can also provide an avenue for the music educator to introduce a new musical passage that will be used for synchronized movement later.

Movement Options

Children can become easily frustrated when they are unable to participate in the musical exercises and games because the movements or responses are too complex for them. Music offers better opportunities to join in, since there are no right or wrong ways to create music. Any instructions for these children should be simplified and broken down into small steps, and children should not be expected to combine a series of steps or responses at one time. Even children who have no cognitive disabilities require simplicity in new exercises. All songs used should have repeated parts, and pictures can be incorporated since children remember the words or phrasing better when pictures are included in the music. Music educators should work with children with behavioral disabilities and provide them a chance to see, hear, move, or touch instruments without any stress on the child to perform.

Reading Rhythm

The bottom number of the time signature becomes important when music educators try to teach children how to read rhythm. The bottom number shows which note gets one beat. In the 4/4 time

- 152 -

signature, the quarter note gets one beat and is counted as 1, 2, 3, 4 within the measure. A mathematical explanation of how the bottom number relates to other notes can be incorporated into the lesson, and children can see how two half notes are counted as 1, 3 while eight eighth notes are counted as 1 &, 2 &, 3&, 4&. This exercise combines a study of math with the basic fundamentals of music, and music educators can lead the children toward reading combinations of the notes and playing or clapping those rhythms.

Perceptive Listening

Music educators can create listening games for children to verify that they are actively or perceptively listening to the music, and not just hearing the notes or focusing on the words. Some music educators create a music detectives club that encourages children to select a piece of music and identify the different portions that are listed on a card. Children can listen to the piece, such as Haydn's Toy Symphony, and check the space on the card next to the trumpet or bird whistle or ratchet as it is played. Once several students have completed this exercise, the music educator can group them together to discuss what was heard. The group can then listen to the piece again and point out the different voices that some may have missed.

Music Introduction

Music educators should be instructed in how to watch children and learn the best and most effective ways to combine their natural inclinations towards music with lessons in the classroom. All instruction should be deliberate, and music educators can assist other teachers who may have little to no musical background, but want to incorporate music instruction in their classrooms. All educators should continue to seek out songs and chants to supplement their own repertoire for musical instruction, and all music educators should learn how to sing and how to play simple rhythmic instruments. Movements to music should be practiced by any adult who will be instructing children in musical performance and expression.

Philosophy Statement

Before beginning in a new classroom or in a new region, music educators should create a philosophy statement to help them keep their instructions organized and assist them in maintaining a learning goal for the children within a year or semester. The music educator should write down what music nurturing is, and how children can learn and be nurtured by music. The desired environment for this nurturing should then be described, along with all the planned activities and possible options for educational focus in which the music educator believes that children should be involved. Once this has been completed, the music educator should write down what future growth and development expectations he or she has for the children.

Self Conscious Children

Not all children between six and nine are comfortable dancing and moving in front of other children or the music educator unless they have been doing so since they were much younger. One of the easiest ways to foster an environment of acceptability is to sing and dance alongside the children, so that they can see others behaving in a particular way without being ostracized or ridiculed. Music educators could also provide areas for creative movement that have higher walls or are separated and somewhat shielded from the rest of the room. The music center can include headphones so that children do not feel they are encroaching on others' quiet time for homework. Room dividers combined with rugs and drapes can also provide some basic soundproofing.

Classroom Computer Centers

Technology is becoming a greater component of today's classroom for all subjects, from science to composition to arts. The music classroom can also be improved by computers and computer-related software and hardware. As young children become more computer literate, they will discover that more companies are creating computer programs for their level of ability and musical development. Music educators should consider including the computer in the music classroom, so that children can compose their own music, have it notated on music paper, and played aloud. Headphones can also be used so that children will not bother others with their compositions. Older children can be allowed to use the Internet for music-related searches and information about current trends in instruments and performing styles.

Staffing Requirements

The staffing requirements for technology in the 1-6 grade music classroom.

Technology is important in the music classroom of the first through sixth graders. Music educators should be encouraged to incorporate technology into the musical curriculum at appropriate levels of development. They should be allowed time to complete technological training in order to keep up with changing trends and should have access to professional services and development through Internet and email. Music educators should be allowed to interact with other music educators to discuss uses of technology, and technical support should be available. They should be permitted time to develop and adapt new music technology for their classroom. An appropriate student/teacher ratio is necessary for any lab setting and can be achieved through the use of aides or teacher assistants.

The staffing requirements for technology in the middle school music classroom.

Music educators in the middle school music classrooms can continue to expand on the technological education of the elementary school. They should receive time to complete training for new trends in music technology and should be allowed to confer with other music educators through the Internet and email. Technical support for the music hardware and software should be available. Music educators should be encouraged to develop new curriculum materials for incorporating music technology in the classroom and should supervise student work on sequencing, notation, and digital or audio multimedia work. An appropriate student/music educator ratio is required for lab work, and aides and teaching assistants can facilitate this situation.

Composing and Arranging

Occasionally students will be required to arrange pieces for a small ensemble of selected instruments or a fuller instrumental sound at church or religious worship or for solo and ensemble performances or features. Music educators can begin this kind of practice with students by using "This Land is Your Land" in its articulated 4/4 time. Focus should be placed on the simple structure. Students should be encouraged to listen to the melodic and harmonic structure of the music and try to feel how other words would sound in the same stressed and unstressed portions of the song. Music educators can even accompany the students and try to fit in the harmonic progressions vocally and instrumentally, so that the students can see how both parts work together.

Block Scheduling

More schools are adopting the block scheduling, and this translates into different areas of concern for music educators. The modified form of block scheduling has shown a stable enrollment in performance classes but with the drawback of decreases in student participation. The quality level of ensemble rehearsals and performances has been reported as declining, and music educators continue to see changes in student enrollment and schedule conflicts. Additional studies show that students have a greater possibility of burnout, that music is being further classified as an extracurricular activity, and that music educators have an increased workload and are showing increased job dissatisfaction. Researchers will continue to seek better ways of designing the teaching format and class schedule, and music educators will continue to facilitate that change.

Gymnasium Concert Etiquette

Not all schools are large enough to have an accommodating stage or performance area, so concerts may be held in the gymnasium. Music educators need to instruct their students how to perform the selected pieces but also how to conduct themselves during the performance in the gym. A quick review with the audience members before the performance is often necessary to establish the etiquette rules. Audience members should remain seated during the performance and, if required to leave, should do so between songs. Music performances are not the same as athletic events, so constant clapping, whistling, or cheering is unnecessary. Small children should be prevented from acting out or running along the bleachers or stands. Once the song has ended, the audience members may show their appreciation by clapping and/or whistling.

Copyright Rules

Most music educators and musicians have questions about the legitimacy of copyright and any unintentional infractions that might occur. For example, all accompanists should play from original music and not photocopied music. The copying of an entire work is an example of copyright infringement and is not considered "fair use" of music. Copies of an entire work for faculty members to follow may only be permitted with the publisher's permission; otherwise, additional copies can be borrowed. Music CDs should not be copied without the publishers permission, even for practice purposes. Performance tapes can only be sold or distributed if the seller has the permission of the publishers for their work and of the parents for their children's performance.

Music Public Domain

The public domain (PD) of the US includes any music and lyrics composed in 1922 or earlier cannot be claimed by any singer or company. these songs can be used by anyone permission from the original publisher, can be used for profit-making enterprises where royalties could be collected. An amended version or derivative of a PD song can be copyrighted by that composer, but the original song remains available for others to use. Recordings and compositions are protected as separate entities, and practically all sound recordings are under copyright protection until 2067. Some songs written after 1922 are considered PD, but it may be best to consult an attorney before using them. International copyrights do not exist, but other countries may offer copyright protection for seventy years or so after the author's death.

Harold Clurman

Harold Clurman was an American theatre critic and director. Clurman believed that in order to create a successful production that all elements of a production had to work together. Clurman was known for reading and rereading scripts several times, each time with a different goal in mind. For example, he read once focusing on character, once focusing on scene and once focusing on technical aspects. Clurman was also known for directorial style in which he allowed his designers to use creative freedom when designing sets. He guided the designers rather than giving them detailed instructions of what he wanted. He used the concept of spines when directing plays. Spines are defined as the main actions that pertain to a specific character or to the play itself. Clurman would help actors to define the spine of their individual character and then he would explain the spine of the play as a whole. He would then tie each of the actor's spines into the play's spine creating a unified performance.

Tragedy Origin

According to Aristotle, tragedy can be traced to the Greek song form called dithyramb, songs that were sung in honor of the fertility god, Dionysus. Greek men would dance while wearing costumes made of goat-skins in order to impersonate satyrs, as these creatures were the constant companions of Dionysus. The song sung by these men was called a tragoedia, which means "goat-song" in Greek. This ritual was expanded upon by the addition of a central male figure to whom the songs were addressed. The central male figure would answer questions sung to him by the surrounding circle of males, or the chorus. The word "chorus" is derived from the Greek word "choros," which means to dance in a circle. There are many differing views on the exact origin of the tragedy, but the above describes the basic consensus among scholars.

Aeschylus, Sophocles, and Euripides

Aeschylus, Sophocles, and Euripides are noted as the most famous of the Greek tragedians. Aeschylus is best known for his trilogy entitled The Oresteia, which is compromised of the plays Agamemnon, The Libation Bearers, and The Eumenides. Aeschylus became known as the father of Greek tragedy, as he pre-dated both Sophocles and Euripides. According to Aristotle, Aeschylus was responsible for changing the ancient form of the tragedy by adding a second actor, diminishing the participation of the chorus, and focusing on dialogue. Sophocles, known for his work Oedipus the King, heightened the tragic form by adding a third actor and downsizing the chorus to less than fifteen members. Euripides was the first playwright to allow women to act in tragedies.

New Greek Comedy

New Comedy was the genre that ruled the Greek stage from the late fourth century through 260 B.C. New Comedy was largely focused on the idea of unrequited or unattainable love. New Comedy also introduced the character of the mercenary soldier returning home from war. Unlike Old Comedy, this form had no characters likened to public figures or heroes. The characters of New Comedy were common people who faced everyday problems. New Comedy completely eliminated the chorus. New Comedy was received well by audiences because the nature of its plays involved universal themes. The use of these common themes allowed for New Comedy to be translated well in other geographic regions, and the new comic form spread to Rome, Italy, and England. This ancient form of New Comedy was the foundation for the comic forms used in both theatre and television today.

Greek Play Preservation

It was the responsibility of the Athenian archons, or magistrates, to maintain records of Greek productions. They recorded names of the upper-class citizens who financed the productions, as well as the poets, actors, plays and contest winners. These records were later published by Aristotle. Athenians had an insatiable appetite for theatre, as their normal viewings we limited to only a few days of the year. In order to satisfy the need for theatre during the off-season, many of the great plays of that time were rewritten by people known as adapters. To preserve the integrity of the original work, the law required that the distribution of any copy of an original work had to be recorded by a public secretary. The library at Alexandria holds copies of various tragic and satyr plays. The most common of the ancient Greek plays seen today are those that were preserved for

- 156 -

use in educational institutions of the Middle Ages, collections that included the works of Aeschylus, Sophocles, Euripides and Aristophanes.

Actor's Social Position

In ancient Greece, the status of the actor was increasingly elevated over time. In the fifth century, acting became a profession and, as such, was viewed with great admiration and respect. Roman actors, however, had a much more contemptible social status. Playwriting was not a sought-after trade; rather, the profession was forced upon a person by heredity. Actors were often slaves or foreign captives who were made to perform in exchange for their freedom. Many Roman rulers passed laws forbidding certain high-ranking officials from entering theatres or consorting with those who participated in theatre. Women rarely appeared in Roman productions, and those who did so were limited to roles as mimes.

Roman Theatre

Roman theatre typically consisted of a daytime production that lasted for approximately two hours. Plays most often occurred immediately before or after the noon meal. Comedy was the dominant form of Roman theatre, using masks, wigs, costumes, and makeup, and audiences were most entertained by outrageous and crude spectacles. Women were forbidden to participate in these plays, which left the roles of any female characters to be played by young boys. The earliest Roman venues consisted of very basic amphitheatres where the audience reclined on the ground, and actors had very few resources at their disposal. As theatre evolved, the Roman stage was comprised of a common street with several houses in the background. Audiences were entertained by flute players during scene changes. Pompey the Great built the first Roman theatre auditorium in the year 55 B.C.

Middle Ages Drama

The drama of the Middle Ages had its origins in religion, as it was born of the Christian church. Whereas the church had outlawed ancient theatre as blasphemous, the new forms of drama were created by the church as a means of spreading their beliefs. In order to best relay the dialogues that occurred in the stories relating to Jesus' life, priests would each read the lines spoken by characters in the story. Soon, priests began acting out their lines to capture the interest of the congregation. These performances were especially common during Easter. The tradition soon extended to Christmas mass where the Nativity story was retold through a theatrical production. The productions began to grow into more elaborate and exaggerated tales that oftentimes bore little of the original intent. Priests could no longer exclusively handle the multitude of roles in a performance and were forced to invite laymen to participate. Eventually, the responsibility of these performances came to rest solely in the hands of laymen, who formed guilds and various organizations to handle each aspect of the productions.

Minstrels

Minstrels traveled from town to town in medieval days offering a source of entertainment. As he wandered between towns on the back of a mule, the minstrel often dressed in festive costumes. Minstrels, accompanied by their harps, would sing about the saints, heroes, and scripture at gatherings and feasts. Appreciative audiences would often award the minstrel with gifts and tokens. The most talented minstrels were hired for permanent service by ruling Kings and bishops. Minstrels served an important role in the development of drama, as they paved the way for the reintroduction of drama in the Middle Ages after Greek drama had been outlawed by the Christian church. As the popularity of minstrels grew, Paris became the headquarters of minstrelsy, allowing the minstrels to band together into groups that could command rights and privileges exclusive to their craft.

William Hallam

William Hallam was a theatre actor-manager hailing from London. Seeing America as rife with possibility for theatre arts, Hallam decided to create a company of players that he could send there. Hallam charged Robert Upton with traveling to America and preparing theatres for his vision; however, Upton took the money Hallam gave him and joined another company of players in America, completely neglecting the mission on which he was sent. Despite losing the aid of Robert Upton, as well as his own financial resources, Hallam decided to continue as planned. While not the first to introduce drama to America, Hallam did much to establish its permanence. One of his most important contributions was putting together a company of players who had the talent to execute a variety of theatrical genres, thus allowing for the company to offer a multitude of productions.

Henrik Ibsen

Norwegian native Henrik Ibsen was not only a modern dramatist, but also a theatre manager and philosopher. Ibsen's work was prone to reflect his changing ideals. For instance, in one work he would proclaim the value of ideals, while in another work he would deem such values worthless. He addressed this contradictory message in his work entitled An Enemy of the People, stating that most truths become obsolete after twenty years. His work further exposed what he saw as the social prejudices of his time. He extolled the value of the individual and each person's right to choose his or her own path in life. Ibsen believed that the true destiny of each man and the ultimate source of happiness lay within being true to one's self. Ibsen's ideas were not well-received during his time, and he was attacked by other playwrights for his seemingly ridiculous ideas.

Theatre of the Absurd

The Theatre of the Absurd, also known as New Theatre and anti-theatre, is a phrase that was coined by drama critic Martin Esslin. In 1962, Esslin published a book bearing the title The Theatre of the Absurd that categorizes the type of play in which the human condition is decried as meaningless. The view that man is meaningless in the universe is a philosophy born of the French writer Albert Camus. Camus claimed that man had to resign himself to the fact that the universe defied logical explanation and could only be seen as absurd in its behavior. According to scholars, World War II readied the minds of playgoers for the themes presented in the Theatre of the Absurd. Esslin identified Eugene Ionesco, Samuel Beckett, Jean Genet, Arthur Adamov and Harold Pinter as the five defining playwrights of the absurdist movement. While this form of theatre was assigned its own title in the twentieth century, absurdist elements can be noticed in works as far back as those of Aristophanes. Absurdist elements can be identified in most plays predating the definition of Theatre of the Absurd, including Medieval morality plays and Elizabethan dramas.

Pantomime

The pantomime played a very indistinctive role in dramatic productions until English actor Joseph Grimaldi reinvented the pantomime clown role in Harlequin. Clowns were a common character in many forms of theatre, especially pantomimes, and generally appeared as the servant of a more important character. Grimaldi had a talent for visual tricks and general buffoonery and brought clowns to life through his elaborate mechanical tricks. In 1717, actor John Rich played the role of Harlequin in the pantomime Harlequin Executed. Harlequin was originally a speaking part, but people like John Rich only used gesture, movement, and facial expression to convey the same sentiments that had previously been expressed only through words.

Adolphe Appia

Adolphe Appia shaped modern day stagecraft through his early theories involving staging, lighting, and the use of space. He believed that space was a dynamic element that could be utilized to convey a much more realistic feel for audiences. Appia studied various operatic scenes in differing light and staging scenarios in order to find the best combinations; however, he soon decided that the opera genre did not offer the fluidity and staging to accentuate the human presence properly. He theorized that stage space would be better incorporated into a performance if it contained steps, ramps, platforms, and drapes, all of which could be unified with actors through the use of lighting. He published books on his theories, most notable of which are The Staging of Wagner's Musical Dramas, Music and Stage Setting, and The Work of Living Art.

Aesthetic Judgment

Aesthetic judgment is a philosophy that questions the legitimacy of a person's notions of what is pleasing to his or her tastes. Early puritanical thought equated beauty with pleasure, and pleasure was seen as evil. As the idea of aesthetic judgment evolved, it became the consensus that a person should not like something because it was pleasurable to his or her senses; instead, liking something should be supported by that person's ability to associate that object with his or her education and knowledge. Philosopher Immanuel Kant proposed that beauty should be judged both for its subjectivity and universality. Scottish philosopher David Hume also published a series of works on the validity of aesthetic judgment. In his essay on the aesthetics of tragedy, he explained that tragedy could be a pleasurable experience because even though it evokes a sense of sadness, it also produces a sense of delight in the viewing of a theatrical production. In such cases, Hume claims, the conflicting emotions of pleasure and displeasure are balanced by each other and, according to his belief, balanced emotion results in pleasure.

Elizabethan Theatre

The story of Robin Hood was popularized in Tudor England by companies of roving players. Productions were held in barns and inns, as public theatre was poorly regarded by English government of the time. The government attempted to stop traveling players from performing in 1572 with the passage of laws forbidding the practice. The government was concerned that performances were apt to incite rebellion among the population and that the players were carrying diseases, such as the plague, from town to town. Only actors hired by noblemen were allowed to perform, and from 1572 to 1574, only four noblemen obtained licenses to begin theatre companies. As in Roman theatre, women were forbidden from participation, and female roles were played by young boys. By 1576, the popularity of the performances had grown to such an extent that actor James Burbage built a theatre in London to accommodate the large theatre-going audiences.

Chinese Drama

Chinese drama is rooted in—and still holds true to–religious tradition. Chinese drama relies heavily on the principles, superstitions and symbols of Taoism, Confucianism, and Buddhism. The use of various combinations of these religious beliefs allow for Chinese dramatists to create extravagant productions often set in unearthly realms. While both Buddhism and Taoism provide a rich supply of symbolism, Confucianism is a much more intangible belief that centers on ancestor worship. Confucianist belief is most often represented in the musical theatre of the Chinese. Buddhist beliefs are often seen represented in acts of buffoonery towards gods and demons of Buddhism. The role of religion in Chinese drama can be simplified in the following way: Confucianism involves morality, the dead past, and the worship of man; Buddhism involves idolatry, the changing future, and the worship of images; Taoism involves superstition, evils in the present, and the worship of spirits.

Noh Plays

Created by Kwanami Kiotsugu, Noh plays were the dominant form of drama in 14th-century Japan. Noh plays featured only men who wore masks when playing the parts of women or gods. This form of theatre is characterized by its rigid structure and unchanging tradition. The plays always began with a traveler who reveals his own name and the destinations to which he will travel over the course of the play. A chorus describes the scenery and the inner dialogue of the traveler as he wanders the stage. Each place the traveler visits is inhabited by the Spirit of the Place, a ghost that must tell a story of suffering. The ancient legend of the sight is revealed through a combination of dialogue among actors and recitations from the chorus. The play ends as the traveler prays for the ghost to find peace, and then a song is sung to honor the gods.

Actor vs. Dramatist

The dramatist must make sure that the venue for which he is writing will physically be able to accommodate the demands of his play. The dramatist must also be mindful of the audience for which he is writing, as well as the abilities of the actors who will be portraying the characters he creates. The ability of the actor is crucial to the creation of a character because an actor can impose his or her own personality onto the character created by a dramatist. Some dramatists tend to write about characters in the abstract and create characters from their imaginations. Other dramatists create characters based on actual people. Ancient dramatists created characters for the specific actor who would play the role, as did both Shakespeare and Moliere. Naturally, a dramatist's work was influenced by the actors for whom they were writing.

The Claque

The claque was an organized group of people who were hired to applaud during theatrical performances. The idea is believed to have originated when the emperor Nero required five thousand soldiers to chant a song of praise after a performance. Sixteenth century poet Jean Daurat used this ancient practice as the foundation for the formation of the claque. Claque is derived from the French term "claquer," meaning to clap one's hands. Daurat's idea to ensure that performances received applause was to give free tickets to any patrons who agreed to show their approval of the show. Eventually, this practice became so popular that a professional organization for claquers was formed. In 1820, a man by the name of Sauton formed a business that supplied claquers to playwrights. It was the responsibility of the theatre manager to request the number of claquers necessary for a performance. The duties of the claquers reached beyond simple clapping. They could laugh at jokes, fake tears, encourage encores, and generally ensure that the audience remained happy.

Gao Xingjian

Chinese-born dramatist Gao Xingjian was educated in the People's Republic, but his love of theatre was nurtured by his mother, who was an actress. His free thinking and love of theatre resulted in his incarceration in a re-education camp for six years. Under threat of persecution from Communist leader Mao Zedong, Gao Xingjian wrote in secrecy, believing that literature was a link to human consciousness. His works were not published until 1980, and in 1981 his plays were performed at the Beijing People's Art Theatre. Because his plays were influenced by Samuel Beckett, Antonin Artaud, and Bertolt Brecht, his work has been dubbed the Chinese Theatre of the Absurd. Based on Beckett's Waiting for Godot, Xingjian's play Bus Stop was viewed as highly controversial and received much scrutiny from Communist Party authorities. Although the Chinese government could not accept the value of his work, Xingjian was awarded the Nobel Prize in Literature in 2000.

Playwright Contributions

Eugene Ionesco-Rhinoceros, The Chairs, The Bald Soprano, The Lesson, The Killer, Exit the King, Hunger and Thirst, A Stroll in the Air.

George Bernard Shaw-Pygmalion, Caesar and Cleopatra, Androcles and the Lion, The Doctor's Dilemma, Candida, Major Barbara.

Christopher Marlowe-Tamburlaine, Doctor Faustus, The Jew of Malta, Edward II, The Massacre at Paris.

William Congreve-The Way of the World, The Old Bachelor, Love for Love, The Double-Dealer, The Mourning Bride.

Gao Xingjian-Absolute Signal, Wilderness Man, Between Life and Death, Dialogue

Lope de Vega-The Star of Seville, The Sheep Well, The Foolish Lady, Punishment Without Revenge.

Calderón de la Barca-Devotion of the Cross, Life is a Dream, The World is a Fair.

John Lyly-brought pastoral to England; created the form of Court Comedy.

Ben Johnson-London-born dramatist; famed for works of comedy and satire.

Hans Sachs-German shoemaker, writer, singer, and songwriter; wrote over 208 plays during the 16th century.

Lope de Rueda-Spanish actor, manager and playwright; invented pasos, the Spanish version of the short farce.

Emile Zola-French writer who supported naturalism.

Honore de Balzac-French writer who is credited as the founding father of realism in European literature.

Henry Becque-19th-century French playwright who incorporated both naturalism and realism into his work.

Aphra Behn-first female English playwright and a British spy.

Gordon Craig

Gordon Craig is credited with being one of the most influential faces of modern theatre. Craig's ideas on theatre can be seen in his 1904 book The Art of the Theatre. While many of Craig's peers believed that stage-directors should be merely interpreters, Craig saw the stage-director as a creator. It is a commonly held notion that dramatists, directors, and actors follow a hierarchy in which the actor is told what to do by the director, who is interpreting the words written by the dramatist. Craig believed that the role of the director superseded that of both the actor and the dramatist. He believed that theatre needed to be unified under the guidance of the director. One of Craig's most controversial philosophies is that theatre can function independently of literature. He contended that because the impulses of the director or the actor were sufficient enough to create a performance, a script was not essential.

Russian Drama

Drama made its way into Russia by way of Poland in the 12th century. Known as Religious Dialogues or Histories, the performances were exclusive to monasteries until 1603 when they began to be performed in universities. The university performances were done in Polish or Latin, the earliest of which was a Latin piece entitled Adam dated 1507, followed by a Polish piece entitled The Life of the Savior from His Entry into Jerusalem dated 1533. While the origin of Russian drama has its roots in religion, Russia had a unique form of theatre: the Vertep. Vertep is a puppet theatre in which puppeteers control dolls using strings attached to various parts of the doll. Vertep plays were used to depict religious stories. The word "Vertep" means "the secret place," which refers to the cave in which the Russian Orthodox Church believes Christ was born. Puppet characters include the Virgin Mary, Joseph, Jesus, and various other figures central to the birth and life of Christ. Through the years, Vertep plays eventually began to incorporate stories of a more secular nature.

Spanish Drama

The Spanish culture was known for its ballads, a form that translates well into a dramatic performance. The ballads of Spain contained legends that were introduced into the area from various locations. Although Spain's battle with the Moors had ended, the culture of the Moors had left a lasting imprint on the Spanish. Travelers from countries north of Spain brought tales of chivalry, knightly quests, and heroic tournaments. These stories, along with oriental influences, all made their way into the already popular Spanish ballads. The ballads became more and more elaborate, requiring multiple singers and detailed costumes and scenery. The addition of these elements transformed the ballad into full-blown dramatic productions. The works of both Lope de Vega and Calderon de Barca characterize Spanish drama at its height.

Theatrical Forms

Interludes, moralities, and farces were all forms of drama that made an appearance in the Middle Ages. During this time, the classical definitions of comedies and tragedies did not apply. For example, all that was required for a production to be a tragedy was the staging of a fight. The morality play was a religious performance that used allegory. It featured characters named after certain qualities that could be seen in mankind: Greed, Pride, Avarice, and Patience. Interludes and farces were the more secular performances of the Middle Ages. They featured a variety of performers, including pantomimes, strolling players, and professional actors. Many of the performers had the ability to act, sing, juggle, perform acrobatics, and do magic. Farces were most noted for comic situations that used characters to whom the audience could relate. Interludes were exactly what the name implies; they were performed between acts of longer plays. Interludes, due to their brevity, were also commonly performed to entertain guests during celebrations and banquets.

Vaudeville

The creator of vaudeville, Tony Pastor, was a professional circus clown. Vaudeville is a type of variety show that involves a number of different types of acts, usually unrelated to each other. Vaudeville acts included singers, dancers, acrobats, comedians, animal acts, impersonators, and magicians. These shows were originally exclusive to bars and dance halls until Pastor altered the style to make them suitable for the stage. In order to achieve the level of success that Pastor wanted, he knew that he had to make the shows appeal to highly-reputed citizens. Therefore, he rejected the lewd acts that were typical of vaudeville shows. He also banned drinking and smoking in the theatre where the shows were held. Edward Albee and B.F. Keith also played a large part in shaping the vaudeville theatre.

Vsevolod Emilevich Meyerhold

Russian-born Vsevolod Emilevich Meyerhold performed the roles of actor, director, and producer during his lifetime. Known for his socialist tendencies, he studied law for a short time but soon abandoned law school for the Moscow Philharmonic Dramatic School, an institution that was co-founded by Konstantin Stanislavski. Meyerhold went on to act in and direct several productions, each of which served as an opportunity for him to experiment with staging methods. He incorporated symbolism into most of his work, as he believed it was a crucial part of any dramatic production. One of Meyerhold's goals was to reinvent commedia dell'arte in a more contemporary style. In addition, Meyerhold believed that emotion could be conveyed through the use of practiced postures and gestures, regardless of the actor's actual emotional state. Meyerhold's acting technique was in direct opposition to Stanislavski's method, and Stanislavski wanted nothing to do with his Meyerhold's work.

The Cannon-Bard Theory

The Cannon-Bard theory was developed by psychologists Walter Cannon and Philip Bard. Their theory suggests that our emotional reaction to external stimuli leads to a physiological reaction. For example, feeling fearful may cause our heart to race and our body to tremble. This theory is in direct opposition of the James-Lange theory, which suggests that emotion is the result of physiological reaction and not the cause. The Cannon-Bard theory states that one must feel an emotion before the body can physiologically react. This theory can be incorporated into acting techniques by having students participate in scenarios that may make them fearful, anxious, angry or excited and then having them describe the physiological symptoms that accompanied each emotion.

Character Analysis

In order to play the part of any character, an actor should undertake a character analysis. The character analysis is a process by which the actor learns about the unique elements and dimensions that comprise the character. For example, a character is composed of vocal patterns, physical appearances, mannerisms, feelings, prejudices, aspirations, emotions, and goals. The actor must study or think about all of these elements and the degree to which each of these elements should be incorporated into the character. To analyze a character successfully, an actor should try to understand that character's relationship with others, his or her psychological thought process, his or her weaknesses and strengths, his or her sense of morality, and his or her history. The actor must also consider the character's place in the story and how or if the character will be changed by the events of the story.

Dynamics of Drama

In The Dynamics of Drama, Beckerman states that script analysis should involve breaking a script into segments. Each segment consists of an impelling agent exerting force to overcome resistance, which results in the completion of a project. A segment can be termed active if the agent is exerting force externally. Active segments are goal-oriented and require the agent to perform an action to complete the project. A reactive segment is produced when an agent must exert energy internally in order to emotionally or psychologically adjust to a change. Reactive segments generally consist of an agent who experiences a change rather than creates one.

Constantin Stanislavsky

German-born Constantin Stanislavsky is one of the most influential figures of the 20th century with regard to the acting process. He began acting at the age of fourteen and moved to producing and directing as he got older. Stanislavsky's approach to acting was developed over a forty-year period. He invented a method called the Stanislavsky System, which was revolutionary in regard to the psychological and emotional aspects of acting. His system became known simply as the Method. The fundamental principle of the Method is that the actor's primary responsibility is to be believed. Method acting uses emotional memory. This approach was a novel idea in the acting world because it required actors to use parts of their own lives, memories, and personalities while acting, whereas previous methods required actors to be blank slates that were always ready to assume a new character's identity.

Body Positions

Full front is a position in which the actor faces the audience, exposing the entire front of the body. It is an open position that allows the actor to be fully seen and heard by the audience. Open positions are those in which the actor's face, at the very least, is facing the audience. Quarter (1/4) right and left positions are those in which the actor stands facing slightly left or right of the audience. Quarter positions are also open positions and allow two actors to be on stage interacting with each other naturally while still allowing the audience to hear and see them. Left and right profiles are positions in which the actor exposes only one side of his or her face and body to the audience. Because profiles are not open positions, they drastically reduce the visibility of the actor to the audience. In between the profile and quarter positions are the three-quarter (3/4) right and left positions. Opposite of full front is the full back position. In a full back position, the actor faces away from the audience.

Heretical Approach

According to the heretical approach to directing, a director's job is to interpret the script in order to create a dramatic production that will be enjoyed by an audience. This approach requires directors to interpret the script and maintain its overall meaning while exercising creative freedom to alter an ending or omit certain scenes. Many times, this approach can be seen in classical works that are translated to opera. English-born doctor Thomas Bowdler used this approach to rewrite the works of Shakespeare, omitting what he saw as the offensive or unsuitable parts. He called his book The Family Shakespeare, as he believed he had transformed Shakespeare's work into a form that a father could read to his children without fear of corrupting them. Directors may use the heretical approach to directing; however, it is most often associated with a prudish censorship that does not lend itself to the theatre.

Director's Role

Due to the work of Konstantin Stanislavsky, it is now common for directors to collaborate with actors in order to create a successful performance. While directors can be encouraged to guide actors, they should also be cautioned not to over-direct actors, as this could lead to dependency. It is usually best for the director to consult with the actor as opposed to instructing the actor, which makes the director a source of inspiration and encouragement for the actor rather than simply his or her advisor. The actor and director both must recognize each other's creative talents and work together to incorporate their visions into a unified performance that leaves both parties, as well as the audience, feeling satisfied. The role of the director with the actor can take many forms.

Sometimes the director will assume one role and maintain it, or he or she may alternate between different roles. These roles can range from being an authoritarian to a visionary to a therapist.

Staging a Play

Staging a play is the process of determining where actors should be physically located at various points in the play with the aim of this exercise being to ensure that the position of the actors achieves the desired visual focus. The actors, props, set, and lighting must all work together to focus the audience's attention to the right place at the right time. Staging a play also involves blocking. Blocking refers to the positions where the actors are located on stage. Staging a play also involves the coordinating stage business, which includes any activity that takes place on stage during a performance such as actors answering phones in a scene.

Stage Lighting

In its earliest days, theatre lighting was limited to the effects that could be harnessed from the sun, moon, and stars. Early theatre was held during daylight hours, and the light that was cast upon the stage was controlled by nature. It can be assumed that theatre stages may have been built with this in mind. It is probable that the stages were built in such a way as to cast shadows in the necessary places while positioning the most intense rays of light in others. Italian theatre began making use of candles for lighting effects in the 16th century, while English theatre began using them in the 17th century. In the 18th century, oil lamps became the lighting method of choice. Gas lighting became available in the 19th century, and the first theatre to use it was the Chestnut Street Theatre in Philadelphia. The invention of electricity in 1879 revolutionized the world of theatre. The first theatre to use electricity was London's Savoy Theatre. In America, Boston's Bijou's Theatre was the first to install electric lighting.

Lighting Designers

Abe Feder was the first to coin the title "Lighting Designer." Feder studied engineering and theatre technology at what is now Carnegie-Mellon University. During his career, Feder was Lighting Designer for over 300 Broadway shows. Feder was also known for his lighting design in architecture, having created the lighting for the Empire State building, the RCA/GE building in Rockefeller Center, and the United Nations building. *Jean Rosenthal* is best known for her lighting design in 1950s and 1960s musicals. She is credited with being the inventor of dance lighting. *Peggy Clark* was the first female to hold the position of president in the United Scenic Artist organization. She assisted in scene design and was Lighting Designer for several Broadway plays.

Stage Lighting Properties

The properties of stage lighting include intensity, color, direction, distribution, texture, and movement. Each function of stage lighting can be achieved in various ways through the manipulation of the properties of light. Visibility can be altered by the use of intensity, color, and direction. Intensity and distribution determine the focus of stage lighting. Modeling is primarily achieved through the manipulation of light direction. Information, like visibility, can be achieved by the use of intensity, color, and direction. For example, daytime scenes have brighter lighting than nighttime scenes. The mood of a play can be altered through the use of the light properties of intensity, color, direction, and distribution. The overall mood of a comedy is often best projected in warm, bright light, while tragedies have darker lighting. The manipulation of all of these functions and properties determines the success of the composition function of lighting, which serves to create a coherent production.

- 165 -

Floodlights

Floodlights are used to flood an area with light. There are three types of floodlights: evenly spread, bottom concentration, and battens. Evenly spread floodlights provide light to a large area with every part of the beam emitting the same amount of light. Floodlights that are concentrated on the bottom emit a heavier light in the lower part of the beam. This is achieved by shaping the reflector part of the floodlight with an epitaxial lamp. Battens are created when floodlights are attached in long strips and used to light specific areas. Battens that are set up on the stage floor are called ground rows. Battens used on the front edge of the stage are called footlights. Battens that are suspended from the ceiling are called border lights or magazine battens.

High School Theatre Arts

Students in high school theatre arts courses study, write, research, critique, create, design, perform, and participate in a variety of theatre-based learning experiences. The plan allows for a total of four years of theatre arts training. The theatre arts curriculum includes courses that provide instruction in performance and design techniques, style, historical motifs, and genres, creating valuable performance-based experiences for students while using appropriate technology and media. Such courses develop critical thinking, creativity, and aesthetic perception, at the same time reinforcing skills in leadership and collaboration. A program of study in theatre arts also generates a heightened sensitivity to the arts as students explore theatre's significance and influence on society.

Student's Acting Progress

At a beginning level, students in theatre arts should be capable of using physical, emotional, and social elements to portray a character in monologues, duets, and improvised scenes. Students should also be capable of recreating a character through observation. Beginning students should have the ability to use their imaginations to improvise a character's thoughts and emotions, along with being able to use improvisational skills to create a character. Students should be able to demonstrate an understanding of how vocal techniques are used to control volume and clarity when speaking. Students should be able to distinguish between the various styles of acting, as well as identify ways to analyze characters. Beginning students should have an understanding of how such technical elements as costume, makeup, props, and lighting can enhance character development. Beginning students should be able to demonstrate through improvised scenes how movement can be used to express the thoughts and emotions of characters.

Advanced students in theatre arts should be able to develop, communicate, and sustain a character for the duration of a published script. They should have an ability to incorporate physical, social, and emotional elements while portraying characters. Advanced students can create characterizations using complete scripts, and they can use their imaginations to develop a character's thoughts and emotions based on the dialogue and relationships conveyed in the script. Advanced students can use improvisational skills to create complex characters. They should be able to develop and analyze various approaches to characterizations and to determine the effectiveness of certain approaches as they are used in full-length scripts. Advanced students should also show proficiency in selecting and applying technical elements to specific characters in full-length productions. Advanced students should have the ability to perform in ensembles while demonstrating the vocal techniques implied in a script and utilizing movement to convey thoughts, feelings, and character development.

Student's Scene Design Progress

Intermediate-level theatre students have had two to three years of theatre classes. They should have the ability to create technical designs, as well as theatre management designs. Intermediate students should be able to collaborate with a group to perform various technical and managerial roles and responsibilities. Students at this level should have the ability to apply their knowledge by participating in tasks involved with advertising, house management, and box office duties. At this level, students should hold various design positions during the production of a theatrical performance. Finally, they should be able to distinguish between the possibility of pursuing theatre scene design as a hobby or as a profession.

Student's Directing Progress

Students at a beginning level of theatre arts should be familiar with the role of a director and be able to identify the responsibilities of a director. Students should be capable of working alone or in groups to demonstrate the leadership and collaborative skills used by a director when creating a production. Students should be able to read a script and identify potential problems that a director might face. Students should also be able to propose solutions to the problems they identify within a script. Students should be capable of demonstrating their knowledge of stage movement, including blocking and choreography. Beginning theater arts students should also be familiar with the historical timelines and trends related to directing.

Student's Overall Progress

Advanced theatre students should demonstrate the creative ability to develop characters from a variety of dramatic texts, both realistic and fictional. They should have the skills to research, reflect, and revise their acting choices for various characters. Advanced students should be able to use dialogue to advance action when writing a script. They should also be able to use basic dramatic structure while writing a script, as well as have the skills to develop complex characters within the drama. In regard to understanding the historical aspects of theatre, advanced students should be able to research and perform a particular historical or cultural piece while using the appropriate dialect and mannerisms throughout the performance. Advanced students should understand the way that theatre has impacted and continues to impact society and culture. Students should also be capable of designing, performing, and directing plays that are representative of specific theatrical styles. Furthermore, advanced students should be able to use the appropriate vocabulary terms to discuss their aesthetic judgments of dramatic works.

Theatrical Presentation

Theatrical presentation involves familiarizing students with a broad range of activities that can be considered theatrical forms. Such forms include music, dance, performance, and visual arts. Students should examine the structure of each kind of dramatic form in order to determine how that particular form relates to the structure of all arts. Students should be given the opportunity to integrate their knowledge of various forms of theatre into an original performance they create themselves. Lessons should provide a means for students to study both traditional and non-traditional methods of artistic production. Lessons should also provide students with knowledge of and hands-on experience in emerging technology in theatrical productions including film, video, and computer applications.

Incorporating Theater

Students in fourth grade should continue expanding theatre vocabulary. They should also build upon their existing knowledge of artistic perspective by learning to identify a character's motives. Students should learn how subtle changes in voice can be used to convey meaning during speaking and acting. Students should be taught how to use artistic expression by participating in activities that require them to express the emotions of actors through the use of gestures. They should also retell stories in various tones, including comic and tragic. Students should have the opportunity to create a character through the use of costumes, masks and props. In regard to the history of theatre, students should be introduced to local theatre history and trends. Students can develop aesthetic judgment abilities by critiquing performances based on the elements of acting they have studied. Besides understanding how audiences impact various types of performances, fourth-grade students should be able to view a dramatic performance and identify the methods employed by the scriptwriter to evoke certain kinds of responses from the audience.

Students in seventh grade should be introduced to more theatre vocabulary. They should develop the ability to identify dramatic elements, including foreshadowing, crisis, rising action, catharsis, and denouement. In order to develop skills in creative expression, students should be allowed to explore character and motivation by participating in rehearsals. Students should learn the value of maintaining a rehearsal script in order to organize their rehearsal times and to keep track of their thoughts and ideas concerning blocking, props, and lighting. Students should be taught to incorporate tension and suspense into their writing. Regarding the historical and cultural aspects of theatre, student should participate in a culture-specific performance in which they design and create the masks, costumes, and sets used in the presentation. Students should also be able to compare and contrast various theatrical styles. With regard to aesthetic judgment, students should understand how cultural influences affect the content and meaning of drama.

Lessons Learned

In first grade, students can learn to cooperate in group activities. They also begin to understand the concept that all things in life have a beginning, a middle, and an end, just like they see in stories. In second grade, students learn problem-solving skills, which can be carried into other courses. In third grade, students are taught to question events and gain information through applying the 5 Ws (who, what, when, where and why). In fourth grade, students learn to use acting as a tool for understanding local history. They also learn to work with a team to accomplish a specific goal. In fifth grade, students learn about the various career options available to professional actors and theatrical technicians. In sixth grade, students learn how theatrical skills are used in the social sciences, such as advertising and marketing. In seventh grade, students learn how the voice can be used to project confidence during oral presentations. In eighth grade, students begin to understand the various jobs available in theatre, and they are encouraged to research the educational requirements necessary for those jobs.

Drama Styles

Classicism is a theatrical style developed by French playwrights in the 17th century. In general, classicism places emphasis on society, reason, and enlightenment. Classicism as a theatrical style incorporates the rules and traditions of ancient Greek and Roman theatre and embodies the theories created by Aristotle regarding the unity of time, place, and action. *Neoclassicism* was a product of the 18th century. As a theatrical style, Neoclassicism is characterized by extravagant costumes and elaborate scenery with stories that involve a high degree of melodrama. Neoclassic theatre had clearly defined genres of either tragedy or comedy. *Elizabethan* theatre is characterized by a large number of characters, several subplots that eventually merge, and a varied mixture of emotion. *Restoration* drama, also known as comedy of manners, is characterized by witty dialogue with themes of virtue and honor. Restoration theatre also features plots involving the sexual behaviors of sophisticated society.

Aristotle

Aristotle identified six elements that define drama: spectacle, sound, diction, character, idea, and action. According to Aristotle, these six elements represent what every drama has in common. Modern critics combine the elements of action, character, and idea into the single element of plot. Action is any physical, mental, or emotional activity performed by a character. The term character refers to the physical, mental, or emotional qualities that are demonstrated by an actor's allowing the audience to see him or her as a unique individual. Idea is defined as the theme which the author is attempting to convey to the audience. These three elements can come together as the plot; however, it is possible for any one of these elements to be dominant. Diction refers to the language of the play. Language is a crucial element, as it reveals both overt and subtle information about the characters and situations in a play. Music refers to the actual music used in a play, as well as all other auditory devices, which can include the rhythm of spoken lines and sound effects. Spectacle refers to the visual elements of a play, including, make-up, costumes, and sets.

Role Playing

In role-playing, participants adopt and act out the roles of characters that may have personalities, motivations, and backgrounds different from their own. Role-playing is also considered to be a technique that allows participants to resolve conflicts and practice certain behaviors. People use the phrase "role-playing" in at least three distinct ways:

- To refer to the playing of roles in a theatrical or educational setting;
- To refer to a wide range of games, including computer role-playing games and play-by-mail games;
- To refer to role-playing games used in therapy.

Role-playing in the form of historical reenactment has been practiced by adults for millennia. The ancient Romans, Han Chinese, and medieval Europeans all occasionally organized events in which everyone pretended to be from an earlier age, with the primary purpose of these being entertainment. Today, historical reenactment is often pursued as a hobby.

Puppets

A shadow puppet is a cutout figure held between a source of light and a translucent screen. It is different from other forms of puppetry, as it is two dimensional. Shadow puppets can form solid silhouettes or can be decorated with various amounts of cutout details. Color can be introduced into the cutout shapes to provide different dimensions, as exemplified by Japanese shadow puppets.

Human carnival or body puppet are designed to be part of a large spectacle. Often used in parades and protests, these figures are at least the size of a human and oftentimes much larger. Because a performer's entire body is covered with the puppet, the appearance and personality of the person controlling the puppet is not known and is generally irrelevant to the viewer. The puppeteer must never be revealed during performances. These puppets are particularly associated with large scale entertainment, such as the nightly parades at the various Disney complexes around the world. Big Bird from Sesame Street is a classic example of a human carnival or body puppet.

Mask

A mask is an artifact normally worn on the face, typically for protection, concealment, performance, or amusement. Masks have been used since antiquity for both ceremonial and practical purposes. Although they are usually worn on the face, they may also be positioned for effect elsewhere in relation to the wearer's own head. The origin of the word "mask" can be traced to three sources: the French "masque," the Italian "maschera," and the Spanish "máscara."

The 5000-year-old Sumerian mask of Warka is believed to be the oldest surviving mask. Looted from the Iraqi National Museum in Baghdad, it was recovered in 2003.

Whiteface Clown

Traditionally, the whiteface clown uses "clown white" makeup to cover his or her entire face and neck with none of the underlying flesh color showing. In the European style of whiteface makeup, the ears are painted red. Features, emphasized in red and black, are delicate. A whiteface clown is traditionally costumed far more extravagantly than the other two clown types, sometimes wearing a ruffled collar and pointed hat which typify the stereotypical "clown suit." The whiteface character-type is often serious, all-knowing (even if not particularly smart), bossy, and cocky. He is the ultimate authority figure. He serves the role of "straight-man" and sets up situations that can be turned funny.

Clowning History

During their history, clowns have been associated with jugglers, who were seen as pariahs of society alongside actors, prostitutes, and lepers, and thus (at least in Europe) wore stripes. At one time, clowns even had strong associations with the devil. Jugglers often used clowning techniques, and the later court jesters often danced, performed acrobatics, and juggled. The character of the clown passed through pantomime, into vaudeville, and on to the touring circuses of the 19th and 20th centuries.

During the 16th century, the commedia dell'arte greatly influenced Europe's perceptions of the clown character. The commedia dell'arte provided audiences with a new form of improvisational comedy that used stock characters, some of whom wore masks based on the grotesque masked clowns of carnivals and mystery plays. The stock characters of the commedia dell'arte originally included the Zanni, servants who moved in and out of the story, oftentimes using acrobatics to disrupt the situations involving their masters; Pantalone, the old miser; and Il Dottore, the banal doctor. The stock character list grew from there to incorporate Arlecchino, a harlequin famous for his patched, multi-colored clothing; Tartaglia, known for his glasses and stuttering; and Pulcinella, who has a ravenous appetite as well as a huge nose. Many of these characters survived into the twentieth century in one form or another.

Character Clowns

A character clown adopts the persona of an eccentric character of some type, such as a butcher, a baker, a policeman, a housewife, or a hobo. Prime examples of this type of clown are the circus tramps Otto Griebling and Emmett Kelly. Red Skelton, Harold Lloyd, Buster Keaton, and Charlie Chaplin all fit the definition of a character clown as well. Makeup for character clowns is a comic slant on the standard human face. Their makeup starts with a flesh tone base and may make use of anything from glasses, moustaches, and beards to freckles, warts, big ears, and strange haircuts.

Circus Clowns

In a circus, a clown might:

- walk a tightrope, high wire, slack rope, or piece of rope on the ground, though in the last case, the clown might be just as likely to wrestle around on the ground with the rope, as if it were a boa constrictor.
- ride a horse, a zebra, a donkey, an elephant, or even an ostrich.
- substitute himself in the role of "lion tamer."
- act as an "emcee", or Master of Ceremonies, the preferred term for a clown who takes on the role of Ringmaster.
- "sit in" with the orchestra, perhaps in a "pin spot" in the center ring, or from a seat in the audience.
- play a part any other circus performer might play. In fact, it is not uncommon for an acrobat, a horseback rider, or a lion tamer to secretly stand in for the clown, with the switch taking place in a brief moment offstage.

Mime

A mime is an actor who communicates entirely by gestures, body movements, and facial expressions. Mimes sometimes imitate a person, especially for satirical effect, as when an actor mimics a politician. The term "mime" can also refer to an early form of comedy in Greece and Rome in which actors combined dialogue with dancing and suggestive gestures.

Free Writing

Free writing is a form of brainstorming in a structured way. The method involves exploring a topic by writing about it for a certain period without stopping. A writer sets a time limit and begins writing in complete sentences everything that comes to mind about the topic. Writing continues without interruption until the set period expires. When time expires, read carefully everything that has been written down. Much of it may make little or no sense, but insights and observations may emerge that the free writer did not know existed in his or her mind. Writing has a unique quality of jogging loose ideas, and seeing a word or idea appear may trigger others. Free writing usually results in a fuller expression of ideas than brainstorming does because thoughts and associations are written more comprehensively. Both techniques can be used to complement one another and can yield much different results.

Important Terms

Acting process: refers to the methods and materials from which an actor draws his or her ability to perform; actors should be able to verbalize the tools they use in their acting processes.

Affective memory: a technique in which an actor reactivates a past experience to gain the emotional and psychological feelings associated with those events and then transferring them to a performance; used when the actor believes the character they are portraying is undergoing an event that emotionally parallels that which the actor experienced in real life.

Atmospheres: defined by Michael Chekhov as the inherent energy within a specific place; actors may imagine they are in a specific location while performing in order to depict the corresponding emotions and actions that would best suit that environment thus creating an atmosphere.

Character acting: occurs when an actor must make a change to their physical person in order to perform a role; may include the use of dialect or accents that are not part of the actor's real persona or using stage makeup to create a specific facial disfigurement.

Articulation: the ability to clearly pronounce words while acting or performing.

Blocking: developing the movements of actors on stage in relation to other actors, scenery, and props.

Catharsis: the purging of an emotion, such as fear or grief, while performing on stage.

Concentration: the ability of an actor to be in character through use of dialogue, attitude, voice, costume, expressions, and mannerisms.

Cold reading: occurs when actors read a script for the first time.

Context: the conditions or climate in which a play was written or meant to be performed.

Cue: a signal that serves as an indicator of another action that is about to occur.

A-D converter: an analog to digital converter; used in computer soundcards; converts a varying electrical signal into binary data.

ALD: Association of Lighting Designers

A1: code used by the Lighting Industry Forum to identify the recommended usage of various lamps; A1 lamps are those recommended for projection.

Absorption: the ability of a surface's ability to absorb sound.

Acoustics: the behavior of sound in certain areas; usually depends upon the size and shape of a space, as well as the presence of sound-absorbing materials.

Acting area: space on a stage or in a performance space in which an actor can move while remaining in full view of the audience.

Bastard prompt: used in situations where the prompt corner must be stage right instead of stage left.

Battens: floodlights set up in compartments that allow the mixing of light colors.

Beamlight: a flood lantern that uses a parabolic reflector to create a high-intensity parallel beam.

Beginners: term shouted by stage management to signify that it is time for the actors who appear in the first scene to come onto the stage.

Bell board: a live sound effects board that can play such sound effects as door bells, ringing phones, and sirens.

Bifocal spot: a profile light that contains two sets of shutters; one set produces a hard-edged light, the other one a soft-edged light.

Border: a piece of cloth used to mask lighting rigs; can also refer to flown scenery from the audience.

Boss plate: a metal plate in stage floor that is used to bolt down scenery.

Breakaway: a prop or part of set that is made to break upon impact.

Breakup: an abstract Gobo that is used to provide a textured light with no distinctive pattern.

Bump: a sudden flash of light often used as a cue.

Burnout: a colored gel that has lost its color or melted with use.

CMY: refers to the colors cyan, yellow, and magenta, which are used to mix colors in moving lights.

Color cal: -the list that specifies all of the colors that will be needed for the lighting plan.

Color filter: a piece of colored plastic that blocks the light of any other colors from passing through except that which is the color of the filter.

Additive color: occurs when two beams of different colors are focused onto the same area.

Subtractive color: occurs when two colors of gels are placed in front of a lantern.

Color temperature: the warmness or coolness of lighting; high color temperature lights appear whiter or cool.

Come down: the closing time of a show.

ERS: acronym for ellipsoidal reflector spotlight.

Effects projector: a lantern that can project such images as clouds or rain.

Animation disc: a metal disc with slots that can be rotated in front of a lantern to give the effect of movement in the light.

Exposition: usually occurs at the beginning of a play; provides background information about the characters or plot of the play.

FBO: acronym for fade to blackout.

Fade: gradual increase or decrease in light or sound level.

False perspective: design technique that makes the set appear larger than it really is.

False proscenium: placing a canvas or flat panel onto a proscenium stage in order to decrease the size of the space to accommodate a small set.

Noise gate: used to decrease background noise by maintaining a specific sound level by muting or increasing a signal in response to the noise level.

OP: acronym for opposite prompt; refers to the side of the stage opposite of the side from which prompts are received.

On the book: term used to refer to an actor who must use a script during a scene.

Open the house: occurs when stage management alerts the FOH staff that the stage is set and the audience can begin taking their seats.

Overlay: refers to the wider spot when there are two followspots on the same performer.

Paper the house: refers to a marketing technique in which tickets are given away to make a show seem to be selling more than it actually is.

Pit net: a net placed over the pit area of the theatre to prevent actors and objects from falling into the area where the orchestra is located.

Places: a term called out by directors when it is time for actors to stand in the appropriate positions to begin a scene.

Platform stage: usually refers to an acting stage that is lifted from the floor in a space that was not created as a theatre.

Preproduction: the time before a production in which the planning is done.

Preview: a performance that occurs prior to opening night.

Principals: the main actors in a production.

Promenade: a theatrical arrangement in which the audience moves around the acting area to see the performance from multiple locations.

Strike: the disassembling of stage sets.

TBC: acronym that stands for to be confirmed; usually seen in a cast list when an actor has not been chosen for a part or if a venue or date has not yet been selected.

Throw: the distance between a light source and the person or item being lit.

Thrust: a stage that reaches forward into the auditorium and has audience seating on at least two sides; also called a theatre in the round.

Thunder run: a channel down which a cannonball can be run to simulate the sound of thunder.

Thunder sheet: a sheet of metal that can be shaken using two attached handles or beaten to simulate the sound of thunder.

Tilt: the up and down movement of a lantern.

Ushers: theatre staff members who lead audience members to their seats; ushers are often seated in the auditorium during performances in case of an emergency.

Visual cue: a cue that is taken based on the action on stage rather than given by a stage manager.

Vomitory: an entrance to the auditorium that is located in the banked seating areas.

Wagon stage: a complex scenery device in which bulky set items are positioned on sliding trucks that are the width of the proscenium arch; trucks are mechanized to allow for quick scene changes.

Walk on: an acting role that requires the actor be physically present on stage but not speak.

Wash: a lighting cover that blankets the whole stage in a certain type or color of light

How to Overcome Test Anxiety

Just the thought of taking a test is enough to make most people a little nervous. A test is an important event that can have a long-term impact on your future, so it's important to take it seriously and it's natural to feel anxious about performing well. But just because anxiety is normal, that doesn't mean that it's helpful in test taking, or that you should simply accept it as part of your life. Anxiety can have a variety of effects. These effects can be mild, like making you feel slightly nervous, or severe, like blocking your ability to focus or remember even a simple detail.

If you experience test anxiety—whether severe or mild—it's important to know how to beat it. To discover this, first you need to understand what causes test anxiety.

Causes of Test Anxiety

While we often think of anxiety as an uncontrollable emotional state, it can actually be caused by simple, practical things. One of the most common causes of test anxiety is that a person does not feel adequately prepared for their test. This feeling can be the result of many different issues such as poor study habits or lack of organization, but the most common culprit is time management. Starting to study too late, failing to organize your study time to cover all of the material, or being distracted while you study will mean that you're not well prepared for the test. This may lead to cramming the night before, which will cause you to be physically and mentally exhausted for the test. Poor time management also contributes to feelings of stress, fear, and hopelessness as you realize you are not well prepared but don't know what to do about it.

Other times, test anxiety is not related to your preparation for the test but comes from unresolved fear. This may be a past failure on a test, or poor performance on tests in general. It may come from comparing yourself to others who seem to be performing better or from the stress of living up to expectations. Anxiety may be driven by fears of the future—how failure on this test would affect your educational and career goals. These fears are often completely irrational, but they can still negatively impact your test performance.

> **Review Video:** 3 Reasons You Have Test Anxiety
> Visit mometrix.com/academy and enter code: 428468

Elements of Test Anxiety

As mentioned earlier, test anxiety is considered to be an emotional state, but it has physical and mental components as well. Sometimes you may not even realize that you are suffering from test anxiety until you notice the physical symptoms. These can include trembling hands, rapid heartbeat, sweating, nausea, and tense muscles. Extreme anxiety may lead to fainting or vomiting. Obviously, any of these symptoms can have a negative impact on testing. It is important to recognize them as soon as they begin to occur so that you can address the problem before it damages your performance.

> **Review Video:** 3 Ways to Tell You Have Test Anxiety
> Visit mometrix.com/academy and enter code: 927847

The mental components of test anxiety include trouble focusing and inability to remember learned information. During a test, your mind is on high alert, which can help you recall information and stay focused for an extended period of time. However, anxiety interferes with your mind's natural processes, causing you to blank out, even on the questions you know well. The strain of testing during anxiety makes it difficult to stay focused, especially on a test that may take several hours. Extreme anxiety can take a huge mental toll, making it difficult not only to recall test information but even to understand the test questions or pull your thoughts together.

> **Review Video:** How Test Anxiety Affects Memory
> Visit mometrix.com/academy and enter code: 609003

Effects of Test Anxiety

Test anxiety is like a disease—if left untreated, it will get progressively worse. Anxiety leads to poor performance, and this reinforces the feelings of fear and failure, which in turn lead to poor performances on subsequent tests. It can grow from a mild nervousness to a crippling condition. If allowed to progress, test anxiety can have a big impact on your schooling, and consequently on your future.

Test anxiety can spread to other parts of your life. Anxiety on tests can become anxiety in any stressful situation, and blanking on a test can turn into panicking in a job situation. But fortunately, you don't have to let anxiety rule your testing and determine your grades. There are a number of relatively simple steps you can take to move past anxiety and function normally on a test and in the rest of life.

> **Review Video:** How Test Anxiety Impacts Your Grades
> Visit mometrix.com/academy and enter code: 939819

Physical Steps for Beating Test Anxiety

While test anxiety is a serious problem, the good news is that it can be overcome. It doesn't have to control your ability to think and remember information. While it may take time, you can begin taking steps today to beat anxiety.

Just as your first hint that you may be struggling with anxiety comes from the physical symptoms, the first step to treating it is also physical. Rest is crucial for having a clear, strong mind. If you are tired, it is much easier to give in to anxiety. But if you establish good sleep habits, your body and mind will be ready to perform optimally, without the strain of exhaustion. Additionally, sleeping well helps you to retain information better, so you're more likely to recall the answers when you see the test questions.

Getting good sleep means more than going to bed on time. It's important to allow your brain time to relax. Take study breaks from time to time so it doesn't get overworked, and don't study right before bed. Take time to rest your mind before trying to rest your body, or you may find it difficult to fall asleep.

> **Review Video: The Importance of Sleep for Your Brain**
> Visit mometrix.com/academy and enter code: 319338

Along with sleep, other aspects of physical health are important in preparing for a test. Good nutrition is vital for good brain function. Sugary foods and drinks may give a burst of energy but this burst is followed by a crash, both physically and emotionally. Instead, fuel your body with protein and vitamin-rich foods.

Also, drink plenty of water. Dehydration can lead to headaches and exhaustion, especially if your brain is already under stress from the rigors of the test. Particularly if your test is a long one, drink water during the breaks. And if possible, take an energy-boosting snack to eat between sections.

> **Review Video: How Diet Can Affect your Mood**
> Visit mometrix.com/academy and enter code: 624317

Along with sleep and diet, a third important part of physical health is exercise. Maintaining a steady workout schedule is helpful, but even taking 5-minute study breaks to walk can help get your blood pumping faster and clear your head. Exercise also releases endorphins, which contribute to a positive feeling and can help combat test anxiety.

When you nurture your physical health, you are also contributing to your mental health. If your body is healthy, your mind is much more likely to be healthy as well. So take time to rest, nourish your body with healthy food and water, and get moving as much as possible. Taking these physical steps will make you stronger and more able to take the mental steps necessary to overcome test anxiety.

> **Review Video: How to Stay Healthy and Prevent Test Anxiety**
> Visit mometrix.com/academy and enter code: 877894

Mental Steps for Beating Test Anxiety

Working on the mental side of test anxiety can be more challenging, but as with the physical side, there are clear steps you can take to overcome it. As mentioned earlier, test anxiety often stems from lack of preparation, so the obvious solution is to prepare for the test. Effective studying may be the most important weapon you have for beating test anxiety, but you can and should employ several other mental tools to combat fear.

First, boost your confidence by reminding yourself of past success—tests or projects that you aced. If you're putting as much effort into preparing for this test as you did for those, there's no reason you should expect to fail here. Work hard to prepare; then trust your preparation.

Second, surround yourself with encouraging people. It can be helpful to find a study group, but be sure that the people you're around will encourage a positive attitude. If you spend time with others who are anxious or cynical, this will only contribute to your own anxiety. Look for others who are motivated to study hard from a desire to succeed, not from a fear of failure.

Third, reward yourself. A test is physically and mentally tiring, even without anxiety, and it can be helpful to have something to look forward to. Plan an activity following the test, regardless of the outcome, such as going to a movie or getting ice cream.

When you are taking the test, if you find yourself beginning to feel anxious, remind yourself that you know the material. Visualize successfully completing the test. Then take a few deep, relaxing breaths and return to it. Work through the questions carefully but with confidence, knowing that you are capable of succeeding.

Developing a healthy mental approach to test taking will also aid in other areas of life. Test anxiety affects more than just the actual test—it can be damaging to your mental health and even contribute to depression. It's important to beat test anxiety before it becomes a problem for more than testing.

> **Review Video: Test Anxiety and Depression**
> Visit mometrix.com/academy and enter code: 904704

Study Strategy

Being prepared for the test is necessary to combat anxiety, but what does being prepared look like? You may study for hours on end and still not feel prepared. What you need is a strategy for test prep. The next few pages outline our recommended steps to help you plan out and conquer the challenge of preparation.

Step 1: Scope Out the Test

Learn everything you can about the format (multiple choice, essay, etc.) and what will be on the test. Gather any study materials, course outlines, or sample exams that may be available. Not only will this help you to prepare, but knowing what to expect can help to alleviate test anxiety.

Step 2: Map Out the Material

Look through the textbook or study guide and make note of how many chapters or sections it has. Then divide these over the time you have. For example, if a book has 15 chapters and you have five days to study, you need to cover three chapters each day. Even better, if you have the time, leave an extra day at the end for overall review after you have gone through the material in depth.

If time is limited, you may need to prioritize the material. Look through it and make note of which sections you think you already have a good grasp on, and which need review. While you are studying, skim quickly through the familiar sections and take more time on the challenging parts. Write out your plan so you don't get lost as you go. Having a written plan also helps you feel more in control of the study, so anxiety is less likely to arise from feeling overwhelmed at the amount to cover. A sample plan may look like this:

- Day 1: Skim chapters 1–4, study chapter 5 (especially pages 31–33)
- Day 2: Study chapters 6–7, skim chapters 8–9
- Day 3: Skim chapter 10, study chapters 11–12 (especially pages 87–90)
- Day 4: Study chapters 13–15
- Day 5: Overall review (focus most on chapters 5, 6, and 12), take practice test

Step 3: Gather Your Tools

Decide what study method works best for you. Do you prefer to highlight in the book as you study and then go back over the highlighted portions? Or do you type out notes of the important information? Or is it helpful to make flashcards that you can carry with you? Assemble the pens, index cards, highlighters, post-it notes, and any other materials you may need so you won't be distracted by getting up to find things while you study.

If you're having a hard time retaining the information or organizing your notes, experiment with different methods. For example, try color-coding by subject with colored pens, highlighters, or post-it notes. If you learn better by hearing, try recording yourself reading your notes so you can listen while in the car, working out, or simply sitting at your desk. Ask a friend to quiz you from your flashcards, or try teaching someone the material to solidify it in your mind.

Step 4: Create Your Environment

It's important to avoid distractions while you study. This includes both the obvious distractions like visitors and the subtle distractions like an uncomfortable chair (or a too-comfortable couch that makes you want to fall asleep). Set up the best study environment possible: good lighting and a comfortable work area. If background music helps you focus, you may want to turn it on, but otherwise keep the room quiet. If you are using a computer to take notes, be sure you don't have any other windows open, especially applications like social media, games, or anything else that could distract you. Silence your phone and turn off notifications. Be sure to keep water close by so you stay hydrated while you study (but avoid unhealthy drinks and snacks).

Also, take into account the best time of day to study. Are you freshest first thing in the morning? Try to set aside some time then to work through the material. Is your mind clearer in the afternoon or evening? Schedule your study session then. Another method is to study at the same time of day that you will take the test, so that your brain gets used to working on the material at that time and will be ready to focus at test time.

Step 5: Study!

Once you have done all the study preparation, it's time to settle into the actual studying. Sit down, take a few moments to settle your mind so you can focus, and begin to follow your study plan. Don't give in to distractions or let yourself procrastinate. This is your time to prepare so you'll be ready to fearlessly approach the test. Make the most of the time and stay focused.

Of course, you don't want to burn out. If you study too long you may find that you're not retaining the information very well. Take regular study breaks. For example, taking five minutes out of every hour to walk briskly, breathing deeply and swinging your arms, can help your mind stay fresh.

As you get to the end of each chapter or section, it's a good idea to do a quick review. Remind yourself of what you learned and work on any difficult parts. When you feel that you've mastered the material, move on to the next part. At the end of your study session, briefly skim through your notes again.

But while review is helpful, cramming last minute is NOT. If at all possible, work ahead so that you won't need to fit all your study into the last day. Cramming overloads your brain with more information than it can process and retain, and your tired mind may struggle to recall even previously learned information when it is overwhelmed with last-minute study. Also, the urgent nature of cramming and the stress placed on your brain contribute to anxiety. You'll be more likely to go to the test feeling unprepared and having trouble thinking clearly.

So don't cram, and don't stay up late before the test, even just to review your notes at a leisurely pace. Your brain needs rest more than it needs to go over the information again. In fact, plan to finish your studies by noon or early afternoon the day before the test. Give your brain the rest of the day to relax or focus on other things, and get a good night's sleep. Then you will be fresh for the test and better able to recall what you've studied.

Step 6: Take a practice test

Many courses offer sample tests, either online or in the study materials. This is an excellent resource to check whether you have mastered the material, as well as to prepare for the test format and environment.

Check the test format ahead of time: the number of questions, the type (multiple choice, free response, etc.), and the time limit. Then create a plan for working through them. For example, if you have 30 minutes to take a 60-question test, your limit is 30 seconds per question. Spend less time on the questions you know well so that you can take more time on the difficult ones.

If you have time to take several practice tests, take the first one open book, with no time limit. Work through the questions at your own pace and make sure you fully understand them. Gradually work up to taking a test under test conditions: sit at a desk with all study materials put away and set a timer. Pace yourself to make sure you finish the test with time to spare and go back to check your answers if you have time.

After each test, check your answers. On the questions you missed, be sure you understand why you missed them. Did you misread the question (tests can use tricky wording)? Did you forget the information? Or was it something you hadn't learned? Go back and study any shaky areas that the practice tests reveal.

Taking these tests not only helps with your grade, but also aids in combating test anxiety. If you're already used to the test conditions, you're less likely to worry about it, and working through tests until you're scoring well gives you a confidence boost. Go through the practice tests until you feel comfortable, and then you can go into the test knowing that you're ready for it.

Test Tips

On test day, you should be confident, knowing that you've prepared well and are ready to answer the questions. But aside from preparation, there are several test day strategies you can employ to maximize your performance.

First, as stated before, get a good night's sleep the night before the test (and for several nights before that, if possible). Go into the test with a fresh, alert mind rather than staying up late to study.

Try not to change too much about your normal routine on the day of the test. It's important to eat a nutritious breakfast, but if you normally don't eat breakfast at all, consider eating just a protein bar. If you're a coffee drinker, go ahead and have your normal coffee. Just make sure you time it so that the caffeine doesn't wear off right in the middle of your test. Avoid sugary beverages, and drink enough water to stay hydrated but not so much that you need a restroom break 10 minutes into the test. If your test isn't first thing in the morning, consider going for a walk or doing a light workout before the test to get your blood flowing.

Allow yourself enough time to get ready, and leave for the test with plenty of time to spare so you won't have the anxiety of scrambling to arrive in time. Another reason to be early is to select a good seat. It's helpful to sit away from doors and windows, which can be distracting. Find a good seat, get out your supplies, and settle your mind before the test begins.

When the test begins, start by going over the instructions carefully, even if you already know what to expect. Make sure you avoid any careless mistakes by following the directions.

Then begin working through the questions, pacing yourself as you've practiced. If you're not sure on an answer, don't spend too much time on it, and don't let it shake your confidence. Either skip it and come back later, or eliminate as many wrong answers as possible and guess among the remaining ones. Don't dwell on these questions as you continue—put them out of your mind and focus on what lies ahead.

Be sure to read all of the answer choices, even if you're sure the first one is the right answer. Sometimes you'll find a better one if you keep reading. But don't second-guess yourself if you do immediately know the answer. Your gut instinct is usually right. Don't let test anxiety rob you of the information you know.

If you have time at the end of the test (and if the test format allows), go back and review your answers. Be cautious about changing any, since your first instinct tends to be correct, but make sure you didn't misread any of the questions or accidentally mark the wrong answer choice. Look over any you skipped and make an educated guess.

At the end, leave the test feeling confident. You've done your best, so don't waste time worrying about your performance or wishing you could change anything. Instead, celebrate the successful completion of this test. And finally, use this test to learn how to deal with anxiety even better next time.

| **Review Video: 5 Tips to Beat Test Anxiety** |
| Visit mometrix.com/academy and enter code: 570656 |

Important Qualification

Not all anxiety is created equal. If your test anxiety is causing major issues in your life beyond the classroom or testing center, or if you are experiencing troubling physical symptoms related to your anxiety, it may be a sign of a serious physiological or psychological condition. If this sounds like your situation, we strongly encourage you to seek professional help.

Thank You

We at Mometrix would like to extend our heartfelt thanks to you, our friend and patron, for allowing us to play a part in your journey. It is a privilege to serve people from all walks of life who are unified in their commitment to building the best future they can for themselves.

The preparation you devote to these important testing milestones may be the most valuable educational opportunity you have for making a real difference in your life. We encourage you to put your heart into it—that feeling of succeeding, overcoming, and yes, conquering will be well worth the hours you've invested.

We want to hear your story, your struggles and your successes, and if you see any opportunities for us to improve our materials so we can help others even more effectively in the future, please share that with us as well. **The team at Mometrix would be absolutely thrilled to hear from you!** So please, send us an email (support@mometrix.com) and let's stay in touch.

If you'd like some additional help, check out these other resources we offer for your exam:

http://MometrixFlashcards.com/CLEP

Additional Bonus Material

Due to our efforts to try to keep this book to a manageable length, we've created a link that will give you access to all of your additional bonus material.

Please visit http://www.mometrix.com/bonus948/clephumanities to access the information.